BILLY DURANT
Creator of General Motors

BILLY DURANT
Creator of General Motors

by

Lawrence R. Gustin

WILLIAM B. EERDMANS PUBLISHING COMPANY
Grand Rapids, Michigan

Printed in the United States of America

Library of Congress Cataloging in Publication Data

Gustin, Lawrence, 1937—
    Billy Durant: creator of General Motors.

    Bibliography: p. 274.
    1. Durant, William Crapo, 1861-1947.   2. General
Motors Corporation.   I. Title.
HD9710.U54G474   338.7'62'20924 [B]   73-2291
ISBN 0-8028-3435-3

Illustrations on pages 1-3, 5, 6, 7, and 9 by Steve Clack.

75-7579

For Rose Mary, Bob and David

Contents

Photo Credits

The majority of photographs are from the files of *The Flint Journal*, the collections of Kenneth Wallace, Sr., of Flint and Crooks Studio, and from the General Motors Corporation and its divisions. Many are found in all these collections and so are not specifically credited. Other photos were obtained from the following sources:

Page 29—Left, Mrs. Catherine L. Durant. Right, courtesy Free Public Library, New Bedford, Massachusetts. 37—Top, Mrs. Joyce S. Cook. Bottom, Clarence H. Young. 44—Carl Bonbright. 52—Gerry Fauth. 70-71—Gerry Fauth. 79—Mrs. Catherine L. Durant. 80—Mrs. Catherine L. Durant. 87—Sloan Museum, Flint. 109—Mrs. Catherine L. Durant and Aristo Scrobogna. 158—Sloan Museum, Flint. 163—Sloan Museum. 177—Chrysler Corporation. 186—Gerry Fauth. 194—Gerry Fauth. 198—Mrs. Catherine L. Durant. 216—W. W. Murphy. 225—Mrs. Catherine L. Durant (both). 226—Manufacturers Association of Flint. 229—Mrs. Catherine L. Durant and Aristo Scrobogna. 236-237—Sloan Museum, Flint. 242—Mrs. Catherine L. Durant. 254—Aristo Scrobogna.

Foreword

This account of the career of William Crapo Durant is based in part on unpublished manuscripts and documents and on interviews with his widow, two of his personal secretaries and others who knew him well.

Among the manuscripts used extensively are Durant's own autobiographical notes. This manuscript of seven short typewritten chapters, plus scattered notes, is not always accurate—much of it was written in the 1930s and 1940s, decades after the events described—but it contains valuable information and some insights into Durant's motives. These notes, and numerous letters and other personal papers, were made available to the writer by Durant's widow, Mrs. Catherine Durant, with the cooperation of his last personal secretary, Aristo Scrobogna, who is the legal custodian of Durant's papers.

Durant is best remembered in Flint, Michigan, a city which owes practically all of its large industrial base—and its historical distinction of being the birthplace of General Motors—to his accomplishments. And the manuscript which really provided the basis for this account is a 600-page *Industrial History of Flint* which was compiled by Frank M. Rodolf in the early 1940s when he was a reporter and librarian for *The Flint Journal.* It is surely one of the best and most complete accounts of Durant's career ever compiled. Rodolf, who left *The Journal* shortly after the manuscript was completed, was located by the writer in New York City. With his permission, and that of *The*

Flint Journal, which copyrighted his manuscript, some of his work is incorporated in this book. A copy of his manuscript is in the Flint Public Library. In some ways, it is a product of *Flint Journal* reporters over a period of more than half a century. Rodolf drew on the articles of his predecessors, and those who followed him also contributed to it. Portions of it were published in *The Journal's* GM Golden Milestone edition of August 14, 1958.

A great many persons gave various kinds of help. Clarence H. Young, assistant director of the Manufacturers Association of Flint, biographer of Charles Stewart Mott, and long considered one of the leading experts on Durant, provided initial interest and considerable guidance, along with a large amount of material from his files. An excellent speaker, Young has kept the memory of Durant's spirit alive in Flint, the starting point of most of Durant's successes. Much of the revived interest in Durant can be traced to Young.

Richard P. Scharchburg, associate professor of social science at General Motor Institute, has constantly been seeking new sources of information about Durant's career and has provided invaluable assistance with guidance, research assistance, and the checking of accuracy. There are periods in Durant's career which have still not been thoroughly cleared up to the satisfaction of either the writer or of Scharchburg, but the research goes on.

George S. May, author, historian and professor at Eastern Michigan University, encouraged the writer and offered research advice and assistance. Dr. May is now writing a comprehensive history of the origins of the automobile industry in Michigan, drawing on many original sources. He and his wife, Tish, spent weeks going through the voluminous records of John J. Carton, Durant's long-time attorney, and made copies of significant letters in this file available to the writer.

Dr. Roger Van Bolt, director of the Sloan Museum, provided much information from the museum's extensive collection of papers and photographs. Richard Crabb, author of *Birth of a Giant*, and Beverly Rae Kimes, who wrote an excellent historical account of Buick in *Automobile Quarterly* in 1968, encouraged the development of the book.

Alfred D. Chandler, coauthor with Stephen Salsbury of *Pierre S. du Pont and the Making of the Modern Corporation*, which is the most detailed account of the years of Durant's presidency of General Motors, read the portion of this account dealing with those years and offered suggestions.

Clark D. Tibbits of Columbiaville, Michigan, has made a personal project of seeking details about Durant's father, who disappeared when Durant was a youth. Late in 1972, he found the tombstone of William Clark Durant, the father, in a cemetery in his hometown of East Lempster, New Hampshire, with the date of his death—previously unknown to the Durant family and historians—1883.

Among those interviewed by the writer or associates were Charles Stewart Mott, who was the last of the pioneer leaders of the auto industry when he died at age ninety-seven in 1973; W. W. Murphy, Durant's personal secretary for more than thirty years, who was interviewed by Richard Scharchburg; Mrs. Jay (Frances Willson) Thompson, whose grandmother was a sister of Durant's mother; Mrs. Joyce S. Cook, former women's editor of *The Flint Journal*, who knew all of the early Flint automotive families; Gerry Fauth, a great fan of Durant's, who collected and thus preserved for the Flint Public Library a vast collection of automobile memorabilia; Carl W. Bonbright, whose father was Durant's sales manager in the carriage days and who, as a small child, rode in the first car built in Flint (Judge Charles Wisner's); Laverne Marshall, who as a teenager chauffeured Durant around Flint; Arthur H. Sarvis, who covered Durant's activities for *The Journal* back in 1910; William S. Ballenger, Jr., son of one of Durant's closest associates in the early days of Buick and Chevrolet; George H. Koskey, whose long and successful industrial career included associations with Walter Chrysler and Charles W. Nash at Buick; and Archie Campbell, a business associate of Durant's in his later years, who provided original material for this account.

Glen A. Boissonneault, editor of *The Flint Journal*, and Rudolph H. Pallotta, the city editor, provided both encouragement and time. Editorial advice was given for various sections of this account by John R. Davis, S. Gordon Gapper, Colin McDonald, Roger Van Noord, and Ed Hayman. William D. Chase, *The Journal* librarian, provided research advice. *The Flint Journal*'s file of clippings and microfilm is one of the most important sources of Durant material. The newspaper's reporters were close to Durant and many early accounts appear to be based on "inside" information.

Persons who consented to read this manuscript for accuracy included Dr. David L. Lewis, professor of business history at the Graduate School of Business Administration at the University of Michigan; Dr. Alfred D. Chandler, who besides being an author is Straus Professor of Business History at the Graduate School of Business Administration at Harvard University; Dr. George S. May; Richard P. Scharchburg; Clarence H. Young; Richard Crabb; Mrs. Catherine L. Durant; Aristo Scrobogna; Gerry Fauth; and Archie R. Campbell.

Among others who provided assistance were Michael L. Kiefer, Bruce MacDonald, George Dammann, G. H. Rideout, Raymond J. Kelly, Jr., Robert W. Donovan, Merle Perry, David G. Gosler, Stanley T. Richards, Edward P. Joseph, and my wife Rose Mary and parents, Mr. and Mrs. Robert S. Gustin.

Most of the photographs used in this book are from *The Flint Journal* and the vast original historical collection of Kenneth Wallace of Flint, with the permission of *The Journal* and Mr. Wallace. Some are from the individual collections of other persons mentioned above, and some are from the files of General Motors.

Some important sources of information are confidential.

General Motors was not involved in any way with the development of this account, although a number of individuals within the corporation were helpful.

Mrs. Catherine Durant and Aristo Scrobogna were interviewed for several days in New York and New Jersey. Mrs. Durant is a gracious, intelligent, and attractive woman who has warm memories of her husband and who displays little bitterness about the events which robbed her and her husband of their fortune. Still, she sometimes finds it painful to discuss the past, and memories of her husband's last years can move her to tears. Scrobogna not only gave the writer complete access to the files he holds but also provided research assistance during a period of more than a year.

Besides the papers and interviews listed above, some important information has come from papers which are available in libraries. The Michigan Historical Collections at the University of Michigan in Ann Arbor contain the Henry H. Crapo papers, which shed light on Durant's mysterious father. The papers of John J. Carton, long-time Durant attorney, are also there. Durant's high school record is on file in the Flint School System administration building; his divorce papers in the Genesee County Courthouse; the handwritten minutes of the Durant-Dort Carriage Company are in the Sloan Museum, Flint.

A large amount of published material was also examined. A complete bibliography appears at the back of the book.

This account is an enlargement of a series, *Billy Durant and Flint: The Beginnings of General Motors*, published in *The Flint Journal* in March, 1972.

L. R. G.

Flint, Michigan

Prologue

The new reporter in town, assigned to Detroit by a major magazine, looked out of his office window toward the huge gray bulk of the General Motors Building across the street. He noticed small decorative stones in the walls near the roof and then caught a detail—the letter "D" inscribed in some of the stonework. He telephoned one of the offices in the half-century-old building. What does the "D" stand for? The secretary didn't know, but she would find out. A few minutes later she returned to the phone. Durant, she said. The initial stands for W. C. Durant.

Those carved stones are about the only public reminder at General Motors of the man who created GM—the largest industrial corporation in the history of the world. It is not surprising that the new reporter was puzzled. William Crapo Durant is no longer exactly a household name; he is seldom mentioned in the same breath with Henry Ford, Walter P. Chrysler, or Alfred P. Sloan.

Yet of all the colorful men who propelled the United States of America into the automobile age, W. C. Durant was perhaps the most unusual—and from an organizational standpoint in the pioneering era, the most important. If Durant had not appeared on the stage in the auto industry's formative years, General Motors would not exist. Neither would the largest-selling automobile, Chevrolet. Quite probably there would be no Buick or Oldsmobile today, and possibly no Pontiac or Cadillac. Charles

W. Nash would not have had the chance to form his own automobile company. Walter P. Chrysler might have stayed in railroads. Alfred P. Sloan's career would have been far different. The list goes on and on. Certainly there would have been a giant automobile industry today had Durant not been involved. But just as certainly it would have had a far different structure.

Durant had a hand, directly or indirectly, in shaping the beginnings of three of the four major American automobile manufacturing corporations that exist today. He founded General Motors and greatly influenced the careers of both Nash, one of the founders of what has become the American Motors Corporation, and, to a lesser extent, Chrysler, founder of the Chrysler Corporation. Of the major U.S. auto manufacturers that survive, only Ford was not significantly influenced by Durant. And at one time Durant came close to controlling Ford, losing out only because banking institutions did not share his faith in the future of the automobile.

Unlike most of the pioneer automotive giants, Durant was not a back-shop tinkerer. While other men put automobiles together, he put organizations together, and he did it with dramatic flair. He was an extremely complex and paradoxical personality, a supersalesman who spoke in a soft voice, a builder of fortunes who cared very little about money and who ultimately died without leaving any. He dreamed great dreams and made them come true because he had unparalleled vision and courage, an iron will, and a legendary charm that made him an adored leader of thousands. Even those who did not always agree with his methods called him a genius, though they also sometimes called him a dictator and a gambler. He was all three.

Even his most loyal followers did not understand him and could not predict his next move. He was too far ahead of them. He was capable of fantastic successes and equally fantastic failures. At times he seemed childlike in his business dealings; at other times he outsmarted the sharpest leaders of finance. He plunged headlong into catastrophes that an average man might easily have seen coming. But that same overriding optimism permitted him to create great organizations.

He had an attitude not common among men of big money—he tried to protect the people who invested with him, even if this protection would break him. Finally it did. And when at last he was unable to save the dollars of his supporters, he himself plunged from multimillionaire to bankruptcy.

By 1940 Durant was back where he had started, working hard in Flint, Michigan, and planning great business expansions. Except that by then he was seventy-eight years old and no longer wealthy, and his business was bowling, not automobiles. He was operating a bowling alley almost in the shadow of the Buick manufacturing complex he had created. Still he had great dreams. Since he was then in bowling alleys—as usual ahead of his time—he planned to build fifty bowling centers across the country. "I haven't a dollar," he said to a visitor to North Flint Recreation one evening. "But I'm happy and I'm carrying on because I can't stop. There's much more to life than money."

One man who frequently visited Durant at the bowling alley was Frank M. Rodolf, at the time a reporter for *The Flint Journal*. More than three decades later, Rodolf, sitting in a restaurant in New York City, recalled: "We talked often, but I remember that he never sat down. He would be running here and there, waiting on customers, talking rapidly all the time. What did I think of him? I thought he was a phenomenon."

Durant could tell a visitor all about how he had founded General Motors in 1908. But that wasn't the beginning, he said. It had all really started back in 1886 on the streets of Flint. Some of Durant's recollections of this period were recorded by Frank Rodolf. Other details were dictated by Durant himself in what he hoped would be his autobiography, a project he never completed. What follows is, in part, Durant's personal story of how he founded General Motors.

Chapter One

The Road Cart

It had started, he remembered, on a September evening in 1886. He was twenty-four years old then, a slightly built, already successful businessman in the old lumber town of Flint, Michigan, and, as usual, he was in a hurry. The board of directors of the city's privately owned gas company was to meet in an hour, and Billy Durant had to get over to the plant, read a meter, and get to the meeting.

His quick, bouncy gait slowed at the city's main intersection, Saginaw and Kearsley streets. He saw his friend Josiah Dallas Dort in the doorway of the hardware at the corner, and there was time for a short chat. And then Johnny Alger, a husky youth who worked for Dort at the hardware, pulled up to the boardwalk in his new two-wheeled road cart.

Alger offered Durant a ride. The cart, he suggested, was an unusual vehicle with a wonderful ride. Durant walked over to have a better look. The cart seemed quite ordinary, if anything a bit flimsy. Alger jumped down and poked a finger at the springs, which were held with stirrup-shaped mounts under the shafts. This was the secret, he said, a unique seat suspension. Durant glanced at his watch; he could use a ride to the gas plant. He squeezed onto the seat next to Alger, waved to Dort, and was on his way.

The seat was barely large enough for two men, and he half expected to be thrown off at any moment. But Johnny was right. The cart did not bounce the rider around as other carts did. And now as he rode to the gas plant, the cart swaying only slightly as Johnny's spirited horse raced along the rough, unpaved main street of Flint, his interest began to rise.

When he stepped down from the cart, he asked Alger where he had bought it. The local agent was H. D. Newman, the tinsmith, he replied. Durant was at Newman's door the next morning. The road cart? Sure, it's being built by the Coldwater Road Cart Company, but Newman could sell him one right here in Flint. That evening, Durant headed for the train station, and by eleven o'clock he was checking into a hotel in Coldwater, a village 120 miles southwest of Flint.[1] Billy Durant, who had sold lumber, groceries, patent medicine, cigars, and real estate in the seven years since he had dropped out of high school, who was now a partner in a thriving insurance agency, had decided to get into the vehicle business.

In the morning he went directly to the Coldwater Road Cart Company factory, a small, old-fashioned carriage shop. He walked in, looked around, saw nobody, opened another door, and found himself in a little carpenter shop, staring directly into the eyes of a middle-aged man with bushy eyebrows. Durant and Thomas O'Brien exchanged introductions. Durant started to talk. He had ridden in one of O'Brien's carts and been so pleased that he wondered whether he might buy a small interest in the business.

"Why not buy it all?" O'Brien asked, almost casually.

Durant was startled. He had very little money.

"It wouldn't take much," O'Brien replied with a shrug.

They stared at each other for a long moment, and then O'Brien excused himself to talk with his partner. Durant plopped himself on a carpenter's bench and waited. A short time later, O'Brien returned with William H. Schmedlen. Durant found Schmedlen to be young, alert, pleasant. They talked for a few minutes about this and that, and then Durant said, "If the business is for sale, what's the price?"

O'Brien and Schmedlen said they would like to talk privately. Within minutes they returned with an offer to sell all the materials in their road cart operation—wood stock, axles, wheels, springs, finished and unfinished vehicles, patterns, dies, the whole works except their tools—for $1,500. The price seemed fair, but was the patent for the spring suspension included? The partners thought they might receive a royalty. Durant hesitated. Finally they included the patent in the deal.

"As I said before, I have very little money, nowhere near enough to make the purchase," Durant continued. "But if you will go down to the office of your attorney with me and execute a bill of sale and assign the patent and deposit all the papers in your bank, I will go to Flint this afternoon and see if I can obtain the money, which must be in your hands within five days or no deal." In that reply, recorded in Durant's autobiographical notes, is much of the spirit that guided his life: Decide quickly, make your pitch, nail down the details, don't worry about the money.

At the attorney's office, the remaining details were worked out. Two days after he had first seen Johnny Alger's road cart, Durant was on a train headed back to Flint with a contract in his pocket for the business of manufacturing them.

In Flint the next morning Durant set out to borrow $2,000. He estimated he would need the additional $500 to move the business to Flint and start operations. He had many connections. His grandfather, Henry Crapo, had once been governor of Michigan. Crapo had died in 1869, but in 1886 the name was still big in town, and several of Billy Durant's uncles and cousins were among Flint's most prominent citizens. Yet Durant would recall that he decided to avoid the several banks in town where his friends and relatives had important positions, reasoning that "if I make a failure of the venture, I will never hear the end of it."

He had no such influence at Citizens National Bank, and so he was soon sitting in the office of Robert J. Whaley, president of the bank, a man he knew only slightly and with whom he had never done business. Durant can be pictured in Whaley's dusty, cluttered office, talking in his notably soft voice, his head thrust forward toward his listener as he talked. He was not quite handsome—his nose was straight but a bit large—but his face looked honest and his dark eyes sparkled. Most of the time he smiled engagingly. The total effect was one of quiet charm and confidence.

Whaley listened to Durant's proposal, then walked him downstairs and directed the cashier to make out a ninety-day renewable note for $2,000 and deposit it in Durant's account. In Durant's mind the loan was so significant that more than half a century later he wrote: "Robert J. Whaley, by reason of his courage and his confidence, is entitled to all the credit for having made possible the creation of a nationwide institution which resulted later in the establishment of 12 industrial institutions in Flint, besides [making it] the birthplace of the largest creation of its kind in the world—the General Motors Corporation."

Leaving the bank, Durant went to the office in downtown Flint where he and I. Wixom Whitehead, an old schoolmate, operated their insurance business. When Dallas Dort walked in, to find out where his friend had been the last few days, Durant announced with elation, "I'm in the manufacturing business," and explained that he had made arrangements to build road carts just like the one young Alger had so proudly displayed.

Dort, a tall, slender, handsome young man, ten months older than Durant, had first met Durant when the hardware store had sold some materials to Durant for a business construction project (one of Durant's many sidelines), and he respected Durant's business acumen. He had also been impressed himself with the road cart's potential. Furthermore, the hardware business was not going well. So he asked if Durant would like a partner. Durant replied that he would be delighted to sell a half interest for $1,000. He had never expected to buy the whole thing in the first place.

Dort went to James Bussey, his senior partner in the hardware store, and told him of his new opportunity. Bussey agreed to release him from his contract and to give him $500 for his share of the business. Returning to Durant with the news, Dort announced that he would take the next train to his home in Inkster and get the other $500 from his mother. "She'll raise the money if she has to mortgage the farm."

If Durant and Dort were pleased with their opportunity in Flint, the reaction to the deal was also favorable in Coldwater. The *Coldwater Semi-Weekly Republican* reported the sale to "W. C. Durand" in its issue of September 14, 1886, and congratulated O'Brien and Schmedlen on their success.

Durant (left) and J. Dallas Dort near Imperial Wheel in Flint, 1908. Together they formed the Flint Road Cart Company, later renamed the Durant-Dort Carriage Company.

Durant and Dort were still in the process of organizing their new Flint Road Cart Company when Durant made his first effort to promote and sell the cart. In Durant's own detailed account:

"When the material from Coldwater arrived and Mr. Schmedlen came over to help us get started—as per our agreement—we discovered among the collection two handsome road carts, one

21

particularly attractive, built from open grain white ash—a perfect picture—which I appropriated as my sample ... but where was I to get my audience to demonstrate my ability as a salesman?

"I discovered that most of the county fairs were over on account of the lateness of the season, but in looking over the list I found a big one called the 'Tri-State,' opening in Madison, Wisconsin, on the following Monday. Why they called it the 'Tri-State' I could never understand except that it made it more impressive. They might just as well have called it the 'World's Fair.' As a matter of fact, it was a very popular and well-conducted state fair. It was Friday—the fair was to open on Monday, and according to the rule, which proved to be quite flexible, the entries had to be in place by noon of that day.

"I wired my entry and shipped my sample by American Express, leaving that night for Madison, via Chicago. Arriving at my destination early Sunday morning, I found everything in

The Flint Road Cart with which Durant and Dort entered the vehicle business in 1886. This one is in the Sloan Museum, Flint.

confusion, but during the day located the president of the association, who happened to be the head of a good-sized implement and vehicle jobbing concern. I had the opportunity of telling him what a wonderful cart we were bringing over from Flint at considerable expense, mentioning a few of the outstanding features, adding that there was nothing on the market that would compare with it. Strange to say, I think he believed me. . . .

"Monday came and no cart. Tuesday also came—but no cart. Inquiry developed that Chicago was the transfer point, that the arrival was delayed. . . . I succeeded in having the committee postpone the prize from Tuesday until Wednesday afternoon.

"The sample was delivered at Crane & Company's warehouse Wednesday morning, where Mr. Crane was shown something that he had never seen before. I did not have to do much talking. THE CART SOLD ITSELF. We went to the office where we looked at the map, outlined the territory and the contract was drawn with an initial order for 100 carts, with a small check to bind the bargain. Then to the fairgrounds, where we arranged for a series of afternoon tests to properly demonstrate the principle [of the spring suspension]. Early in the afternoon the committee put in an appearance. I let them run the show with my help, with the result that we were awarded the blue ribbon.

"While it was originally intended to call the cart 'The Flint,' we later adopted the slogan 'Famous Blue Ribbon Line' of carriages, built by Durant and Dort, which name was never changed. The company after a few years took first place in volume production and held that position until the horse-drawn vehicle passed out of the picture, supplanted by the automobile."

Leaving the fair with his orders and his blue ribbon, Durant shipped his handsome cart to Milwaukee, where he called on George C. Cribbs & Company. Cribbs was impressed and wanted a carload (thirty-five carts) every ten days. Durant explained that he was just getting started. They worked out a flexible contract, specifying that deliveries would be made as soon as possible.

On his way back to Flint, Durant called on J. H. Fenton of

Chicago, who had a wide reputation as a supplier of horse racing sulkies. Fenton looked at the cart, suggested a few minor changes to lighten the weight, and asked that his model carry the name Fenton Favorite.

Clearly, Durant's first instincts had been correct. The little road cart from Coldwater had impressed every important carriage man who had seen it. All he had to do, it seemed, was display the cart and take orders for delivery! Completing his first sales trip, William Crapo Durant was on a train headed for Flint with orders for more than 600 carts. The Flint Road Cart Company had yet to build one.

Durant thought about this on the train. He had done a fine selling job—now it was time to produce. But despite Schmedlen's help, the new company was not ready to build its own carts. By the time the train arrived at the Flint station, he had decided on a course of action. The next morning he knocked on the door of William A. Paterson's carriage factory.

Paterson operated Flint's largest carriage business, employing

First $1,000 entries by Dort and Durant in Flint Road Cart Company bank book on September 28, 1886, the earliest document in the vehicle industry which eventually led to the creation of General Motors. The Citizens Bank of Flint obtained the book from Mrs. W. C. Durant in 1971, at the suggestion of Clarence H. Young.

a dozen workers and producing two buggies a day. The company was the pride of the city: Paterson carriages had a wide reputation for craftsmanship. Durant told Paterson that he was new to the carriage business, that he had orders for 600 carts but no hope of producing them on his own. Would Paterson be interested in building 1,200 carts exactly like the sample? Paterson replied that he would, for $12.50 each, crated at his factory. Durant figured he could sell them at retail for nearly twice that. A contract was signed.

Durant and Dort then formally entered into a partnership, on September 28, officially organizing the Flint Road Cart Company with a $2,000 bank account. At first they rented a little shop in Brush Alley in downtown Flint and used the Durant & Whitehead insurance office as a headquarters. Within a short time they moved their operations into a one-story frame building rented from Paterson behind St. Paul's Episcopal Church downtown. Two months later *The Flint Journal* reported that the company was "getting out lots of patent road carts these days, and the building just south of the Waverly House, which is being used as a storeroom, is being packed full."

Chapter Two

King of the Carriage Makers

When Billy Durant's grandfather, Henry Howland Crapo, arrived in Flint in January of 1856, he found a settlement of 2,000 people which had incorporated as a city only a few months before. The city had started in 1819 as a trading post on the Saginaw Trail at a ford of the Flint River, but settlement was not significant until after a tavern was built in 1830.

Alexis de Tocqueville, visiting the Flint River settlement in 1831, during his travels through the American wilderness to gather material for his *Democracy in America*, recorded two observations: He was frightened half out of his wits when he stumbled against a settler's pet bear in the dark ("What a devilish country where they use bears for watchdogs"), and he found this settler as learned a man as any French aristocrat, though his dwelling was crude and his furniture sparse (de Tocqueville spent the night sleeping on the floor of the man's cabin). That settler was apparently representative of the early men of Flint, many of them from New York State and New England. The Yankees were resourceful and well-educated farmers who brought with them small stakes of cash and worked hard to create a community of businesses, churches, and schools in the wilderness.

Henry Crapo's family had not been unanimously enthusiastic about his decision to move out to what they considered to be a wilderness frontier. Most of them would have preferred to remain in civilized New Bedford, Massachusetts, the old whaling port where Crapo was a leading businessman. Crapo had been New Bedford's elected town clerk, treasurer, and tax collector, he had invested in whaling ventures, and he was manager of an insurance company and owner of a nursery specializing in fruit and ornamental trees. He was already in his fifties when he became so heavily involved in Michigan forest land that he felt he had to move to Flint permanently.[1] Most of the family joined him there in 1858.

Crapo did well in Flint. He became one of the city's leading lumber barons, operating three mills and building the first

This photo of Governor Henry Howland Crapo and his family was taken about 1855. From left, front row, are Henrietta (Mrs. Ferris F. Hyatt); Rhoda (Mrs. James C. Willson); Wilhelmina (Mrs. Charles W. Clifford); Governor Crapo and his wife; Emma (Mrs. Harrow Page Cristy); Lucy (Mrs. Humphrey Howland Crapo Smith); and Lydia, who died unmarried in 1861. Back row, from left, are Mary (Mrs. John Orrell); William Wallace Crapo; Rebecca (Mrs. William Clark Durant, mother of William Crapo Durant); and Sarah (Mrs. Alphonso Ross).

railroad into the city. By 1860 he was mayor, and from there he advanced quickly to state senator. In 1864 he became the Republican nominee for governor and won the election. He was reelected in 1866. Crapo's business and political leadership qualities were enormous. A century after his death in 1869, Henry Crapo was still regarded by local historians as one of Flint's most important historical figures.

Crapo's family included nine daughters and one son, but by 1858 some of the children were married and so did not follow the rest of the family to the Michigan frontier. One Crapo daughter, Rebecca, had married a William Clark Durant in New Bedford November 29, 1855 (Thanksgiving Day), and lived in Boston with her husband. Durant was an elected clerk with the National Webster Bank of Boston. They had two children. A daughter, also named Rebecca, but nicknamed Rosa, was born in Boston November 24, 1857. A son, William Crapo Durant, was born at the family home, 40 Springfield, in Boston's Dorchester District December 8, 1861.

Although Henry Crapo spent most of his time during the 1860s in Flint and in the governor's office in Lansing, and Billy Durant and his parents lived in Boston, the boy did on occasion visit his illustrious grandfather. As early as June, 1863, when Billy was sixteen months old, he and his sister stayed with the Crapos in Flint while their parents visited Chicago.[2]

Crapo was interested in the boy. As a present for Billy's third birthday he signed a certificate naming the child a major in the 57th Regiment of the Michigan Cavalry Volunteers—official-looking, but fake. He "promoted" Billy to colonel when he was seven. But the old man's affection is especially evident in several letters to the boy. From his sickbed on April 11, 1869, he wrote:

> My dear little grandson, 'Willie' C. Durant,
>   Grandpa has received both of his very good letters and is very proud of them as he is of his noble boy. . . . Grandpa has not been outdoors in about seven months and has not "set up" more than 6 or 8 times—a few hours at a time—in all that period. . . . I am very glad indeed that you like your Michigan sled and wagon, and hope you will have a great deal of pleasure playing with them. . . .[3]

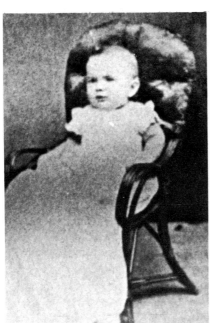

William Crapo Durant, 1862, and (right) at about age three. Someone, perhaps his mother or father, wrote on the back of the photo, 'L'Enfant terrible.'

The Governor was much concerned, however, that his son-in-law, Billy's father, was neither a good husband nor a good father. In letters to his son, William Wallace Crapo, the governor criticized William Clark Durant sharply and at length, complaining that the man was "imbued with a mania for stock speculation," that he drank heavily and argued with Rebecca in front of the family on visits to the Crapos, and that he had a penchant for "reckless ventures" and "wild speculations." Crapo lectured Durant sternly, and Durant was penitent under the gaze of the fiery old governor. But Crapo took steps anyway to change his will so that the money he left to Rebecca could not be controlled by her husband. In one letter the Governor lamented:

Soon he will be an old man with a son to be provided for and settle with some kind of business, and this last is not anything that can be done by simply saying, "Willie go here" or "Willie go there." The habits of the boy are to be formed, both by parental training and parental example, in order to give him proper notions of business, and that ...must be done if done at all when the boy is a boy; otherwise he will have neither taste nor desire for any fixed business when he commences as a young man, nor will he settle down to anything.

When Crapo died on July 23, 1869, the Durants came as a family from Boston for the funeral. Billy was seven. But soon Rebecca and her husband parted, and in 1872 she arrived in Flint with her two children to settle permanently.

These family strains help explain the deep love that developed between mother and son. Rebecca concentrated her attentions on her children, and Billy—"My Willie," as she called him—seems to have been the favorite. To the end of her life, at age ninety in 1924, she and her son remained very close. In later years Durant traveled hundreds of miles by train to be with her for a few hours at the summer home, "Barney's Joy," he had built for her at Pentwater, Michigan. And she stayed in an apartment in New York when he was living there, so they could lunch together often. When she died he insisted that her house in Flint be maintained exactly as she had left it. And it was, until the house was razed in 1928.

Years later a business associate said of Durant: "One characteristic which will outweigh Billy's sincerity, kindliness and faith in his fellow man is his love for his mother. Of the dozens with whom I have spoken concerning him, most have singled out that particular trait as the most indicative of the man."[4] Durant himself explained: "She always thought I was a wonderful boy. And I have tried not to disappoint her."[5]

By moving to Flint Rebecca was assured of building a strong family life for her children, even though William Clark Durant was no longer around. The Crapo family abounded in strong personalities. There was first of all the great paternal figure of Governor Crapo, whose influence was reflected in his daughters and son. And William Wallace Crapo, Billy's uncle, was not only

75-7579

an important businessman who spent some time in Flint, but later a long-term congressman from the family's home state of Massachusetts.

Among his aunts and uncles were a number of other prominent citizens. Of these, Dr. James C. Willson, husband of Rhoda Crapo, was apparently an influential father figure when Durant was in his teens. Dr. Willson was a widely respected general practitioner, and he became general manager of the state school for the deaf (located in Flint) and chairman of the board of Flint's major hospital (Hurley). He was a civic leader and philanthropist, a man of strong character and simple religious faith, a man who could take a fatherless boy in hand.[6] Rebecca and her children lived with the Willsons for three years after their move to Flint.

After the death of Mrs. Henry Crapo in February, 1875, and the distribution of the estate—estimated originally at between $500,000 and $1 million—Rebecca was able to purchase a large home across the street from the new high school but still just around the corner from the Willsons. The home became a showplace. It had hand-carved furniture with velvet cushions, curtains of Brussels lace, and crystal chandeliers from New Bedford. It was also one of the first homes in Flint equipped with electric lights.

As for Billy's father, he drifted in and out of Flint on occasion and as late as October, 1877, when Billy was sixteen, was still writing letters to William Wallace Crapo on the stationery of a Detroit lumber wholesaler and of the Detroit YMCA. He wanted W. W. Crapo's help in purchasing land in Michigan's Upper Peninsula.[7] After that, he dropped from sight. Catherine Durant, W. C. Durant's widow, said that as a young man Billy once went to New York and hired detectives in a futile attempt to find his father. Whether the family actually learned of his death in 1883 or not, Rebecca was listed as his widow in the Flint City Directory by 1886.

Billy's boyhood is recorded in bits and pieces, since he did not talk of it often. He attended Professor VanDerVelpen's class at the Flint Conservatory of Music, apparently playing cornet in one production. He was a drum major in a local marching band. He played some sandlot baseball, though he was not much of an

The house at Church and W. Second streets in Flint which Rebecca made home for her children, William and Rosa. It was razed in 1928.

Rebecca Durant made her Flint home a showpiece. The chandeliers were shipped from her original home town of New Bedford, Massachusetts.

athlete. When he was sixteen, he was elected manager of the Flint Athletics, the second amateur baseball team organized in Flint. The manager, pitcher, and catcher were elected by popular vote of their teammates. In their first recorded game, the Athletics were whipped by the Brown Sox 25-0.

He attended Flint High School, where he did reasonably well in such courses as algebra, geography, Latin, French, physiology, and rhetoric.[8] One of his earliest known signatures is in a classmate's autograph book: "There is a happy time, not far away (examinations), Yours truly, W. C. Durant, June 17, 1878."[9] At one point the family thought he might become a lawyer or a preacher (his family was Presbyterian). But just after his seventeenth birthday, a half-year short of graduation, Durant suddenly dropped out of school. His last grades are dated January 31, 1879. He came home, announced to his

Rare undated photo of Durant, probably as a teenager.

mother that he was not going back, and said he was going to start to work.

The most likely place of employment was the Crapo Lumber Company in Flint, founded by his grandfather in connection with his many lumber interests and operated at the time by William Wallace Crapo. A job was arranged, and Billy laid out his best clothes for his first day. After all, the grandson of Henry Crapo should look the part when he set out in the business world. A rude awakening awaited him at the office. Instead of getting a desk or selling job, he was sent out into the lumberyard. The foreman hesitated only a moment when he learned the young man's name. Then he ordered him to take off his coat and start piling lumber. His wages were the average for new unskilled help—seventy-five cents a day.[10] At night he clerked in a downtown drug store whose owner made and sold patent medicine. Durant became so interested in the idea of selling the medicine that he soon gave up both the mill and clerk job and traveled the surrounding country selling the panacea to the farmers.

He was starting out in the business world at a time of difficult readjustment in Flint. The prosperous lumbering era, which had brought Henry Howland Crapo from the East and had boomed the city from 2,000 to 8,000 inhabitants in thirty years, was over, the great pine forests now depleted.[11] Flint in the 1880s was merely holding its own.

The city's great lumbering families remained, however. This was partly because of their vast land holdings, partly because Flint had developed into a pleasant place to live. It was considered an attractive little city with its large homes, wide, tree-lined streets, fine schools and churches, and interesting collections of books and art. So the lumbering families stayed, and looked for new outlets for their fortunes. Lumber money financed the transition from harvesting raw materials to engaging in manufacturing. Woolen and cotton mills, furniture and farm implement factories, and a variety of other enterprises were started. Some were successful, some were not.

Begole, Fox & Company, which had operated one of the largest lumber mills, searched about for a new use for its idle buildings and chose wagon-making. The company became known as the Flint Wagon Works in 1882, joining William A. Paterson's carriage company and W. F. Stewart's carriage body-making enterprise in the growing vehicle industry.

Another enterprise boosting the local economy was the manufacture of cigars. Durant got into the selling end of the cigar business while still a young fellow living with his mother (he was listed as a laborer in the city directory). The idea of selling cigars on the road did not appeal to Rebecca, but the cigar man offered to pay four dollars a day, plus traveling expenses of two dollars a day, and so Durant took some samples and started out. Ignoring his employer's order to stop at all the towns between Flint and Port Huron, Durant took the train directly to Port Huron, went to see everyone in the town who sold cigars, and explained that it would be to their advantage to buy them directly from the manufacturer, who was headquartered only fifty miles away in Flint.

When Durant got back to Flint, his employer was waiting. How much were his expenses? Eight dollars and fifteen cents a day, Durant replied. The man threw up his hands in despair. How could he make any money if his salesmen were spending that much for traveling, he scolded. Durant replied that in the two days he was gone he had gotten orders for 22,000 cigars!

As the cigar business expanded, so did Durant's responsibilities. Soon he had replaced three salesmen.[*] "They finally gave me a salary of $100 a month—$1,200 a year and I had been working in a lumber yard at seventy-five cents a day," he said. "But the cigar business expanded too much and lost money." [12]

About this time Durant began working as secretary for Flint's privately operated waterworks. Part of the job was to collect overdue bills. Water service was so poor that many customers were simply refusing to pay.

Durant soon became a familiar figure to Flint residents. He went to every house, interviewed wives as well as husbands, wrote down their complaints, and tried to solve them. After about eight months of intense work, he had the waterworks back on its feet.

[*]Durant is credited in E. O. Wood's *History of Genesee County, Michigan*, with completely reorganizing the cigar firm, the George T. Warren Company, and building it into one of the largest concerns of its type in the state.

But this was only a part-time job. Although the record of his work with the utilities is not entirely clear, he was apparently an officer with both the city's privately owned gas works and electric light company. He was credited with bringing together a number of fire insurance agencies, in partnership with I. Wixom Whitehead, and within two years building one of the largest agencies in central Michigan. Already he was finding success through consolidation. Whitehead handled most of the inside work, Durant most of the selling. Durant branched out into real estate, and then construction. In 1884 he was also listed as one of three proprietors of the Casino roller skating rink in Flint. [13]

In 1885 he bought from a relative a rambling, two-story frame house at Garland and Fourth streets in Flint. There, on June 17, at the age of twenty-three, he married Clara Miller Pitt, one of two daughters of Ralph S. Pitt, ticket agent at the Flint and Pere Marquette railroad station. Clara, with her bobbed, softly curled hair and large, beautiful eyes, was an attractive young woman. A large number of friends and relatives attended the wedding, and the gifts—including an upright piano from Clara's father—filled an entire room. William and Clara ducked a fusillade of "rice and old shoes" thrown by the guests, the society columns reported, as they ran from the door to a carriage decorated for good luck. They took the evening train to Detroit, from there heading east for the honeymoon.

The Durants settled in the house on Garland to raise their family. Their first child, Margery, named after Clara's mother, was born in 1887; their second, and last, Russell Clifford (Cliff), in 1890.

Durant was working for the insurance company and also for the utilities in 1886 when his trip to read a meter was interrupted by the encounter with Johnny Alger and his road cart—an evening that led to his visit to Coldwater and to the start of a fabulous career.

Durant and Dallas Dort were able to survive in their first few months in the road cart business only because William A. Paterson agreed to supply their new company with its initial production of carts. Paterson had not easily reached his position as the best carriage maker in the region. A native of Canada, he

William Crapo Durant as a young entrepreneur, probably about the time he started with the Flint Road Cart Company.

Durant's first wife, Clara (Pitt) Durant, and their children, Margery and Russell Clifford.

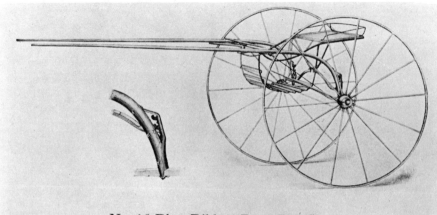

No. 15 Blue Ribbon Drop Bar Cart

GAR—Axle, straight taper, 1 inch, coached. Springs, half elliptic, 39 inches long, hung over axle attached to three hook adjustable hangers on shafts. Wrought seat arms.
SHAFTS—Selected hickory, 24 inches apart at tips, 41 inches apart at cross bar, 77 inches long from tip to cross bar.

SEAT—27 inches front, 24 inches rear, 14 inches deep.
WHEELS—Sarven, 1 x 48 inches high only. Steel Full bolted.
PAINTING—Rubine red or Brewster green.

Blue Ribbon Drop Bar Cart, similar to first road cart.

had been raised by a stern uncle, learned the carriage trade in Guelph, Ontario, and become associated with craftsmen while working on Concord wagons and Wells-Fargo stagecoaches in New England. He tried out his trade in Pontiac, Michigan, and then moved north to Flint in 1869, the year of Henry Crapo's death. Paterson did hard manual work to get his nest egg, later set up a blacksmith shop, and by the 1880s was operating the biggest carriage business in a city that had produced some wagons as early as the mid 1830s.

With the big orders from Durant and Dort, Paterson borrowed money and expanded his business. Soon he decided to produce his own model of road cart, and so did the Flint Wagon Works on the city's west side. The Flint Road Cart Company was going to have to build its own. Durant and Dort bought parts from local shops and hired assemblers. Business boomed. In its first full year of operation, the Flint Road Cart Company turned out 4,000 carts.

Next Durant looked around and saw that lightweight four-wheel buggies were popular, but that no large company was producing a substantial, good-looking one at a reasonable price. Durant was upset that Paterson had jumped into the road cart business but, as he pointed out, time and success are a great healer, and so he went back to Paterson, who still had the best factory and organization in Flint. Durant made a contract with Paterson for an initial order of 200 buggies—double Paterson's annual production. "I had an advantage in the deal because I knew Mr. Paterson needed money," Durant wrote. "He was considerably in debt to the Genesee County Savings Bank (in which our people were interested), having become over-extended in the erection of a fine hotel and a large office building, and a cash deal looked good to him."

Durant lined up a big contract for the buggies in Chicago, only to find that Paterson chanced upon the same buyer and told him that since the product was made in his factory, the buyer could save money by buying direct from him. That did it. Durant and Dort decided that from then on, they would build all their own vehicles. They leased half of an idle Flint cotton mill—it was new, but had never operated—and in ten days were building practically the same buggy they had been buying from Paterson.[14] They leased the rest of the cotton mill, then bought it outright, and finally enlarged it—all in two years. Soon they were taking over other empty buildings around town, one a former farm implement factory, another an old table-building plant. The Flint Road Cart Company was in the buggy business and on its way.

In 1889 Fred A. Aldrich, a printer-editor, accepted Durant's offer to join the business for twelve dollars a week. Aldrich became the company's secretary and remained a life-long friend of Durant. Dort held the title of president. As for Durant, he was, as Dort said, "the firm's leading force and genius," but he wanted to avoid a president's title and duties, a trait which would show up many times in his career. "Elect me janitor or office boy," he would say when offered a presidency. Instead, Durant was treasurer. He was becoming very interested in the manipulation of money.

In 1890 Durant noticed the industriousness of a young man and hired him as a laborer in the road cart plant. There are at least two stories about Durant's "discovery" of Charles W.

Nash. One is that Nash was first noticed while cutting grass at the home of Durant's mother. Another is that Nash was working in the W. C. Pierce hardware in Flint. Durant may have cleared it up on January 29, 1942, when he wrote to Nash: "I remember so well meeting you in the hardware store, at which time I was very much interested in you. . . . I suggested that you come over to the factory and you promptly accepted."

Nash started out in the blacksmith shop and then stuffed cushions for buggy seats. He was paid according to how many cushions he stuffed, and he worked so hard and fast that other laborers began to grumble. He was making them look bad. "I need the money," he explained, and no one knew the value of money and the ethic of hard work better than Nash. At the age of seven, he had been "bound out" by his father to a farmer near Flint, where he was supposed to work for room and board until he reached adulthood. But at twelve he ran away from the farm, hired out as a laborer on other farms in the area, and worked in the hardware store in Flint.

After he started work at the factory, he continued to seek any odd job that would pay a few cents. One day he was asked if he would like to make some extra money by picking plums at Dort's home. He would, and handled that chore so well that Dort was as attracted to him as Durant had been earlier. Soon Dort was giving Nash more responsibilities and their relationship became as close as father and son.[15]

The company which Durant had put together almost casually with local young men was developing into a rich blend of managerial talents. Dallas Dort was an excellent administrator—conservative, practical, civic-minded, personable. Aldrich was meticulous and hard-working in handling the office details, a diplomat who could smooth over the occasional quarrels between Dort and Durant. Nash, starting at the bottom but moving up quickly into positions of authority, was a fount of common sense in working out manufacturing problems, a developing leader of men, a man who had known nothing except poverty and work from childhood and so carried into the factory an instinct for saving money and working hard.

As for Durant, he was ever the optimist, visionary, promoter, supersalesman. Billy Durant could arrive in a strange town, find the best salesmen, and hire them away from whatever they were doing. He could sell a customer a cart, a salesman a career, or a company a sales territory. Within a few years he had developed a sales organization of national proportions. Perhaps it was this talent, more than any other, which made Durant a dynamic force in the vehicle industry for more than forty years.

Durant had a theory about salesmanship: "Assume that the man you are talking to knows as much or more than you do. Do not talk too much. Give the customer time to think. In other words, let the customer sell himself." That system works best, of course, when you have a good product. Durant did have it in the low-priced road cart with the wonderful suspension. "Look for a self-seller," Durant would say. "If you cannot find one, make one."[16]

On September 9, 1893, the Flint Road Cart Company was incorporated with $150,000 capitalization. The original $2,000 in borrowed capital had been multiplied seventy-five times in less than seven years—mostly out of profits. The name was changed to the Durant-Dort Carriage Company on November 6, 1895.*

During the 1890s, the Durant-Dort Carriage Company grew rapidly, and Durant became interested in a number of side ventures. In 1892 he became treasurer of a company which manufactured a revolving hat display case. Durant and Dort also became interested in a bicycle company and persuaded local investors to back it. When the company failed, as the bicycle fad diminished, the investors lost their money. Durant decided, however, they should be repaid out of the Durant-Dort coffers. After all, he reasoned, the company's officials had urged the men to invest, and therefore Durant-Dort was responsible. On several other occasions, Durant again protected investors. The impact locally was significant. Durant was becoming a million-

*Flint may have come close to losing the business in 1891. The headline in *The Genesee Democrat* on June 30 said, FLINT ROAD CART WORKS TO GO TO SAGINAW, and the story quoted the unnamed proprietor as follows: "We regret to leave Flint but the inducements offered us in the way of . . . improved facilities were such that from a business standpoint we couldn't afford to disregard them." Perhaps it was only an effort to get more inducements out of Flint. Fortunately for the future of that city, however, the move did not take place.

aire, but he was also establishing a reputation for being loyal to those who followed his advice. It was soon evident that the best investment in Flint was a business backed by Durant. You might get rich. On the other hand if the investment was lost, Durant would make good.[17]

Durant and Dort expanded in the 1890s with four subsidiaries: Webster Vehicle in 1892, Victoria Vehicle in 1894, Diamond Buggy in 1896—all of these in Flint—and Imperial Wheel in Jackson, Michigan, in 1898.

Diamond Buggy offers an example of how Durant operated. During the Christmas holidays of 1895, he got the idea that Durant-Dort should develop a new line of sensationally cheap vehicles that would be sold for cash, not on credit. Immediately

Some of these officials of the Durant-Dort Carriage Company in Flint became automotive pioneers. From left, front row, are W. C. Durant, A. B. C. Hardy, W. C. Orrell and Fred A. Aldrich. Back row, from left, are James A. Slocum, Charles D. Wesson and Charles Webster. In the center is J. Dallas Dort.

he called Dort, who was not enthusiastic. Durant wore him down in a two-hour telephone conversation. Then, having won his point, he called A. B. C. (Alexander Brownell Cullen) Hardy, manager of the Wolverine Road Cart Company of Davison, near Flint, just as Hardy was sitting down to a turkey dinner on New Year's Day, 1896. The turkey got cold as Hardy went immediately to Flint for a conference. Hardy was hired within a week as manager of the new Diamond Buggy subsidiary.[18] And with Durant and Hardy plunging into production and sales, Diamond Buggy cleared 150 percent profit in five months.

The carriage business was highly competitive. The Durant-Dort Carriage Company, seeking to increase the quality and reduce the price of its products, decided to try to control its own parts and supplies. Durant explained:

"We started out as assemblers with no advantage over our competitors. We paid about the same prices for everything we purchased. We realized that we were making no progress and would not unless and until we manufactured practically every important part that we used.

"We made a study of the methods employed by the concerns supplying us, the savings that could be effected by operating the plants at capacity without interruption, and with practically no selling or advertising expense. Having satisfied ourselves that we had solved our problem, we proceeded to purchase plants and the control of plants, which made it possible for us to build up, from the standpoint of volume, the largest carriage company in the United States."

A particularly urgent problem was the creation of trusts in the carriage supply companies. One day a supplier in Cleveland tipped off Hardy to the trust plans, urging him to place a large order at once because a trust was about to take over his business and only orders placed before the takeover would be handled at the current price. Durant-Dort officials also learned that trusts were trying to corner the wheel industry and the spring and axle and linseed oil industries (the last important for paints and varnishes) with the purpose of gaining a monopoly.

Durant took on the trusts as a challenge. Immediately he went to West Virginia to buy axle-making machinery and arranged to have an axle plant set up in Flint. He placed many

Rare photo of the Durant-Dort officers in their Flint office, a building still standing. The photo was probably taken in about 1898. From left are J. Dallas Dort, W. C. Durant, sales manager Charles Bonbright, an unidentified secretary, and Fred A. Aldrich.

thousands of dollars worth of orders with other suppliers at prices so low that the trusts later tried to cancel them with all sorts of inducements—unsuccessfully. Durant-Dort established the Flint Axle Works in 1900 and the Flint Varnish Works in 1901. Dort, who in 1898 left the company and went to Arizona for two years because of his wife's health, helped out by purchasing large tracts of timberland in several southern states to assure the business's wood supplies. All of these moves placed Durant-Dort in an enviable position to compete with any vehicle firm that had to pay trust prices for materials.

The grueling days and sleepless nights of the trust crisis suited Durant perfectly—he habitually worked late, getting by on four or five hours of sleep a night, and the challenge continually charged his system with new energy. But Hardy, taking over as president in Dort's absence, was burdened with all the details and was at the point of collapse. Once he went to an out-of-town hotel to relax, but Durant had him on the phone so often that he gave up the idea of a rest and went back to work. Finally, even Durant could see that his colleague was exhausted, and ordered him to go to Europe for a rest. Hardy attended the Paris Exposition and enjoyed the trip so thoroughly that upon finding the business pressures just as great when he returned, he told Durant that he was quitting. He resigned from the company and took his wife on a leisurely eleven-month tour of Europe in 1901.

While Hardy was in Europe, he began to study the advanced automobiles being turned out there. From his new position he could see what wasn't nearly so evident in Flint, isolated as it was from other cities by distance and bad roads. The automobile was definitely something to be reckoned with. The more he looked, the more convinced he became that the horseless carriage craze was more than a latter-day bicycle fad. In fact, he began to wonder if the automobile might not eventually mean the end of the carriage business.

Back in Flint, however, the carriage business continued to grow. Steel arches over downtown Saginaw Street carried the slogan, "The Vehicle City." Flint's Big Three carriage makers—Durant-Dort, the Flint Wagon Works, and W. A. Paterson—were producing more than 100,000 carriages, buggies, and carts annu-

Flint was proclaimed The Vehicle City long before the first automobiles appeared—the city produced more than 100,000 horse vehicles a year.

The Durant-Dort Carriage Company Factory 1 in Flint, 1905.

ally. Some cities may have been manufacturing more—Cincinnati, for example, claimed 160,000 units produced in 1900—but no one company was as large in terms of volume as Durant-Dort and its subsidiaries.

At the company's peak, Durant-Dort was not only an assembly company, but was making its own wheels, axles, paints, varnishes, and buggy tops and controlled its own sources of lumber. Besides its plants and subsidiaries in Flint, it had interests in Blount Carriage and Buggy, Atlanta, Georgia; Atlanta Wheel and Axle, East Point, Georgia; Dominion Carriage, Toronto, Canada; Pine Bluff Spoke, Pine Bluff, Arkansas; Hughes-Purcell Paint, Kansas City, Missouri; and hickory forests and mills in Tennessee and Arkansas. Estimates of production during this period range from 75,000 to 150,000 vehicles a year, but production figures for the carriage industry are difficult to pin down.

No. 605 Blue Ribbon Limousine Buggy

In Flint alone Durant-Dort manufactured 56,000 vehicles in 1906, the peak year, according to Nash. That year the company had a factory force of 1,000 and was building up to 480 vehicles a day. It also produced up to 200,000 sets of wheels, 75,000 sets of axles, and 60,000 gallons of varnish a year. The carriages were not built on assembly lines. Components were assembled on wheeled racks and wheeled from one work station to another, from one processing room to another. Paterson had innovated some mass-production techniques; Durant-Dort, with its greater volume, refined them and added new ones.

Besides its Famous Blue Ribbon line, Durant-Dort produced vehicles for farm implement companies and mail order houses. Among the names of its vehicles were the Eclipse, the Standard, the Victoria, the Moline, and the Diamond. There was a Poppy line for the California market. Variety seemed endless. Individual markets required individual treatment. In the East, customers liked somber colors, mostly black. In the West, the style was for gay color combinations with fancy pin-striping. Between twelve and eighteen coats of paint were required on each vehicle, a process that required weeks because of the slow-drying paints of the day.

At the turn of the century, the Durant-Dort Carriage Company was a humming machine with its combination of a great sales network, efficient assembly operation, and company-owned subsidiaries. And as Durant-Dort flourished, so did the other carriage companies. The Flint Wagon Works hit peak production of 35,000 vehicles a year. Paterson's production reached 23,000.

Meanwhile in Europe A. B. C. Hardy crawled under French automobiles to see how they were made. He flagged down motorists so he could study their cars in detail. And when he returned to Flint late in 1901, he went to the directors of the Durant-Dort Carriage Company with the warning. "Get out of the carriage business before the automobile ruins you."

Nobody listened.

Chapter Three

The Horseless Carriage Comes to Flint

By 1900 the horseless carriage had come to stay. Scores of organizations and individuals across the United States were building automobiles of some kind, and a few—notably the Olds Motor Works of Lansing and Detroit—were headed toward serious manufacturing.

W. C. Durant was not impressed. Automobiles, he said, were noisy, dangerous, smelly contraptions that disturbed tranquility and frightened horses. When his beautiful young daughter Margery ran to him in 1902 with the exciting news that she had just ridden in a Panhard, her father scolded her for taking a foolish risk.[1]

By this time Durant was apparently losing interest in the carriage business as well. To a man of Durant's temperament, the fact that the Durant-Dort Carriage Company was running smoothly and making great profits meant that it was becoming rather dull. Durant liked to create organizations. When they were going well, he would just as soon let someone else take over the details and look for a new challenge. Dallas Dort was again president of the company, following Hardy's departure, and Charlie Nash was running a taut factory operation.[2] In fifteen years Durant-Dort had grown from a $2,000 investment into what would soon be a $2 million concern. It was producing more vehicles than any other manufacturer in the country, if not the world.

Durant was a millionaire at forty, and he was eager for new

adventures. He discovered New York City, and then the stock market. The intricacies of the market, the large amounts of money changing hands, the risky nature of that business, all appealed to his gambling instinct, his need for dramatic tension. He was spending so much time in New York that he began to feel guilty about neglecting the carriage business, and considered retiring from it. In 1901 he asked to be dropped from the Durant-Dort salary list. But on September 14 the directors refused the request by unanimous vote, possibly the first time the company had ever overruled a request by its founding genius. So Durant continued to attend at least a few board meetings in Flint each year and even used his lengthy New York visits to purchase Christmas gifts for the office staff.[3]

Durant's marriage may have had something to do with his spending more time in New York than in Flint in the early 1900s. His alienation from Clara had already begun, and their relationship continued to deteriorate with his long absences from home.[4] Durant's mother Rebecca tried to cheer her only son with long and affectionate letters. Two days before his forty-first birthday she wrote: "How quickly the years do pass. Are you alone, with not one of us to help you celebrate your birthday? I hope it's bright with sunshine for this one day—for New York has so little of heaven's own light. . . ."[5]

Six months later, in May of 1903, Durant's sister, Mrs. Rosa Willett, died in New York, and Rebecca's letter to Durant reflects both her deep sorrow and her warmth.

> My Dear Dear Boy,
> Could I take your hand in mine—feel your loving touch, your helpfulness—and sympathy—it would express more than I can write for even today my heart is full—my eyes overflowing with tears. But I must tell you myself what a comfort your letter has been. Those last sad duties are always hard—but with your brother love—and deep pity for the unfortunate sister—and the mother far away—yet to know the closing chapter of the life story—so sad—of her child—once young and happy—cared for loved—now laid at rest. . . .

About this time Durant might well have cut his ties completely with Flint, except to visit his mother and his children.

Although Judge Charles Wisner is generally considered to be the builder of Flint's first automobile, Dr. H. H. Bardwell's horseless carriage shown here, assembled in 1901 or early 1902, apparently got more exposure on the city's streets. Wisner, Bardwell, Hardy, and James Whiting were interested in automobiles for several years before fellow Flint citizen W. C. Durant caught the automobile "bug."

But the citizens of Flint were beginning to get involved in situations that would have a dramatic effect on his career. In late 1900 a Flint judge by the name of Charles H. Wisner, working in a carriage house behind his home, built the first automobile made in Flint. It was a noisy one-cylinder vehicle that was down for repairs much of the time. H. H. Bardwell built Flint's second car in 1901, and it got more exposure on the streets of Flint.

By 1902 Judge Wisner felt that his car was in good running order, and he asked Durant if he would be interested in it as a manufacturing possibility. Durant was not very interested, but the judge was a friend. So one Sunday when Durant was in Flint, he and Wisner started out at 5 a.m. and drove the car

A. B. C. Hardy's Flint Roadster, of which fifty-two were manufactured in 1902-03. It was the first automobile manufactured in Flint and one still exists, on display at the Sloan Museum, Flint.

around the city all morning. Eventually they stalled at a raised crosswalk at Church and Court streets, where any moment crowds would be assembling to attend the nearby churches. The very thought of all their friends finding the judge and the carriage king stuck in an automobile at the center of town struck them as so funny that they laughed until they had to sit down on the curb. So much for the Wisner car—though they did finally manage to push it over the crosswalk and drive on.

But by this time there were also a few other horseless carriages on the streets of Flint. Even William A. Paterson owned an electric. And Arthur Jerome Eddy of Chicago, a multi-talented fellow who had grown up in Flint and who was acquainted with Durant, was popularizing the automobile by driving between Flint and Chicago and making even longer trips. In 1902 he published a book called *Two Thousand Miles on an Automobile,* and in it commented: "Any woman can drive an electric automobile, any man can drive a steam; but neither man or woman can drive a gasoline; it follows its own odorous will and goes or goes not as it feels disposed."

A. B. C. Hardy, back from Europe and excited about what he had learned of the automobile, was so convinced he was right about its future—and the local carriage makers wrong—that he decided to manufacture a car himself. Local bankers shied away, so Hardy used mostly his own money to set up the Flint Automobile Company late in 1901 (it was capitalized at $5,000), starting in a building on N. Saginaw Street that in the 1850s had housed Flint's first true vehicle factory, the wagon shop of Abner and Frank Randall. Soon afterward he moved into an old harness factory next to the Flint Specialty Company, which was turning out the world's largest production of whip sockets for the carriage industry—up to one million a year. Hardy aimed at the low-price market, perhaps influenced by the success of Durant and Dort in the road cart and carriage business. By late 1902 he was building Flint Roadsters priced from $750 to $850, flashy little cars that sparkled with red paint, red leather, and polished brass.

Hardy bought bodies from the W. F. Stewart Company in Flint—the old carriage supplier was branching into automobiles for the first time—and axles from Charles Stewart Mott's Weston-Mott Company in Utica, New York. He built his own one-cylinder, eight-and-a-half horsepower engines. By late 1903 he had produced fifty-two cars. Suddenly, however, he was confronted by the Association of Licensed Automobile Manufacturers, a group of automobile producers licensed under the 1895 patent of George B. Selden. The Selden interests used his patent for a motorcar to collect royalties from early automakers. Members of the Association agreed to pay the royalties; and the Association retained the right to license new manufacturers. A share of the royalties was returned to the Association.

The Association demanded a fifty-dollar royalty for each of the fifty-two cars Hardy had sold. Hardy thought about it, then gave up. Facing fifty-two federal court injunctions, one for each car sold, he went out of business and left Flint in a fury. He headed west, to Waterloo, Iowa, where he got a job as general manager of a carriage company. He remained there until 1909, when he was summoned back to Flint by his old boss, W. C. Durant. Henry Ford eventually fought the Selden patent interests, and in 1911, after years of litigation, beat them, the court deciding that the patent did not apply to most American automobiles. But that was far too late to save Hardy and his gaily painted little Flint Roadster.

While Hardy was building cars, a man named James H. Whiting was watching. He would visit Hardy at his factory, talk with him, look around, perhaps dream a little. A lot of men dreamed about building cars, but Whiting was not like the rest of them. He was quiet, conservative, older than most of his contemporaries in the Flint carriage industry, a solid, wealthy citizen, and manager of the Flint Wagon Works.

Whiting had once operated the Whiting & Richardson Hardware Store in downtown Flint, where Dallas Dort was working under new management when he talked with Durant on that eventful night in 1886. Whiting had left to manage the transformation of the old Begole, Fox & Company lumber business into the Flint Wagon Works in 1882. Despite his conservative outlook on business in general, Whiting was only a step behind

*James H. Whiting. He moved Buick from Detroit to Flint in 1903, turned
it over to Durant in 1904.*

Hardy in his interest in automobiles. Often when he went to
carriage shows in New York and Chicago he would slip over to
the automobile shows and spend much of his time looking at
cars and talking with manufacturers. Just as he had seen the
need to get out of lumbering and into vehicle manufacturing in
1882, he was in 1903 beginning to think of a shift from
horse-drawn wagons to horseless carriages. Flint depended on
carriages for its economic life. If the automobile was coming,
then Flint, and particularly the Flint Wagon Works, had better
get involved. Men in other communities around the country
were being swept up by the automobile craze—by 1902 hundreds of companies, most of them tiny, were producing some
kind of car. The fact that Whiting knew nothing about automobiles did not deter him in the slightest. He had money and a
vehicle factory—a good engine man might be all he would need
to make the transition.

So in 1902 and 1903 Hardy was building automobiles, Whiting was thinking a great deal about them—and W. C. Durant was

55

spending a lot of his time in New York City playing with the stock market.

The market was not a full-time avocation; Durant was also working on his latest business idea. In 1902 he tried to pull off a consolidation of some of the country's major carriage concerns. He discussed his plans with Whiting and Paterson and with major promoters in New York. He considered more than fifty possible consolidation formulas. Consolidations had worked well within the Durant-Dort framework; they could save even more money, he argued, on a national basis. Many of these multi-million-dollar schemes were casually sketched out on napkins, envelopes, and tablecloths, and so no record of them survives.[6] Durant's big plans came to nothing, however. It turned out that the carriage men were individualistic souls who wanted to run their own businesses. Consolidation might have meant more money, but it also meant losing at least some control, and they would have none of that.

In Flint, James Whiting's position as a man of means who was interested in automobiles was widely known by 1903. Perhaps it was inevitable that one of the hard-pressed automobile companies would eventually come to see him. The first men who did were Benjamin Briscoe, Jr., and his brother Frank of Detroit, who wanted to unload a company in which they had an interest. Its founder had built approximately two automobiles in three years of trying. The name of the firm was the Buick Motor Company.

The story of Buick to this point was one of a small group of talented inventors who developed superior engines, but who in the process spent more money than they ever made. They were doing basic research instead of producing for the market, and they were backed by men who could not afford that kind of luxury. The leader of this group was David Dunbar Buick, born in Scotland forty-nine years earlier, brought to the United States at the age of two, a man who had already distinguished himself in the plumbing-fixture business. He had patented a method of affixing porcelain to cast iron, a secret until then guarded by a German cartel, and the invention helped make possible the development of modern bathtubs and other bathroom and kitchen fixtures. Buick and William Sherwood, his partner in the Detroit plumbing-fixtures business, might have become wealthy by taking larger advantage of this breakthrough. Instead Buick got bored with plumbing, began tinkering with gasoline engines, and progressed from building marine engines to automobile engines under a succession of companies—the Buick Auto-Vim and Power Company, the Buick Manufacturing Company, and the Buick Motor Company.[7]

By April, 1901, David Buick had built, or at least partially built, the first Buick automobile, which he offered to sell to Walter L. Marr for $300. Whether Marr bought it or not is unknown, but in this period Buick, Marr, and Eugene C. Richard, an excellent engineer, developed the soon-to-be-fa-

Rare portrait of David Dunbar Buick.

William A. Paterson, who operated Flint's finest carriage company in the 1880s and built the first road carts for Durant and Dort.

mous "valve-in-head" engine. The valve-in-head engine, unlike the L-head engine in general use at the time, was built with the valves directly over the pistons. This resulted in a more compact combustion chamber and a faster fuel-burn rate—in general a more efficient machine. The Buick engine was thus more power-ful for its size than any other, and eventually the entire industry made use of its principle. The little engine was certainly an important factor in the eventual success of the Buick auto-mobile. It was patented in Richard's name, and he is credited with its initial development. But Marr, a brilliant engineer who built many kinds of engines and several of his own cars, became identified as the chief figure in its later development.

Despite the engine breakthrough, David Buick was having problems. He and Marr quarreled, and Marr left to work on some of the first Oldsmobiles and then to build his own Marr Autocar. Buick got into debt to the Briscoe Brothers, successful Detroit sheet metal manufacturers who made garbage cans and also parts for some of the new automotive companies. Unable to pay his debts and seeking more credit from the Briscoes, Buick agreed to their demand that his company be reorganized. The Buick Motor Company was incorporated May 19, 1903, and the Briscoes were to get $99,700 and David Buick only $300 worth of its capital stock of $100,000. Under this curious contract David Buick had the option of purchasing the Buick stock merely by paying back what he owed the Briscoes—the sum of $3,500. But if this were not done by September, when Ben Briscoe was scheduled to return from a trip to Europe, the Briscoes would take over the business management.

Ben Briscoe wanted desperately to get into automobile manufacturing, but by this time he was fed up with the endless, high-priced tinkering of the Buick group. All he wanted was to get his money back or, failing that, to take over the Buick plant and use it to team up with Jonathan D. Maxwell in an automobile venture. In early July, 1903, the two decided to form another company, the Maxwell-Briscoe Company, to manufacture the Maxwell car. Now Briscoe wanted nothing more than to unload the Buick and get his $3,500 back before his self-imposed September deadline.

There is more than one account of what happened next. Briscoe's version is that a salesman mentioned that the Flint Wagon Works was interested in building automobiles. The story in Flint is that Frank Briscoe learned of Whiting's interest from Dwight T. Stone, a young Flint real estate agent who had married a cousin of the Briscoes. Either way, in the middle of the summer of 1903, Ben Briscoe conferred with James Whiting and the other Wagon Works directors: Charles M. Begole (son of a former Michigan governor, Josiah Begole), George L. Walker, William S. Ballenger, and Charles A. Cumings. Briscoe's story is that the Wagon Works bought the Buick Company that very day, though the details required several months of negotiations. Briscoe, assured now that Buick's debt to him would be paid, turned over the details to David Buick, and went off to Europe to study how to build better radiators.

While he was gone, Whiting and the directors of the Wagon Works continued to investigate the Buick prospect. More people were losing than profiting in motor cars in 1903, but Flint had everything at stake in vehicles. The penalty for ignoring the automobile could be a company and a city-wide disaster. Besides, Whiting had been bitten by the automobile bug. The romance and excitement of the idea of building cars overrode his basically conservative nature. Also, Buick could build stationary farm engines at first while automobile manufacture was studied. In early September, just before the Briscoe deadline, an agreement was reached: The Flint Wagon Works would buy the Buick Motor Company and move it to Flint. Reportedly the deal was clinched for $10,000, which the Wagon Works directors borrowed on a one-year note from a local bank.

Two major news events in Flint were reported on Page One of *The Flint Journal* on September 11, 1903. One was that the annual convention of the Michigan Master Horse Shoers had come to a close after proposing the establishment of a state college of horse shoeing. The other was that the Buick Motor Company was moving from Detroit to Flint and that ground had been broken that morning for a new plant near the Wagon Works at the west end of Kearsley Street. The newspaper noted that Buick was "a splendid new manufacturing industry" with paid-in capital stock of $50,000. It would employ at the outset a hundred skilled mechanics and machinists and would manufacture stationary and marine engines, automobile engines, transmissions, carburetors, and "sparking plugs." The reporter also noted that there had been rumors for several weeks that the Flint Wagon Works was considering the idea of building automobiles,

> and when Secretary Whiting was asked this morning by The Journal if the organization of the new concern was the first move in this direction, he smiled pleasantly and suggested that for the present the engines and accessories would be built by the new factory and that the broader opportunity was one for further consideration.

Two days after the Buick announcement, *The Journal* expressed in an editorial the hope that Buick would be a producer of automobiles as well as of engines:

> Flint is the most natural center for the manufacture of autos in the whole country. It is the vehicle city of the United States, and in order to maintain this name by

which it is known from ocean to ocean, there must be developed factories here for the manufacture of automobiles.

The automobile plant already in operation here [Hardy's Flint Automobile Company, which would go out of business five weeks later] is turning out a very superior machine and is building up a good reputation which can be drawn on as time proceeds.

By mid-December, 1903, the new one-story Buick factory, south of the Wagon Works, was operating with twenty-five employees. But only engines, not automobiles, were being made. Arthur C. Mason, who had been hired away from Cadillac in Detroit, was in charge of operations. Some Buick histories say that sixteen or more Buick automobiles were built in 1903, but none was produced in Flint that year, and it has never been clear how many were ever produced in Detroit before the move to Flint. Perhaps only one, certainly very few. In contrast, the Olds Motor Works in Lansing produced 4,000 cars in 1903, and Henry Ford, just getting started, built 1,708. Cadillac built 1,895, and more than a dozen makes were advertised in Detroit newspapers.

On January 19, 1904, the company was reorganized as the Buick Motor Company of Flint, with $75,000 capitalization instead of the $50,000 originally intended, and half of that sum, $37,500, was paid in. David Buick and his son Thomas were to get 1,500 shares between them—but only after dividends from the stock repaid all the debts they had accrued in Detroit before incorporation. Other large stockholders were Whiting, as president—1,504 shares; Charles M. Begole, vice-president—1,068; George L. Walker, director—725, and William S. Ballenger, treasurer—707. The officers at first were the same as in the Wagon Works, except that David Buick was secretary. Shortly after the move to Flint, another truce was reached between David Buick and Walter Marr, who was then persuaded to come to Flint, where he perfected the valve-in-head engine.

By the spring of 1904, the inevitable occurred. Buick and Marr pleaded with Whiting to let them build a car, instead of just engines. Whiting didn't need much persuading, and told them to go ahead if they could build one that really performed.

Downtown Flint in 1903, the year Buick moved to town.

The first two-cylinder engine was ready for installation on May 27. By early July the first Flint Buick was ready for a road test.

The car was basically a sturdy chassis with two uncomfortable seats and a two-cylinder, 12-horsepower valve-in-head engine. On Saturday, July 9, 1904, the car left the Buick plant with Walter Marr driving and Thomas Buick, David's son, along for company. They drove to Detroit and returned the next Tuesday, July 12. Details of the first test run were published on Page One of *The Flint Journal* the following day:

> Bespattered with flying real estate from every county they had touched, but with the knowledge that they had made a "record," Tom Buick and W. L. Marr of the Buick Motor Works, who left for Detroit on Saturday to give the first automobile turned out by that concern a trial on the road, returned to the city late yesterday afternoon. The test of the machine was eminently satisfactory and, in fact, exceeded expectations.
>
> In spite of the muddy condition of the roads the trip home was made in the remarkable time of 3 hours and 37 minutes, or at the rate of a trifle less than a mile in two minutes, on the basis of the distance traversed as figured by the gentleman in charge of the machine. Through a

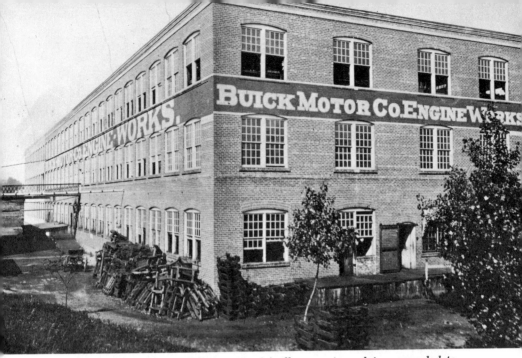

First Buick factory in Flint was originally one story, later expanded to three floors. The first phase was started in September, 1903, and in operation by December. The first Flint Buicks were produced in this plant near the Flint Wagon Works on the city's West Side. Early engines for Chevrolet, manufactured by Mason Motor Company, were also produced there.

mistake they failed to take the right turn when near Lapeer and it was necessary for them to make an extra 15 miles. This increased the total distance of the run to nearly 115 miles, as they passed through Pontiac, Orion, Oxford, Lapeer and Davison, not following the direct route.

"The machine made the run without a skip," said Mr. Marr today, "and reached here in the best of condition. We took hills handily with our high speed gear and the machine sounded like a locomotive. It simply climbed. In one place we raced with an electric car and showed them the way. We went so fast at another time that we could not see the village 'six-mile-an-hour' sign."

The machine used in making the trip is the $950 tonneau put out by the Buick company, and is equipped with a 12-horse power engine that can develop from 18 to 21 horse power on a pinch. It was provided with a "testing" body and was stripped of anything that would add unnecessary weight. Its long rakish looking body, covered with mud, gave it the appearance of a speeder and attracted much attention along the route of the run.

Upon its return to the city the machine and its occupants, mud and all, were photographed by C. R. Quay.

The success of that test sold at least seventeen cars before a complete one was built. Dr. Herbert H. Hills of Flint was permitted to drive the test car several times and received the first delivery of a new Model B, the first-production Flint Buick, although according to his diary he was seventeenth on the list of buyers. Because he lived in Flint, he was promised the first car if he would permit its use for demonstration.[8] The car was delivered to him August 13, 1904.

With production of Buicks getting underway in July and early August, James Whiting might have been very pleased with his new company. Instead he was deeply worried. The fact was that Flint Wagon Works' original investment in Buick, $37,500, had been used up. Apparently Buick was deeply in debt to several Flint banks. Creditors were screaming for the company to fulfill the orders its salesmen had taken for stationary farm engines, and the Association of Licensed Automobile Manufacturers, the Selden interests who had closed up Hardy's business, may have been ready to stop the production of Buicks just as they were getting started. If Buick folded, Flint would lose another foothold in the automobile business. Whiting kept his own counsel for weeks, but finally determined that it was no use—he would have to go outside his resources and those of the Flint Wagon Works.

On a train trip to a carriage show in Chicago, Whiting confided his problem to Fred A. Aldrich, secretary of the Durant-Dort Carriage Company. It was not unusual for competing Flint vehicle makers to discuss problems. While all of the firms competed ferociously with each other, if one of them had a serious problem, such as a major fire, they would draw together as a family until the company with the problem was ready for competition again. Flint's 14,000 citizens were proud that their city was recognized from coast to coast as "The Vehicle City."

Aldrich told Whiting that if there was one man who could save the day, that man was W. C. Durant. Whiting knew him well. Whiting had been building wagons for four years when twenty-four-year-old Durant decided to get into the vehicle business. In eighteen years Durant had surpassed not only Whiting's Wagon Works, but every vehicle builder in the country as well. Durant had a reputation as a supersalesman, he always seemed to be able to get his hands on money when he needed it, and he loved a challenge. There were only two problems. Durant was in New York at the moment, and he detested automobiles.

After his talk with Aldrich, Whiting went to see Dallas Dort. Dort listened as Whiting unfolded his problems, and then he agreed with Aldrich's advice. It was true, Dort said, that Durant wasn't fond of automobiles and, indeed, Dort felt the same way. But this seemed to be not just another automobile company in trouble—it looked like a crisis with city-wide ramifications. Now Durant was a loyal Flint citizen, Dort observed, just

Walter Marr (at the wheel) and Tom Buick, son of David Dunbar Buick, arrive in downtown Flint after the historic test run to Detroit in the first Buick built in Flint. The date was July 12, 1904.

as he and Whiting were. And Durant would be back in Flint shortly.

Most of Flint did not know it, but the future of the city seemed to hang in the balance as Whiting waited for Billy Durant to come home.

Dr. Herbert H. Hills bought first production Flint Buick in August, 1904.

Chapter Four

Buick: Rags to Riches

It was late in August, 1904, when Billy Durant, a self-made millionaire at the age of forty-two, stepped off the train at Flint. He had heard something about James Whiting's problems with his new automobile company. Could he be of service?

They talked. The Buick was a fine automobile, with a powerful little engine. All that was needed was a sharp young businessman to take command—and some more money. Always, it seemed, Buick needed more money.

Durant admitted that he felt pretty much the way Dort and Nash did about automobiles. "I thought it was terrible the way those noisy contraptions, especially the old steam engines, shocked people and frightened horses. My cousin, W. C. Orrell, had one and I was mighty provoked with anyone who would drive around annoying people that way. I was not in the least bit interested in managing an automobile concern."

But he would take a look anyway. On September 4, Dr. Herbert Hills took him for his first ride in a Buick.* He was also

---

* Recalling Durant's first ride in a Buick, Dr. Hills told the *Flint News-Advertiser* nearly half a century later (January 7, 1953):

"One day I called Durant and asked him if he and his family would like to go for a ride in my new Buick. He said they would, and we started off with Durant and me in the front seat, and Mrs. Durant and their daughter in the rear. We drove out W. Kearsley Street, then one of the few paved streets in Flint, and Durant kept firing questions at me about how the car ran and if I liked it or not. We didn't talk about anything else the whole time. Later Durant told me that drive had influenced his decision to become general manager of Buick."

Durant's calm, confident personality is expressed in this portrait.

driven around by Whiting and Arthur Mason. Why, he wondered, did they drive only on the smoothest streets? Durant liked what he saw, but he wanted to drive it himself.

So he took the car out alone. He rammed it down the muddy, rutted roads of the Flint countryside, roads which the locals were convinced were the worst in the country. Sometimes there were mechanical failures, sometimes the Buick got stuck. But on the whole, Durant was impressed—the Buick stood up pretty well, and its engine did seem to get it through terrain that stopped other cars. There was something else. The automobile attracted public attention. It gathered crowds just as the little road cart had done.

One day in October, Durant and Whiting drove around Flint in a Buick, and then sat in the car in front of Whiting's house. They talked for more than an hour. Then Whiting walked into the house and announced with relief to his family: "Billy's sold."[1]

A lot of factors were involved in that decision. Durant was impressed with the performance of the engine and he liked the look of the car. Influential men of Flint were turning to him for help and he did feel a strong loyalty to the city. For the first time he began to see that the automobile had a future. The stockholders of Buick were so desperate that they were willing to turn over controlling interest to him. And perhaps most important, the Durant-Dort Carriage Company had a large, idle factory in Jackson, Michigan. It had once housed the Imperial Wheel Company, but Durant-Dort had moved that firm to Flint, and the Jackson plant was a large white elephant.

By November 1, 1904, an agreement had been reached. That day Durant was elected to the Buick board of directors. Whiting resigned from the presidency to devote more time, it was said, to the Flint Wagon Works, though Durant had plans for his services. Durant, just as he had in the carriage company, declined the presidency. Instead, Charles M. Begole was elected president, and George L. Walker became vice-president. The Buick directors immediately announced that Buick capital stock was being increased from $75,000 to $300,000, with plans for an early increase to $500,000; that Buick production would be greatly expanded; and that assembly operations would be moved to the factory in Jackson.

This was big news in *The Flint Journal* that day, as was an announcement that the owners of the Flint Gas Light Company were selling to other interests for $325,000. Durant is said to have talked the sellers into subscribing a large share of this money to the new Buick stock issue.[2] It helped that he had once been treasurer of the gas light company.

On November 19 Buick's capital stock was increased to $500,000 and Durant received $325,000 worth as his individual property. The other stockholders received the balance of $175,000 in stock. Durant later transferred $101,000 worth of his shares to Whiting and $22,000 worth to Begole in exchange for their personal management of the Buick company. Whiting helped him operate Buick in Jackson and Begole helped manage both the Jackson and Flint operations, both also retaining their positions with the Flint Wagon Works.[3] Durant turned

The first driveaway of Flint Buicks took place—according to the date on this photo—November 7, 1904, at Saginaw and First streets. If the date is correct, virtually all of the Buicks built up to this time are in the picture. The two on the right are not fully assembled. These are Model B Buicks, of which about twenty-eight were built in Flint in 1904 before assembly was moved briefly to Jackson.

over most or all of the rest of his Buick stock to the Durant-Dort Carriage Company, partly in payment for use of the Jackson factory, partly because, as he pointed out, he was promoting Buick on the carriage company's time. From the start, Durant-Dort was heavily involved in the financing of Durant's automobile ventures.

Immediately after being handed control, Durant turned his attention to a group of creditors who were trying to make large claims against Buick for nonfulfillment of contracts for stationary engines. You can press your claims, he told them, and you might force Buick into bankruptcy and collect next to nothing. Or you can string along with reasonable demands and eventually get your money back or your engines. He needed time to get Buick on its feet. It was a compelling argument, and the creditors backed off.

Now it was time to get the assembly operations moved over to Jackson. But first, there was the matter of the automobile show opening in New York. Durant decided to display a Buick and see what he could do. A few weeks after the show ended, Durant's wife Clara wrote to a friend: "William has just returned from the auto show in New York, where he sold 1,108 machines. The Buick is certainly a success."[4] At that time

QUAY PHOTO

Buick had built fewer than forty cars! Just as in 1886, when he sold 600 road carts before building one, Durant's optimism was far ahead of his ability to deliver. Once again he was displaying his unusual talent as a salesman. As Walter P. Chrysler later wrote: "I cannot find words to express the charm of the man. He has the most winning personality of anyone I've ever known. He could coax a bird right down out of a tree."[5]

Not that there weren't times when Durant, too, had his doubts about Buick. Early in the game Arthur C. Mason, Buick's engine superintendent from the beginning in Flint, was developing a new high-speed engine. Durant promoted it with the slogan: "We do with two cylinders what others are trying to do with four." He was elated over the new engine until one day, while walking from the Flint plant to his home, he was met by one of the town's leading citizens.

"What's all this talk about this new motor?" the man wanted to know.

Durant explained that Mason was experimenting with an engine of 4,000 revolutions per minute at a time when the average was 1,800 r.p.m. Durant's notes continue: "After a short visit, [the man] made no effort to conceal his apprehension and put himself on record against the whole automobile venture and against the high speed motor in particular. He stated that I was gambling my whole established carriage business for a visionary and passing fancy. As I had great respect for his opinion, I began to feel that there might be something in his warning."

To check out Mason's engine, Durant hired a motors expert named Simmons, who came to Flint and studied the engine and the factory. Simmons' analysis was not encouraging. "This thing," he said, pointing to Mason's new engine, "is basically unsound and extremely dangerous. It's quite likely to explode. In fact, I would suggest the purchase of a bushel basket with every one sold in order to be able to pick up the pieces."

Mason had listened quietly, but with mounting anger, as Simmons made his report. Finally he could contain himself no longer. He stepped up to the motor, started it, and placed his head alongside the engine block. "If it explodes," he said, "I might as well go with it."

Simmons took his fee and walked out in a huff. "Needless to say," Durant observed, "Mason's work was crowned by a great success and was largely responsible for Buick's quick recognition as a leading motorcar. And his theory was adopted by automobile manufacturers all over the world." Durant concludes his account of the incident with this analysis of Buick's success: "Power, the achievement of Mason's long experiments and hard work, became synonymous with Buick. We played on that one item: Power! Power to outclimb, power to outspeed anything on wheels in our class. With Buick we sold the assurance that the power to perform was there. Power sold Buick and made it what it is today."[6]

By early 1905 Buicks were being assembled in Jackson. Finally the car would get into significant production. From 1900 to 1903 Buick had produced at least one, perhaps several, prototypes of the Model A Buick in Detroit; in 1904 between twenty-eight and thirty-seven Model B's were produced in Flint. But in 1905 large-scale production began in Jackson with the Model C, hardly changed from the Model B. The Model C had a 22-horsepower engine and sold for $1,250. Twenty dollars more bought a celluloid front curtain, forerunner of the windshield.

Not everyone in Flint was entirely pleased with Durant's handling of Buick. His associates in the Durant-Dort Carriage Company had trouble understanding his intense interest in automobiles when the carriage company was doing so well—1906 was Durant-Dort's biggest year. Others were unhappy that Buick assembly had been slipped out of Flint and over to Jackson, though Flint still built transmissions and engines at the little Buick factory near the Wagon Works.

One day Dallas Dort and Charlie Nash went to see Durant at his home in Flint, hoping to persuade him to stay in Flint and get actively involved with the carriage company again. When they walked into the house, they found him pumping happily away at a player piano. When he stopped playing, he began to talk in glowing terms about the future of automobiles. All of this was too much for Nash. "Dallas," he said, turning to Dort, "I think Billy has gone crazy."[7]

In 1905 Nash and Dort were still firmly wedded to the carriage industry. Eventually, however, both followed Durant

1905 BUICK MODEL "C"

PRICE,F.O.B.—$1,200

WEIGHT—1,850

WHEELBASE—89   TREAD—58

ENGINE—2 cyl.—4¼ x 5 - 159.0 disp.
H.P.—Max. brake 22 S.A.E. 18.2
Valves—In head, removable cages.
Cooling—Water with pump.
Carburetor—Schebler.
Lubrication—Force feed lubricator.
Ignition—Splitdorf coil, storage
battery, and Rajah spark plugs.

CHASSIS—Frame—Angle iron.
Springs—¾ elliptic in front,
semi-elliptic in rear.

REAR AXLE—Chain drive.

TRANSMISSION—Planetary type—2 speeds
forward and 1 reverse.

CLUTCH—High speed friction cone type.

BRAKES—Double external contracting on
differential.

STEERING—Pinion and sector.

WHEELS—Wood spoke. Clincher rims.

TIRES—30 x 3½

BODY—5 passenger touring.

MISCELLANEOUS—This car was practically
the same as the 1904 Model "B".
Production was 750 cars. It was
built in Jackson, Michigan.

into automobiles. Nash became president of Buick in 1910, president of General Motors in 1912, and achieved lasting fame by establishing the Nash Motors Company in 1916. And Dort— whose heart nevertheless always remained with horses and carriages[8]—formed the Dort Motor Company in 1915, manufacturing cars until shortly before his death in 1925. As for the Durant-Dort Carriage Company, the greatest carriage producer of them all, it was finished by 1917.

Durant realized that manufacturing Buick engines, transmissions, and bodies in one city and then shipping them for assembly to another was a woefully inefficient procedure. It was expensive and it meant that he was constantly traveling between the two cities. He knew he had to build a large new factory, and for that he would need cash. The financial leaders of Jackson could not be persuaded to raise money for Buick. So he cast an eye toward Bay City, Michigan, with its handy port on Lake Huron. He said he offered to move Buick to Bay City if the town could raise $100,000.[9] The money wasn't raised. The proposal may have been only a feint anyway, to shock Flint's financial leaders into action. If it was, it worked. The four Flint banks each pledged $20,000 through subscriptions by their directors, for which they would get a 25 percent bonus of Buick stock. They would pledge a total of $80,000 in cash and get $100,000 in stock. But they extracted an agreement: Durant would have to discontinue his operations in Jackson and move the whole Buick business back to Flint.[10]

One Flint bank failed to raise its share, so the Genesee County Savings Bank provided two $20,000 subscriptions, the second coming from a special account which had originally been started when the bank sold some surplus material. The account had grown through the years as occasional notes were paid after having been written off, and in 1905 it totaled more than $20,000. It may have been just enough to bring Buick back to Flint.[11]

It is small wonder that Durant had no trouble selling the Genesee Bank on the Buick investment. Those pledging $2,500 each were Dallas Dort, Arthur G. Bishop, James C. Willson, George C. Willson, W. C. Springer, J. H. Crawford, and W. C. Orrell. Other signers were W. A. Atwood, who pledged $1,500,

Flint April 24/1905

We, the undersigned, hereby subscribe for the
number of shares of stock of the BUICK MOTOR COMPANY
(par value $100 each) set opposite our respective
names (to be issued to such parties and in such amounts
as we may designate) and agree to pay therefor at the
rate of one hundred dollars ($100.00) per share to
the Treasurer of said Company on or before *August 1st*,
1905. This subscription is made with the understanding
that the BUICK MOTOR COMPANY will discontinue its
Jackson plant and locate its entire business at Flint,
commencing construction work upon its new buildings
as soon as plants can be prepared and the weather will
permit.

Name	Shares	Amount
J. D. Dort	25	$2500.00
A. J. Bishop	25	2500.00
James A. Wilson	25	2500.00
W. C. Spencer	25	2500.00
J. H. Crawford	25	2500.00
R. C. Orrell	25	2500.00
W. A. Atwood	15	1500.00
Gringe C. Wisson	25	2500.00
W. W. Crapo	10	$1000.00

and William Wallace Crapo, who pledged $1,000. Crapo and Dr. James C. Willson were uncles of Durant, George Willson and Orrell were his cousins, Dort was his partner in the carriage company, and Bishop was such a close associate that Durant later named him to the board of General Motors.

Within a short time other Flint carriage makers and individuals also joined as big financial supporters. Durant-Dort, as a company, pledged $100,000, for example.[12] Decades later, when he was writing his memoirs, Durant recalled that "in the small town of Flint, where I started Buick, in 48 hours I raised $500,000. Few of the subscribers had ever ridden in an automobile."

On September 11, 1905, exactly two years after Whiting announced that Buick engines would be built in Flint, Buick's capitalization was raised from $500,000 to $1.5 million. John J.

One of the agreements which helped to raise enough money to return Buick assembly from Jackson to Flint and to start building the largest automobile factory in the world. This group of Genesee Bank directors included Durant's business partners and relatives.

A driveaway of Model C Buicks in downtown Jackson in 1905. While the main assembly operations of Buick returned to Flint in 1906, Buick trucks were still being assembled in Jackson as late as 1912.

Carton, the Buick attorney, had some difficulty finding enough assets to justify the increase in stock. Finally he itemized a few inventions "not patented for business reasons" and assigned dollar figures to them. Although the papers were approved by state officials, the Michigan Legislature took note of the entry and adopted a law prohibiting the listing of such intangibles in the future. After that, however, Buick didn't need them.[13]

The money raised, Durant prepared to move Buick assembly from Jackson back to Flint. But he was not quite through with Jackson. In 1906 he organized the Whiting Motor Car Company as a Buick subsidiary (with James H. Whiting as president; Charles M. Begole, vice-president; Durant, secretary and treasurer) and the Janney Motor Car Company, both at Jackson.[14] The Whiting Company was dissolved in 1907, apparently without building a car, but James Whiting resurrected the name in 1908 and built Whiting cars at the Flint Wagon Works until 1911. There is no record of Janney's being incorporated, though it apparently did get into operation. It was shortly absorbed by Buick.

Durant's association with Jackson had one lasting result. While living in the Otsego Hotel there—his marriage was breaking up—he met a schoolgirl, Catherine Lederer. She was twenty-five years his junior, daughter of a railroad clerk, and a friend of his children, Margery and Clifford.

Catherine's first memory of her "Willie" is of when he was with his children in Jackson. Margery and Clifford lived with their mother in Flint, but often visited their father. One day Durant sent Catherine two tickets to the theater. She attended with a girl friend. At the end of the performance, Durant walked down the aisle and asked if he could drive the girls home. He drove the other girl home first, and then Catherine. A few days later he went to Catherine's house and asked her mother if he could call on Catherine. Mrs. Lederer replied that she did not think it would be proper, since Durant was still married. "Of course, that made no difference," Catherine Durant later recounted, referring to her mother's objections.[15]

On May 27, 1908, Durant and his first wife, Clara, were divorced in the Genesee County Circuit Court. "The hearing was held in open court before Judge Gage of Saginaw, in the

Durant met his second wife, Catherine Lederer, during his stay in Jackson. She was a friend of his daughter, Margery. They were married in New York in 1908 on the day after his divorce from Clara was final. The second Mrs. Durant today lives in a small apartment in New York City.

absence of Judge Wisner, who had gone north on a fishing trip," *The Flint Journal* reported. Testimony in the divorce case said that Durant had ignored his wife for ten years or more, had failed to write to her in 1906-07 when she was seriously ill, had brought on his wife's illness by neglecting her, and had repeatedly stated he would not live with her.[16]

It is interesting to note that some of the testimony on behalf of Mrs. Durant was given by Dr. Edwin R. Campbell. Dr. Campbell had been the Durants' personal physician for twelve years. Elderly citizens of Flint today remember him as a dashing, handsome man and the city's most prominent obstetrician. It was said that to be well born a child had to be delivered by Dr. Campbell. He made his winter rounds in a red sleigh, his lap

79

Catherine Lederer Durant

covered with furs, and all the young ladies and many of their mothers were properly impressed. In 1906 he married Margery Durant, one of Flint's most eligible girls. And starting in 1908, the very year he testified against Durant in the divorce case, he became one of Durant's closest business associates.

In the divorce settlement Clara received $150,000 in cash and securities and the family home on Garland Street in Flint. It was later reported that in addition she received more than $2 million in an out-of-court settlement. She subsequently remarried and moved to California.

The day after the divorce was final Durant married Catherine Lederer in New York City.

In order to move Buick assembly from Jackson back to Flint, Durant needed a new factory. He had a site—the 220-acre Hamilton Farm on the north edge of the city near some of the Durant-Dort subsidiaries. He had purchased it for $22,000. Durant, who now saw the great future of the automobile more clearly than any of his contemporaries, decided that since he intended to be the world's largest producer of automobiles, he would need the largest automobile factory in the world. Soon the oak forests on the Hamilton Farm were leveled, and in their place the largest automobile factory in the world—fourteen acres under roof—was under construction.

But the trees had not yet started to fall when Durant made his first effort to develop a supply network, as he had earlier in the carriage business. On June 4, 1905, he sent a letter to Charles Stewart Mott of the Weston-Mott Company of Utica, New York, which built axles for Buick and other auto manufacturers. Would Mott be interested in relocating or setting up a branch in Flint?[17]

Two days later Mott replied. He was not interested in building a branch axle factory—it would be too difficult to supervise from long range. He might, however, consider locating the whole business in Flint if the opportunities were attractive. Following this up, Mott went to Jackson to discuss the prospect with Durant and was taken with Durant's confidence and drive. Durant promised Mott he would visit him in Utica, but didn't get around to it until September 1, when he and Dort arrived there by train.

Charles Stewart Mott was persuaded by Durant to move his axle-manufac-
turing business from Utica, New York, to Flint in 1906. Mott was a
General Motors director from 1913 until his death at age ninety-seven in
1973. As founder of the Mott Foundation, he became Flint's great
philanthropist. He also served three terms as mayor.

That night Mott, his partner William Doolittle, and their wives accompanied Durant and Dort on the train back to Flint. They spent the Labor Day weekend looking over the city and talking with community leaders. Mott and Doolittle were not particularly excited by the city itself, but they were very impressed with its community leaders and also with the inducements offered them to move—the citizens of Flint would subscribe $100,000 in new capital, Weston-Mott would be given a site adjacent to the new Buick plant, and there would also be a big axle contract with Buick. That weekend Mott and Doolittle decided to transfer the Weston-Mott Company to Flint.[18]

Construction of the Weston-Mott and Buick factories took place simultaneously. For a time more people were employed building factories in Flint than building Buicks in Flint or Jackson. Weston-Mott's plant was completed in the summer of 1906, and by February 1, 1907, the move to Flint was complete. On that day C. S. Mott moved his family to Flint.* Bill Doolittle also made the move, but died a short time later. Mott's decision to move to Flint to serve Buick showed how far Buick had advanced under Durant's leadership. Two years earlier Weston-Mott had been shipping axles to Buick C.O.D. because Buick's credit was so poor.

Durant had another noteworthy visitor while living in Jackson. R. Samuel McLaughlin, son of Robert McLaughlin, who had built the largest carriage company in the British Empire (though not as large as Durant-Dort), became interested in building automobiles about 1905. He met Durant, an old acquaintance from the carriage days, when he went to Jackson to buy two Jackson cars. Durant suggested that if the Jackson car didn't prove to be an attractive manufacturing possibility, McLaughlin might be interested in the Buick.[19]

McLaughlin was, in fact, disappointed in the Jackson car. He drove a Buick—and liked it at once. He was now interested in building Buicks in Canada. But he and Durant could not agree on financial arrangements, though they parted friends, and McLaughlin went home to Oshawa, Ontario, to build his own car. His venture there got into trouble, however, when his engineer became ill. He then went back to Durant and an agreement was reached for the use of Buick engines in McLaughlin cars. Between 150 and 200 McLaughlin cars were built with Buick engines in 1908. Out of his association with

---

* If Durant had done nothing more for Flint than bring C. S. Mott to town, he would have done enough for the city. In 1908, 49 percent of Weston-Mott's stock was exchanged for stock in the new General Motors Company, and in 1913 Mott exchanged the other 51 percent for GM stock. He used that stock as a basis for other investments and created a huge personal fortune. And he was to create out of that fortune the Mott Foundation, which has become one of the largest in assets in the country. The Mott Foundation has benefited Flint and its citizens in education, parks, and health facilities and in many kinds of programs. C. S. Mott, three times mayor of Flint, was still a director of General Motors when he died at age ninety-seven on March 18, 1973. He was the last of the pioneer leaders in the automotive business.

William H. Little was Durant's production manager at Buick from 1906 to 1910, and later gave his name to the Little automobile, a predecessor of the Chevrolet.

Durant, McLaughlin later was granted the right to build both Buicks and Chevrolets in Canada, and the nucleus of General Motors of Canada was formed.* McLaughlin later wrote gratefully of Durant's cooperation, describing Durant as a daring, far-seeing man, "in my opinion, the greatest in the auto industry of that time."

After Buick returned from Jackson to Flint, William H. Little, who had been building the Ilion Buckboard car at Waltham, Massachusetts, came to Flint as Buick's general production manager. Little was a big, colorful man. He used to drive downtown to the Dresden Hotel for lunch, and invariably he would skid his car around on the pavement to park at the curb. Mott recalled that on one occasion Little's car slid more violently than he intended and the curb took off all four wheels.

---

*In many ways Mott and McLaughlin had similar careers. Both were benefactors of their local communities—Mott in Flint, McLaughlin in Oshawa, Ontario. Both had long lives—McLaughlin died at age one hundred in January, 1972, while still board chairman of GM of Canada. Both could trace the impetus of their careers to Durant and Buick.

Stories about Little abound. One day in 1906 Durant told him there had been complaints about Buick's brakes. Could Little do something about improving them? Little demanded that his engineers develop new brakes immediately. By noon the next day they were ready for a test. The following morning Durant was picked up at the Dresden and taken to a field behind the Buick factory. Little got into the driver's seat, Durant was in the back seat. As Richard Crabb tells the story in *Birth of a Giant*, Little built up speed, then jammed on the new brakes. They locked, and Durant was thrown head first into the front seat and then onto the ground. Little was almost in a state of shock. He and others ran to Durant's aid. Durant picked himself up, brushed off the dust, and said, softly:

"Well, you certainly got some brakes, Bill."

"Get in, Mr. Durant, and I'll drive you back to the plant."

"No thanks," said Billy. "I'll walk."

Buick production rose from 725 in 1905 to 1,400 in 1906, and Durant boasted in a letter that Buick had 100 dealers, including many of the largest in the country, and was building fifteen to seventeen automobiles a day. The business was an enormous success, he explained, because "we are manufacturing a machine of rare merit at a very reasonable price; our motor being conceded by all gas engine experts to be one of the greatest improvements in gas engine practice ever designed."[20] About 1,200 of the 1906 sales were of the new 2-cylinder Model F, which included a storage battery and vibrator horn as standard equipment.

Buick production tripled to 4,641 in 1907, despite the fact that a financial panic created a depression across the country. People were not buying cars, and many automobile companies closed their doors. Durant, juggling bills from suppliers and forcing them to extend credit, ordered his factories to produce at full tilt, storing new Buicks in barns, warehouses, and fields. Luckily, the panic was short, and Durant's gamble paid off handsomely. When people were ready to buy cars again, Buick was the only automaker with plenty of cars on hand. After that Durant seemed never to worry about business cycles, figuring he could ride out any temporary recession.

"He was one hell of a gambler," Mott said, shortly before his death. "To this day, I don't know how he was able to handle it financially, but he did it." Mott was also impressed with Durant's selling ability. He told a story of traveling with Durant from Flint to Utica, stopping in Detroit to change trains. With a little more than an hour to wait, they walked to a nearby Buick dealership and Durant asked how business was going. The dealer said he was having trouble clinching several deals. Durant got the name of one of the prospects, asked Mott to wait for him in the dealership, and was back with a sale in time to still make the train connection.

By 1906 Durant had a reputation of almost legendary proportions in Flint. He may have been "Willie" to his mother and "Pops" to his daughter and "Billy" to a few close friends, but he was "The Man" to the working men of Flint. Writers of the time said that the workers almost worshipped him, awed by his quick mind and by the way he dashed about creating great industrial complexes out of oak forests.

His colleagues were also impressed. At a private dinner gathering in Detroit in November, 1906, Durant was honored with the following bit of doggerel published on the program. It was called "When William Comes to Town" and included these stanzas:

The Model F was introduced in 1906 but was basically unchanged from the Models B and C. It had a 2-cylinder engine and sold for $1,250.

A special lightning cannon ball
Brings William into town—
Her steam gauge shows a sudden fall
When William gets to town.
Flint streets take on a lively air
Quite like a fete or fair
And traffic has all it can bear
When William comes to town.

Blue Ribbon boys are busy wights
When William comes to town
And Buick stock takes dizzy flights
When William comes to town.
Imperial Wheel emits a squeal
And varnish up or down
Flows hurriedly and worriedly
When William comes to town.

Telegraphers get next their keys
When William comes to town
Drones are converted into bees
When William comes to town.
Partners with work and worry mad
With countenances sad
Exclaim, "My God, we'll be so glad
When William leaves the town."

Buick production kept doubling and tripling. In June, 1908, the company set an industry record for any month when it built 1,409 vehicles in Flint and 245 in Jackson. In 1908 Buick production reached 8,820, placing it in the number one position—outbuilding Ford (6,181) and Cadillac (2,380), its two closest competitors, combined.* Durant had made the transition from the largest carriage maker to the largest automobile manufacturer in a little more than three years. There seemed to be no stopping Buick. In 1909 production reached 14,606 and in 1910 it soared to 30,525.[21]

---

*The Buick and Cadillac figures are for the calendar year, those of Ford for the fiscal year. Production and sales figures for many of the early automakers vary widely, even on official lists, and some credit Ford with manufacturing more than 10,000 cars in 1908.

In achieving such success, Durant had proved again that he was more than a supersalesman. He was a leader and organizer without parallel among the early auto manufacturers, not excluding Henry Ford. Realizing that his talent was in organization, promotion, and sales, not in production details, he hired the most talented men in manufacturing he could find and told them to buy the best material available for the Buick.

One such man was Harry A. Shiland, a Massachusetts automobile dealer. Shiland had gone to Durant and told him that while Buick had the most powerful little engine in the land, this fact was hard for the owner to appreciate since other things were chronically going wrong—chains broke, transmissions froze, and the carburetor acted up. He suggested other suppliers for these parts, and Durant immediately accepted his advice. He also hired Shiland as Buick sales manager.

Shiland helped Durant create a great national sales network, recommending that branch distributing houses be set up across the country. Durant bought the idea and toured the country to help establish such branches, using the great Durant-Dort carriage sales network as the nucleus for the Buick sales organization. By 1908 Buick was the most widely displayed car in America.

One of their promotions, however, didn't quite pay off. Shiland and Durant both entered Buicks in the second Glidden Tour. This 1,200-mile run, organized by Col. Charles J. Glidden, was a well-publicized event and offered a good chance to show off their product. The Buick entries were equipped with new steel bushings, instead of the usual bronze, because they were quieter. But disaster struck quickly when the new bushings in Shiland's car froze up, forcing him out of the race. And Durant was disqualified for stopping to aid another driver. The men were disconsolate over the way they had fared, but at least they had learned of the problem with the bushings before many cars had been equipped with them.

Help for Buick came from unlikely sources. A young fellow named Bob Burman (spelled Burnham in some early sources) graduated from painting carriage wheels to testing some of the first Buicks. Laverne Marshall of Flint remembers that Burman seemed to take great delight in tearing up a car. That was all right with Durant: the best way to perfect the Buick was to have it driven until something failed, and then to have engineers correct the problem.

Buicks had hardly gone into major production before Burman decided to try one in a race. Borrowing a car, he headed for Detroit—only to have the transmission fall out as he neared the city. Undaunted, he called a friend to the scene with a new transmission, worked all night to install it, and arrived at the Grosse Pointe race track just as the race was about to start. Barney Oldfield, one of the contestants, recalled the incident:

> We saw this small car chugging along toward the track. It hadn't been officially entered. Some cars that had been entered did not show up. Henry Ford couldn't get his car started for a while. . . . As we wanted more cars in the race, we agreed to allow the newly arrived entrant to compete. That small car was really rolling after it got started. Burman took awful chances on the turns. But he won the contest, and beat Ford and me. . . . The driver was to go on to world fame driving Buick cars. After he broke my world speed record at Daytona Beach in 1911, in the Mercedes he bought from me, he was crowned "The world's speed king," and he was that. . . . As a mechanic working with a fellow named Marr, Burman did more to establish the early Buick cars for their stability and power than any engineers of those days. . . .[22]

After Grosse Pointe, Burman entered two more races, and won those as well. In the East, Buicks were suddenly in the news, setting one-, three-, six-, and eight-mile records. Another won a hill-climb in Pennsylvania.

Durant became enthusiastic about the victories and the resultant publicity, and ordered Walter Marr to start developing racing engines and cars. Marr, the man with a Van Dyke beard and a wry sense of humor, was an engineering perfectionist. He kept Buick moving forward with new ideas and new patents, and it was said that new engines had to be taken away from him to start production because he was never satisfied with the motor of the moment. Marr even mixed his own fuels for experimental use. Once he had the signal from Durant, he plunged enthusiastically into racing. He not only developed hot

Buick racers and production models were tested on track north of the Buick complex.

Buicks became famous, winning all kinds of racing and hill-climbing events in the Durant era, 1904-10. Wild Bob Burman, who was said to be the best of all Buick race drivers, even defeated this plane in a speed festival at Daytona Beach, Florida.

new engines, but drove cars himself in hill-climbs all over America. Buick was winning so many hill-climbing trophies that it was said a steep hill was often referred to as a "Buick Hill."

Durant placed William H. Pickens in charge of the Buick racing team. To this team of Burman, Lewis Strang, and a group of lesser names, Pickens added two young men of Swiss-French upbringing, the Chevrolet brothers, Louis and Arthur.

Louis Chevrolet, a solid chunk of a man, six feet tall, 210 pounds, his features dominated by large, intense eyes and a bristling mustache, had come to the United States in about 1900. He had been born in Switzerland on Christmas Day, 1878, the son of a farmer-clockmaker, and since boyhood had shown a gift for invention and engineering and an inclination for racing. Shortly after his family moved to Beaune, a small town in Burgundy, France, ten-year-old Louis began to enter local bicycle races—and generally won. As a teenager he manufactured a bicycle he called the Frontenac and he invented a wine-barrel pump. The first automobile he saw completely captivated him. Eventually he worked for several French auto companies, and in 1905 he began racing Fiats in the United States. Before the year was out he had beaten Barney Oldfield three times. [23]

A fearless driver and consistent winner, Louis Chevrolet was well known across the country when one night in Wilkes-Barre, Pennsylvania, he was racing against Lewis Strang of the Buick team. Both of their cars broke down. Chevrolet's car was beyond repair, so Pickens asked Louis to help fix the Buick. The men had almost no tools, but by working all night, pouring a new bearing around a piece of gas pipe and then shaving it down to size, they got the car ready for the next day—and the Buick won.

Pickens insisted that Chevrolet come to Buick to help design race cars. Chevrolet agreed to come, but as a racer instead. With Louis Chevrolet, Lewis Strang, and Wild Bob Burman, Pickens had the country's best stable of drivers. (Arthur Chevrolet became Durant's personal chauffeur. As Durant himself pointed out, Louis was a more successful racer, but Arthur took fewer chances.) In two racing seasons, the Buick team won half of America's road races, collecting more than 500 trophies. Durant

Stars of the Buick racing team—from left, Walter Marr, Buick's great engineer and sometimes driver; Wild Bob Burman; and Louis Chevrolet.

One of Buick's most popular cars in the early days—the Model 10. The Model 10, introduced in 1908, ran easily with its smooth little four-cylinder engine coupled to a 2-speed planetary transmission. It also looked cute and it enjoyed racing success across the country. Its $900 price in 1908 included acetylene headlights and a bulb horn.

was so pleased that he presented the three with a $10,000 bonus to split at the end of the 1909 season.

Sometimes late at night or very early in the morning, the drivers would try out their powerful cars on the streets of Flint. Leo Murphy of Flint recalls an early Sunday morning when he watched Burman and Chevrolet test drive a Buick racer on N. Saginaw Street. They would drive down to the Saginaw Street bridge, make a U-turn and head north, and then make another U-turn and roar back again. On one of the U-turns the car overturned—but came up on its wheels. The men sped up a side street, possibly to Chevrolet's house on Root Street nearby, and did not return.

After the victories of 1909, Durant published a small pamphlet to boast:

> It is with keenest pleasure that we again present to our friends and patrons and to the public in general a brief review of the victories won during the past year.
>
> No other automobile manufacturer in the world can claim as many glorious achievements. Our models 10 and 17, although much smaller than a great many of the competing cars entered in the year's races, have proven in 167 different events their superiority over the other makes.
>
> Buicks have proven their superiority. In the future, as it has been in the past, the name Buick will be synonymous with high quality and low prices.

Durant's interest in racing, his search for quality, his eye for simple beauty, and his natural instinct for products that would sell probably came together best in the Model 10 Buick introduced in 1908. It was said to have been originally developed as the Janney. The Model 10 was attractive, easy to operate, and fast for its size. Painted in "Buick gray," the car had an eighty-eight-inch wheelbase and was equipped with a four-cylinder engine and a two-speed planetary transmission. Its price of $900 included acetylene headlights and a bulb horn. For fifty dollars more you got a top. More than half of Buick's new cars in 1909 were Model 10s, and 10,000 Model 10s were sold in 1910.

As Buick boomed, so did Flint. Workers poured by the

thousands into the city, turning the pleasant nineteenth-century community into an overcrowded, hard-drinking boom town. Flint became the fastest growing city in America. It was swamped with prosperity. In 1908 the city had 4,499 factory wage earners—in 1909 it had 10,265. In 1910 the number reached 15,000. Between 1906 and 1910, 3,000 houses were built in Flint. Between 1900 and 1920, the city's population soared from 13,000 to 91,000. Housing was a major problem. Hundreds of families lived in shacks and a few in piano crates and chicken coops. The same bed that was rented by night to a day-shift worker would be rented by day to a man who worked nights. Oak Park was a tent colony. In 1910 an estimated 1,000 workers and their families were camping along the Flint River. Seven square miles were added to the city early in 1910. Farms were subdivided right and left. Four schools were built. All public facilities were overtaxed. One factory foreman had a $400 living room suite delivered to his tarpaper shack. It wasn't that the wages were poor—$2.20 a day was pretty good in 1910. It was just that the city couldn't handle the boom.

On Buick pay nights the sidewalks and saloons overflowed with life, the steel arches over downtown Saginaw Street were lit with many colors, and the streets were filled—mostly with horses. Only 100 cars were licensed in Flint at the start of 1910, though more than 30,000 were built in the city that year.

A newspaper reporter in Detroit wrote of the activity in Flint:

> One must see for himself; one must get into the atmosphere of the tremendous undertakings; one must himself walk over the literal miles of factories in process of construction before one begins to grasp the immensity of the manufacturing undertaking that has made Flint, next to Detroit, the automobile center of the world.
>
> Consider that within a year, 1,800 homes have been built in Flint! Consider that with all the building material, men and money that can be rushed to Flint, resulting in a condition wherein builders jostle one another over whole sections of vacant property, many workingmen and their families still live in tarpapered shanties and tents, and you will have one aspect of the great new life that has come to the state.

By 1910, Flint looked like a mining boom town as thousands of workers poured into the city to work for Buick. When no rooms were available workers sometimes lived in shacks and piano crates. Buick's new North Side complex can be seen in the background.

During the Buick boom, tent cities sprang up in Oak Park, near the Flint Buick factory, and along the banks of the Flint River.

> Whence has Durant this ability to use his boyhood
> village as a commercial center for the country? Oh, ask
> something easy. Who knows anything about the springs of
> genius?[24]

By 1908 David Buick was gone. A good technician but a
quiet man and a dreamer, he was thoroughly disenchanted with
the fever pitch of operations at the company which bore his
name, and he got out. "There wasn't an executive in the place
that ever knew what time it was," he complained. "We worked
until we had the day's job done and were ready for tomorrow
and then we went home—and not until then."[25]

When David Buick had made his agreement with Whiting and
the Wagon Works, part of the contract stated that he would get
his stock interest in the reorganized company only when the
stock allocated to him had paid some of his debts out of the
dividends. At the time he decided to leave the company, the
dividends had not nearly paid back the debts, but Buick officials canceled them when he surrendered all of his stock interest. The stock would have been worth nearly $10 million a
decade later, Ben Briscoe once calculated, but Briscoe admitted
that the company did pay Buick "a considerable sum," though
not legally obliged to do so.[26] Reportedly Durant gave Buick
$100,000 to invest as he chose. David Buick chose badly. His
investments in later years went sour and he died in relative
obscurity in 1929.

Meanwhile the expansions went on. The Buick and Weston-
Mott plants were hardly completed on Flint's north side when
the W. F. Stewart Company was induced to build its largest
body plant nearby. Already close by were the Imperial Wheel
Works, the Flint Axle Works, the Flint Varnish Works, and the
J. B. Armstrong (springs) Manufacturing Company. All but
Armstrong were Durant-Dort subsidiaries, and all soon became
automobile supply plants. In six years the area of the old
Hamilton Farm had become the industrial heart of Flint.

The frenzy of Buick activities in production, development,
sales, and racing was so great that it would seemingly have
required all of Durant's time to cope with it, and then some.
But the wizard was on to bigger things. Before 1908 was out, he
had founded a new company—General Motors.

Chapter Five

"I Must Have a Consolidation"

As he dined one evening in Flint with his daughter Margery, Durant was called to the telephone. It was Benjamin Briscoe, Jr., in Chicago.

> Briscoe: "Hello, Billy, I have a most important matter to discuss with you and want you to take the first train to Chicago."
>
> Durant: "What's the big idea, Ben?"
>
> Briscoe: "Don't ask me to explain; it's the biggest thing in the country. There's millions in it. Can you come?
>
> Durant: "Impossible, too busy, sorry. But I can see you here. Why don't you take the 10 o'clock Grand Trunk arriving at 7 o'clock tomorrow morning. I will meet you at the station and we will have breakfast together."*

Briscoe agreed. The two met the following morning in Flint, breakfasted at the Dresden Hotel, then went to Durant's office at Buick. Briscoe—who had sold Buick to Whiting in 1903 and

---

* Durant's recollections of the phone call and ensuing events are recorded in his autobiographical notes in a chapter titled "The True Story of General Motors." He recorded the date of Briscoe's call as May 15, 1908, which is incorrect. The initial discussions may have taken place as early as 1907. By January, 1908, the talks were at a serious stage. George S. May gathered this sequence of meeting dates for consolidation talks from the diary of Ransom E. Olds: Detroit on January 17, 1908; New York on January 24-25; again in New York on May 11, and apparently still again at the end of May. The details of the consolidation talks in this chapter are given largely as Durant remembered them, though I have in some cases changed his sequence of events to conform with other evidence.

who had since become president of Maxwell-Briscoe Company—confided that George W. Perkins, a partner in J. P. Morgan and Company and a financial backer of Maxwell-Briscoe, was exploring the idea of a large automobile merger. Would Durant be interested?

"Briscoe had no well-considered plan but he wanted to get my ideas," Durant wrote. "He suggested calling a meeting of about 20 of the leading concerns, naming Packard, Peerless, Pierce-Arrow, Stoddard-Dayton, Thomas, etc. What did I think of it?

"I told him frankly that I did not believe the plan was workable. The proposition in my opinion was too big, too many concerns involved, too many conflicting interests to be reconciled." Durant felt that Briscoe should modify his plans and try for a merger of a few auto companies who were trying to produce in volume in the medium-priced field. He proposed the Ford Motor Company of Detroit, the Reo Motor Car Company of Lansing, Buick, and Maxwell-Briscoe. "I suggested he first see Henry Ford, who was in the limelight, liked publicity and unless he could lead the procession would not play," Durant continued.

In 1908 Henry Ford was gearing up for production that nearly equalled Buick's—and would soon surpass it. The Reo Motor Car Company was headed by Ransom E. Olds, who had driven steam horseless carriages around Lansing as early as 1887, when Durant, fifty miles away in Flint, was just getting started in the Flint Road Cart Company. R. E. Olds had walked out of the Olds Motor Works in 1904 in a management dispute, and by 1908 was in charge of Reo (the name derived from his initials).

Briscoe met with Olds in Lansing, and found him receptive to the consolidation idea. He talked to Ford, who was at least willing to discuss it. Several weeks later, Durant, Olds, and Ford were invited to meet with Briscoe in the old Penobscot Building in Detroit. Durant wrote:

"In the public reception room were gathered the principals, their close associates and advisers. The room was small, no place to discuss business. I sensed, unless we ran to cover, plenty of undesirable publicity in the offing. As I had commodious quarters in the [old] Pontchartrain Hotel, and as the luncheon hour was approaching, I suggested that we separate and meet in my room as soon as convenient. I had the unexpected pleasure of entertaining the entire party until mid-afternoon."

Once the group was assembled in Durant's room, Briscoe urged that a consolidation plan be developed that could be presented to J. P. Morgan and Company. But he had no specific plan. There was a painful pause.

Durant tried to fill the gap. "If we put a value of $10 million on Ford, would Ford consider $6 million a reasonable figure for Reo?"

Henry Ford said he didn't have the slightest idea of the value or the earning capacity of Reo. Durant then asked Ford and Olds, if Ford were valued at $10 million and Reo at $6 million, would $5 million for Maxwell-Briscoe seem reasonable?

Briscoe, slightly irritated, asked about Buick. Durant replied that the report of the appraisers and auditors and the conditions and terms of the agreement would be his answer.

But at least Durant's questions had broken the ice. The men began to ask questions of each other. How would the company be managed? Who would be in charge? Briscoe thought the purchasing, engineering, advertising, and sales departments of the four companies should be combined, and that a central committee should rule on all operating policies.

Durant thought Briscoe's plan would lead to complications. There should be no interference, he felt, in the internal operations of the individual companies. All he wanted was a holding company.

"Durant is for states' rights," Briscoe replied with a laugh. "I am for a union."

There was more general talk—though Henry Ford remained silent. Briscoe said he would report back to the Morgans and that probably the auto men would be invited to confer in New York in the near future.

About a week later the group was called to meet in the law offices of Ward, Hayden, and Satterlee in New York City. Herbert L. Satterlee was a son-in-law of J. Pierpont Morgan, and because Morgan had been an early investor in Maxwell-Briscoe, Ben Briscoe felt obliged to use Satterlee as the attorney through which discussions would continue. Briscoe later wrote that had he been able to use an attorney suggested by Ford, Job Hedges, the outcome of the talks might have been different.[1]

At this meeting questions were asked about who had what share of the market, whether anything could be gained by consolidation, and whether there were any objections to an automobile combine. Henry Ford had one objection. The tendency of consolidation, he felt, was to increase prices, which he believed would be a serious mistake. Durant noted that Ford "was in favor of keeping prices down to the lowest possible point, giving to the multitude the benefit of cheap transportation."

The meetings in New York continued into the spring and summer of 1908, though the exact sequence of events is lost in the conflicting chronology recorded by Briscoe and Durant. At one meeting, according to Briscoe, Ford Business Manager James C. Couzens said that Ford would join the consolidation only if it received $3 million in cash for starters. Ransom Olds is then supposed to have said that if Ford was to get $3 million, Reo had to get the same.

Durant, on the other hand, later said that no specific amount of money was mentioned. In his version, Henry Ford was asked at a meeting in Satterlee's office how much of the preferred stock of the new combine he would take. Ford replied that when he was first approached by Briscoe, he told Briscoe that he would sell his company for cash, not for stock in any consolidation. This surprised the financial backers and the attorneys. They had expected a large subscription from Ford. Satterlee asked Durant to step into an adjoining room. What was all this about? Durant replied that it was news to him. Why not ask Briscoe?

Durant's account continues:

"Briscoe, when questioned, said that Mr. Ford had correctly stated the case, but that he had shown such an interest as the matter progressed that Briscoe, whether rightly or wrongly, inferred that Mr. Ford had changed his mind and would go along with the others.

"Mr. Satterlee was quite put out and after giving the matter a few moments' thought, went back into the other room and very diplomatically stated that there had been a misunderstanding, but that the matter of finance was entirely up to the bankers, and when they had perfected their plans, another meeting would be called."

Ford and R. E. Olds were at this point out of the talks. Durant and Briscoe, however, still had hopes of forming a Buick and Maxwell-Briscoe combine. And by the end of June, 1908, they had almost reached an agreement with their financial backer, specifically George Perkins of J. P. Morgan and Company, on a combination to be called the United Motors Company. On July 1 Ward, Hayden, and Satterlee told Buick's attorney, John J. Carton of Flint, that "the certificate of incorporation of the United Motors Co. has been duly filed and unless something unforeseen arises, its stock will be ready to be issued within a

The end of the day at the Buick and Weston-Mott factories in Flint. By 1908, Buick and Ford—which introduced the Model T that year—were neck-and-neck in a race for production leadership. For at least half the year, Buick was definitely in first place.

few days." The attorneys advised Carton to prepare the stock of Buick for delivery against the stock of United Motors.[2]

The next day, Durant wrote to Carton from Buick's Boston sales branch, also indicating that the consolidation was close to reality, but adding:

> Had a long, hot session with our friends in New York yesterday and was pretty nearly used up at the finish. If you think it is an easy matter to get money from New York capitalists to finance a motor car proposition in Michigan, you have another guess coming. Notwithstanding the fact that quoted rates are very low, money is hard to get owing to a somewhat unaccountable feeling of uneasiness and a general distrust of the automobile proposition.[3]

The Flint Journal of July 3 reported rumors that Buick and Maxwell-Briscoe had merged and that Durant was general manager of the new consolidation. But Durant was out of town, and Buick officials refused to comment.

As the talks seemed to be nearing a successful completion, Satterlee asked Durant and Briscoe if they would object to the combine's being named the International Motor Car Company instead of United Motors. Perkins liked that name, since he was also involved with the International Harvester Company and the International Mercantile Marine. There was no objection.

Meanwhile, Buick's business was booming. As the demand for sales increased, production was stepped up; new additions to the Flint plant were now under construction. Durant was working late into the night in Flint, while at the same time trying to negotiate a successful conclusion to the merger talks in New York. In the midst of all this, he decided to try to involve the Olds Motor Works of Lansing in his plans. He knew little about the Oldsmobile, except that it was one of the most famous automobiles in the country and that the company was having a hard time at the moment.

The Olds Motor Works dated to 1899, having evolved out of an earlier Olds company, when Ransom Olds secured financial backing from S. L. Smith, a copper magnate. They had erected a factory in Detroit, but it had burned in 1901 and the operations were centered again in Lansing, the original Olds base of operations. In 1901 Olds built 425 curved-dash runabouts and within four years was turning out more than 5,000 cars a year. Ransom Olds left in 1904 after a dispute with Smith's sons, Frederic L. and Angus Smith. Then the Olds Motor Works started to go downhill. With more elaborate models that didn't catch on, production fell from 5,000 in 1904 to 1,055 in 1908.

Fred Smith recalled that Durant arrived in Lansing after midnight one night, roused the Olds officials from bed, and at 3 a.m. galloped through the Olds plant on a fifteen-minute tour.[4] Then they talked until dawn about the sale of Olds to the proposed combination, working out a plan for Olds to join the combination after the Buick and Maxwell-Briscoe merger had taken place.

According to Durant's account, S. L. Smith told him that he was the only creditor of Olds and that he valued the business at $2 million. Durant asked if he would take $2 million of the preferred stock of the new combination. "Mr. Smith asked what the preferred stock was worth and if I thought there would be any market for it. I told him that until a statement was issued, the preferred stock would have no market value, but if he would take $2 million preferred with no bonus of common, I would agree to buy the stock from him within one year at a net to him of $1.8 million."

The Smiths, excited about the prospect of Morgan financial backing, agreed to join in the venture. On July 21, 1908, Fred Smith confirmed in a letter to Durant an agreement to transfer three-quarters of the Olds stock for stock in the proposed combine.[5]

Shortly afterward Perkins was planning a business trip from New York to Chicago and asked if Durant would ride as far as Albany on the train with him. Durant wrote: "In his drawing room, we had the opportunity of getting acquainted. I told him of my 20 years' experience in the carriage business and in reply to his questions gave him my views as to how the combination should be handled—and I think I sold him the 'holding company' idea. Mr. Perkins asked what I thought of the proposed name—International Motor Car Company—to which I replied that I considered it most appropriate. He then said, 'I think we should protect it, and if you wish to join me, I will, upon my return to Chicago, file an application for a New York charter.' This I agreed to. . . ."

Whether the Durant-Perkins meeting on the train resulted in closer agreement, as Durant thought, or in the beginning of the end of the Morgan interest in the deal, as Smith wrote, remains unclear. According to Smith, Perkins became alarmed with Durant's insistence that he himself be in charge of the consolidation's finances. Whatever the reason, the talks soon ran into difficulty. After his conversation with Perkins, Durant returned to New York. As he walked into Satterlee's office, he was met by Curtis R. Hatheway, a young attorney with the firm. The Morgans, said Hatheway, were anxious to talk to Durant. Durant was escorted to the office of Francis Lynde Stetson, the Morgan attorney.

Stetson was cordial. He said he had heard some fine things about Buick. He went on to say that he understood Durant was in complete control of Buick stock, with authority to execute an agreement. Durant replied that this was correct, that the stock was deposited in a Flint bank. Durant and Carton had some time before prepared for the consolidation by drawing up an agreement to be signed by Buick stockholders, authorizing Durant to act for them in an exchange of stock between Buick and the planned new company—the exchange to be on the same terms for other stockholders as it would be for Durant. Durant wrote that every share of Buick stock was endorsed under this agreement and deposited in a Flint bank, with a vice-president of the bank as trustee.

"Mr. Stetson asked if the depositors had knowledge of the new securities or any details regarding the new company, the size of the capitalization, etc. I told him the stockholders had confidence in me and that the matter was entirely in my hands.

"Mr. Stetson said he doubted if a title of that kind would be sufficient and said he thought it might be necessary to have the Buick stockholders execute a new set of papers. I questioned the wisdom of changing or even suggesting a change in the agreement. Mr. Stetson insisted that he must have a better title and could not approve the exchange on the terms and under the conditions of the deposit agreement. I told him I was acting on the advice of my attorney and that I would get in touch with him immediately.

"Up to that time, I was what you might say 'quite warm' for the merger, but after my interview with Mr. Stetson, I am frank to say that I cooled off slightly."

Carton replied to Stetson's challenge on July 29, 1908:

> So far as the transfer of the stock of the Buick Motor Company is concerned, it seems to me to be a perfectly plain transaction. . . . The stock of course is owned by individual stockholders who have a right to sell it or transfer it on any terms they see fit the same as they would any other property owned by them. They have agreed to sell and transfer their stock for an equal amount of the preferred stock of the International Motor Company plus an amount equal to fifty per cent of the common stock of that company and I can see no reason why they cannot transfer that stock to the International Motor Company direct or to some other person for the purpose of exchanging it. . . . I can see no reason why the details of the organization should be voluntarily made known to the individual stockholders of the Buick Motor Company. If any should refuse to sell their stock without the knowledge of these details then it would be a matter to be taken up with that individual stockholder but I do not think that will be required in view of the consent which they have already given to the sale and transfer.[6]

While the fuss over the Buick stock continued, another problem came up. The Morgans were upset about an article in the *New York Times* which went into some of the details of the negotiations. Hatheway wired Durant that the Morgans "now refuse to cooperate," but that he would try to restore the situation. Durant replied on August 1 that he had not seen the article, "but I take it that it must have been very 'severe' to have so greatly disturbed our friends at this late date."[7]

The offending article was a one-column item in the *Times*, July 31, 1908, which began:

PLAN A $25,000,000
MOTOR CAR MERGER

The first big combination in the automobile world is now in the making, the plans calling for a company to be known as the International Motor Company with $25 million capitalization, $11 million common and $14 million preferred stock.

The story went on to state, quite correctly, that Buick and Maxwell-Briscoe were to be combined first, with others to follow in consolidation. Several members of the Morgan company were among the underwriters, the article observed, though the banking house was not itself involved in the transaction. The merger could be ready for operation by September. No source was cited for the information.

On August 4 Briscoe returned to New York from a trip and was surprised to find the situation with the Morgans "in somewhat of a chaotic state." He wrote to Durant:

> It seems that on account of the publication of the details in Friday's "Times" that the people on the "corner" [the Morgans] are very upset. Why they should feel it as deeply as they do I can't quite fathom myself ... [and] the position taken by Mr. Stetson, that a full disclosure to each stockholder must be made whose stock is exchanged, will, I imagine, somewhat interfere with your plans. Articles have been appearing in Detroit and Flint papers which have evidently emanated from Buick stockholders. . . . It has always appeared to me that one of the surest ways to get publicity is to deny things, or to refuse to confirm or deny them, and this has been too much our attitude in regard to the publication of the matter. . . . I recognize that the procrastination in pushing the matter through has been very disappointing and disconcerting to you, as it has been to myself. I think that the time that it has taken to get where we have has been quite unnecessary and I am of the opinion ... that it would be possible for you and myself, and perhaps one or two others that we could attach to us, to take hold of this matter and work it out without waiting on anybody. We have both concluded that a million dollars in cash would be enough to finance the proposition and I will eat my shoes if we can't raise a million dollars between us.[8]

According to Durant's account, Ford and Ransom Olds were still involved in the negotiations at this point, but when Ford announced that he wanted money, not stock, the talks fell apart and "everyone except myself left the sinking ship." Yet, given the letters, newspaper articles, and the accounts of other participants, it appears more likely that Ford and Olds had dropped out weeks earlier. The Morgans may have lost interest because of the argument over the Buick stock, or because of the publicity, or because they had perceived that Durant was not about to turn over financial control to the Morgans and be content with managing Buick. Whatever the reason, by the end of August the Morgans appeared no longer interested in working with Durant. Herbert Satterlee asked Durant what he intended to do.

"I told him that I had come to New York several months earlier, and had been led to believe that the consolidation sponsored by the Morgan firm was being seriously considered and had so informed my people; that the Buick stock had been deposited and if released could never again be collected in the same form—nor would I have the courage, or care, to make another attempt. I must have a consolidation.

"Mr. Satterlee said, 'Mr. Durant, you only have the Buick, how can you have a consolidation?' I replied that I would have no difficulty in securing another company, as a matter of fact I had one in mind at the moment—the Olds Motor Works of

Copy of contract in which owners of Buick stock agreed to convert to "International Motor Company" stock. But the consolidation plans fell through and Durant, in September, 1908, created General Motors.

Received of the National Bank of Flint, Buick Motor Company common stock certificates for a total of____four____shares belonging to____Mary E. Busenbark____ of____Flint, Mich.____, which I agree to sell and accept in payment therefor an equal number of shares of the International Motor Company's seven per cent preferred stock, together with one-half as many shares of its common stock, all of which International Motor Company stock so received by me I agree to deliver to the holder hereof on surrender of this receipt.

Dated, August 1, 1908

W. C. Durant

Lansing, Michigan. The company—one of the oldest in the business—was controlled by Mr. S. L. Smith of Detroit, and was being operated by his sons, Fred and Angus Smith, whom I knew intimately. While that company was not a financial success, I believed it had possibilities. Mr. Henry Russel, vice president of the Michigan Central Railroad, a great friend of Mr. Smith, was president of the Olds Motor Works. I was acquainted with Mr. Russel and said I would wire him immediately asking if he would meet me in Lansing the following Saturday, mentioning the fact that I would like to discuss a possible merger of Olds and Buick, which I did.

"Satterlee asked about the capitalization and how the common stock was to be issued. I told him I had in the Buick organization a competent engineer, by the name of Walter Marr, with whom I had worked closely for several years; that the engineering success of the Buick was due largely to his efforts; that he was a crank on carburetors and had taken out numerous patents; that he was very fond of me, had named his only son after me, and I was quite sure he would set aside for my use a sufficient number of patents and applications against which the common stock could be issued.

"Satterlee then asked what I intended to call the company. I told him that in view of the collapse of the 'consolidation,' I assumed Mr. Perkins would have no use for the name 'International Motor Car Company' (owned jointly by us) and believed I would have no difficulty in arranging with him to take over his interest. Mr. Satterlee was not so sure that Mr. Perkins would care to surrender his interest and I suggested that he go over to the bank and talk the matter over with him. In about half an hour he returned and stated that Mr. Perkins preferred to reserve the name 'International Motor Car Company' for possible use at a later date.

"We then looked over the list of names which we had previously prepared when we were seeking a name for the consolidation and when we came to General Motors I selected that name and as of that moment the General Motors Company came into being."

The name was one of several on a list Durant left with the

Cable Address.
Northward, New York.

J. Langdon Ward
Henry W. Hayden
Herbert S. Satterlee
Carlos R. Hathaway
W. Kintzing Post
Thomas M. North

Law Offices of
Ward, Hayden & Satterlee,
Equitable Building, 120 Broadway, New York.
Telephone, 3945 Cortlandt.

Sept. 10th, 1908.

W. C. Durant, Esq.,

    Hotel Manhattan,

        New York City.

Dear Mr. Durant:-

Referring to our conversation during the past two days, we find it impracticable to use the "International Motor Company", incorporated by us recently under the laws of the State of New Jersey, for the purpose of taking over the stock of certain motor companies or to use that name in such connection, at present. It will be impossible to secure the underwriting by the parties with whom we have been in touch, until the inventories, appraisals and audits of all Companies have been finally completed. This would necessarily mean a delay of nearly two months, if not more, and would entirely preclude the plan of perfecting an organization and working out its details before the end of this year. We are convinced that not until after election can the new capital which we had in view be secured for the enterprise and it therefore seems best to incorporate another Company with similar powers, under another name, in New Jersey. We might use the "United Motors Company" were it not for the fact that there is already a "United Motor Car Company" in that State. We suggest the name, "General Motors Company", which we have ascertained can be used.

109

attorneys. On September 10, 1908—six days before incorporation—he received a letter from Ward, Hayden and Satterlee:

> We find it impractical to use the "International Motor Company". . . . We might use the "United Motors Company" were it not for the fact that there is already a "United Motor Car Company" in that state. We suggest the name, "General Motors Company," which we have ascertained can be used. . . .[9]

Chapter Six

"Never Mind,
We're Still Running"

Now that Durant had a name for his holding company, he moved quickly to form a combination. Immediately after the International Motor talks collapsed, he packed his papers and the next day left New York for Lansing.

Assured that the Olds officials in Lansing still wanted to merge with Buick, Durant told Ward, Hayden, and Satterlee to file the incorporation papers. On September 15, 1908, the law firm wrote to Durant that "we have seen to it, as far as we were able, that no publicity will attend the filing of the papers."[1] Its word was good. Almost nobody noticed when Curtis R. Hatheway filed articles of incorporation for the General Motors Company of New Jersey with the New Jersey secretary of state's office on September 16, 1908—which today is recognized as the birthday of General Motors. Capital stock was only $2,000 and the names of the incorporators were unfamiliar: George E. Daniels, Benjamin Marcuse, and Arthur W. Britton. They met on September 22 and elected themselves interim directors, with Daniels president. Durant, moving behind the men he used as incorporators, increased the capitalization to $12.5 million on September 28.

On that day President Daniels announced that "Mr. W. C. Durant is present and is prepared to make a business proposition to the company." Durant said he was "advised" that General Motors had been incorporated and further that among its purposes was to build automobiles. That being the case, he proposed to sell Buick to General Motors.[2] Durant was actually in control of both Buick and General Motors, so there was no need for negotiations. On October 1, General Motors bought Buick for about $3.75 million, all but $1,500 of it in an exchange of stock. The sale price was considered conservative.

On October 10 the original General Motors officers were succeeded by William M. Eaton, a prominent businessman in Jackson, Michigan, as president; Durant as vice-president, and Hatheway as secretary. Once again Durant had spurned the president's title, even though he was the founder and the active operator of the business. Eaton could handle the administrative details—Durant had more important work. General Motors bought the W. F. Stewart Company body plant adjacent to Buick in Flint for $240,000 and leased it to Buick. On November 12, General Motors purchased the entire outstanding common stock of the Olds Motor Works for a little more than $3 million, all of it in an exchange of GM stock except for $17,279 in cash.

Considering that General Motors had paid $3.75 million for Buick, then the country's leading automobile producer, this seemed an exorbitant price for the Olds Company, based on its worth that year. Durant acknowledged as much when, looking over the Olds books after agreeing to the purchase, he was asked by Henry Russel, president of Olds, if he had "found anything" (meaning of value). Durant replied that he had not, to which Russel replied, "Neither have I." But Durant knew there was still magic in the Oldsmobile name. Oldsmobile had prestige as one of the first quality producers. Roads across the country were dotted with Olds billboards. The song "In My Merry Oldsmobile," written in 1905, was still popular. The public could easily be sold if the right model were built.

Durant wasted no time in finding one. "Buick was building a very popular small car, the Model 10, which had a powerful four-cylinder valve-in-head motor and gave a wonderful performance when compared with other cars in its price class," he wrote. "The next day I sent to the Oldsmobile factory by truck one of these [Model 10] bodies in the white, following with my engineer and production manager.

"Arriving at the plant, I had the body placed on two ordinary saw horses and asked the plant manager if there was a cross-cut saw. When it was produced, I asked to have the body cut lengthwise from front to rear and crosswise in the center from side to side (bodies at that time were made of wood), giving me an opportunity to widen and lengthen the body, changing the size and appearance completely.

"When finished, it was a handsome creation, painted and trimmed to meet the Oldsmobile standard and priced to the trade at $1,200 ($200 more than the Model 10). This gave to Oldsmobile dealers a very handsome small car without interfering in any way with the Buick Model 10. A happy solution to the problem—placing the Oldsmobile Division of General Motors immediately on a profitable basis."

Despite his activity Durant was still not talking publicly about General Motors through the end of 1908. Although a number of speculative articles had appeared in newspapers since

Durant (in cap at wheel, facing camera) in the Oldsmobile which is believed to have competed in the 1907 Glidden Tour. The photo may have been taken in 1908, however, as that is the year Durant's new General Motors company took over Oldsmobile.

the middle of May, it was not until late December that the name General Motors was widely connected with Durant. On December 28 a one-column article on Page One of *The Flint Journal* carried word from New York that the "formation of the General Motors Company for the purpose of absorbing all the principal concerns manufacturing low-priced automobiles has created a flurry there." The article said that three-quarters of the stockholders of the Olds Motor Works and a "fair-sized proportion" of the stockholders of Buick in Flint had assented to the proposed merger. *The Journal* reported that "when seen in regard to the foregoing dispatch today, W. C. Durant, general superintendent of the Buick Motor Company, said there was nothing in regard to the matter which he could give out for publication."

Of course Buick stockholders in Flint knew of Durant's activities. In a letter to William S. Ballenger dated September 14, 1908, two days before the incorporation, Durant stated, "I have made arrangements so that about the first of the month you can exchange your Buick stock for stock in a new company to be known as General Motors (it having been decided inexpedient to use the name International Motors)."[3]

At the same time he was forming General Motors, Durant made another important move. As he was helping set up a Buick sales room in Boston—the city of his birth and early childhood—a young man came to see him. The fellow showed him a gadget that had some merit, but wasn't suited for Buicks. But it was so well designed that Durant thought the man might be able to produce other products he could use. His name was Albert Champion.

"Have you a factory?" Durant asked.

"No, just a shop," replied Champion.

"What are you making?"

"Magnetoes and spark plugs."

"We don't use magnetoes, but I am interested in spark plugs. Can you make a good one?"

Durant wrote that he was having trouble finding a spark plug suited to Buick's high-speed, high-compression, valve-in-head engine. Only one company made such a spark plug for Buick, and was charging thirty-five cents apiece. Durant told Champion that if he was quite sure he could make a spark plug for Buick, he was welcome to go to Flint with Durant. Durant would start an experimental plant, and if Champion could make good, he would get an interest in the business.

Champion was interested, but a few days later informed Durant that his backers would sell neither the business (Durant had offered $2,000) nor the name, the Albert Champion Company.

"I'm not interested in the name," Durant replied. "I'm interested in spark plugs." He wrote: "As soon as I could arrange it, I took Albert Champion to Flint, found a small building near my office, and put him to work. While I was busy with the Buick sales organization—traveling all over the country—Cham-

Durant moved Albert Champion to Flint in 1908. Champion began and developed what later became the AC Spark Plug Division of General Motors.

pion was busy with his spark plug experimental work. . . . He finally succeeded in submitting to our engineers a spark plug of real merit, and after passing the severest test, it was accepted and made a part of the Buick equipment. The price paid to the Champion department was 25 cents, a saving of 10 cents each over the previous price. It was not long before Buick was using 1,000 spark plugs a day, a saving on this item alone of $100 a day. The investment and expenses of the operation to that time amounted to approximately $36,000."

On October 26, 1908, the Champion Ignition Company of Flint was incorporated, and the next year it became a subsidiary of General Motors. Durant gave Champion $25,000 in stock of its initial $100,000 capitalization. Champion rewarded Albert Schmidt, his most important associate, with $7,500 in stock, which made Schmidt rich within a decade.

Champion had been born in Paris April 2, 1878. By age twelve he was an errand and office boy for a Paris bicycle manufacturer. He became interested in bicycle racing, won the middle-distance championship in France, and went to the United States in 1899 for a series of races. He won the American and world championships, returned to France to study automobile manufacturing, and returned to the United States in 1900. He tried auto racing, almost lost a leg in a racing accident, and then organized the Champion company. His original backers kept the name and moved the company to Toledo at about the same time Champion joined Durant. In Flint, Champion became known as one of the most colorful and flamboyant figures in a town full of them. He lived to see both his new company, later named the AC Spark Plug Division (using his initials), and the company he had left, the Champion Spark Plug Company, become giants in their field. He was a multimillionaire when he died in 1927 while on a visit to Paris.

By the start of 1909 Durant was ready to move in a big way. General Motors was formed with Buick and Olds, and Champion was at work in Flint. Durant's aim was nothing less than to gain control of some of the biggest and best automobile companies in America. But he also wanted to get in on the ground floor with companies just starting. They could be purchased by exchanging small amounts of stock, and who could tell what their patents, products, and inventions might bring? The automobile industry was in its infancy, the public was fickle, the only sure road to power and success was to have a wide range of products. Wrote Durant: "I figured if I could acquire a few more companies like the Buick, I would have control of the greatest industry in this country. A great opportunity, no time to lose, I must get busy. I felt confident, because of the hazardous nature of the automobile business, that if money in sufficient quantity could be obtained, a reasonable number of good companies could be induced to sell out or become members of a central organization that would provide engineering and patent protection and minimize the hazards which were constantly developing."

Here was Durant, in 1908, while the country's banking interests looked on cars as little more than a national fad, already seeing the auto business as the greatest industry in the land. When Durant predicted that some day 500,000 automobiles would be built and sold in a single year, the bankers thought he was mad. Durant did not care what they thought. He knew he was right. As one interviewer reported, "Durant sees—actually sees—90,000,000 people just aching to roll along the roads of this country in automobiles, and he wishes to fill that void."

One of the first companies he went after in 1909 was the Oakland Motor Car Company of Pontiac, Michigan, thirty miles south of Flint. The Oakland Company had been organized in 1907 by Edward M. Murphy, a man of extraordinary business drive and organizational ability. Durant described Murphy as "a high-type, energetic progressive man about my age." Oakland's Model K was a powerful four-cylinder car which in 1908 had won hill climbs all over the country. But when Durant appeared on the scene, the firm was still small and had money troubles.

Durant sent one of his associates, W. L. P. Althouse, to visit with Murphy. Althouse told Murphy and his associates that they were engaged in a hazardous undertaking, depending entirely upon one man—the engineer—to produce a well-designed, safe, and attractive motor car. If the engineer failed to do this in any one year, the company could be ruined. On the other hand, if they would exchange their stock for General Motors stock, their eggs would be in several baskets and they would enjoy the protection of a variety of engineering groups and automobiles.

Murphy's associates listened thoughtfully, concluded that Althouse had a point, and exchanged their stock for GM. But Murphy himself could not be budged, and consequently GM did not gain control of the company. This was a challenge for Durant: "Then I became very much interested. I cultivated Murphy and paid attention to what he was doing, saw him frequently, offered suggestions as to where important materials at very much lower prices could be obtained, and helped him in many ways.

"One Saturday afternoon when I was rushing for Detroit to catch a train to New York, I stopped for a few moments at the Oakland plant. I did not get out of my car. Murphy came down from his office at my invitation to tell me how the business was progressing. I was about to leave when he asked me if I would do an errand for him in New York.

"Returning in a few moments, he brought down a large package which he gave to me to handle in accordance with instructions therein contained. Upon my arrival in New York, I found that his entire Oakland holdings, the savings of a lifetime, were to be exchanged, giving the General Motors Company the control of Oakland Motor Car Company.

"A few days after the stock was transferred in accordance with his instructions, I received a telegram announcing Mr. Murphy's passing.

"The exchange having been made, the E. M. Murphy estate received a handsome fortune, whereas if the exchange had never been effected, the Oakland stock would have been practically worthless by reason of an engineering error which was made a few years later exactly as set forth by Althouse when negotiating with Murphy's associates."

Oakland—which eventually became the Pontiac Division of General Motors—was small game compared with some of the companies Durant sought to control in 1909—Cadillac, Ford, and the E. R. Thomas Company.

Already in 1909 Cadillac had a wide reputation for quality. This was primarily because Henry M. Leland was Cadillac's guiding force. Leland, a distinguished-looking man with his snow-white hair and beard, demanded precision machining in every part he manufactured. He had worked on Springfield rifles and Colt revolvers in the East, had been employed for twenty years by the highly regarded Brown and Sharpe Manufacturing Company of Providence, Rhode Island, and had moved to Detroit in 1890. Leland formed his own company, Leland & Faulconer, which soon earned a high reputation as a manufacturer of precision gears and castings. After the Olds fire in 1901, he was asked to build engines for Olds as it tried to get production going again. Olds was so happy with the first engines Leland & Faulconer produced that when Leland offered an improved version, he saw no reason to purchase it.[4] Leland then sold the improved engine to the Detroit Automobile Company.

In 1902 the Detroit Automobile Company evolved into the Cadillac Automobile Company, and in March, 1903, two Cadillacs were completed, using Leland motors. Because Leland's engines were of higher quality than the car's body and chassis, Leland was persuaded to take over management in 1904.

Cadillac production rose to 4,307 cars in 1906, but fell to 2,696 in 1907, partly because the public was losing interest in Cadillac's one-cylinder cars and was not attracted to Cadillac's larger models, and partly, no doubt, because of the financial panic of 1907. Another factor was that Buick, up in Flint, was really starting to catch on. In 1908 Buick produced 8,847 cars, compared with 2,012 for Cadillac.

Sometime in the fall of 1908, Ralph L. Aldrich, brother of Fred A. Aldrich of the Durant-Dort Carriage Company, stopped in at Durant's office in Flint. Durant asked Aldrich, a Detroit insurance and real estate man, if he knew anyone connected with Cadillac. Aldrich said he was well acquainted with Henry M. Leland and Wilfred C. Leland, Henry's son. Durant said he would pay Aldrich $10,000 if he could arrange a meeting with Durant and the Lelands to discuss the sale of Cadillac. Durant explained that his relations with the Lelands were not very cordial because the two-cylinder Buick was a keen competitor of the "one-lung" Cadillac.

Aldrich left for Detroit and two weeks later called Durant to say that the meeting had been set up in Detroit—at the Cadillac Hotel. Durant took a train to Detroit and waited for Wilfred C.

Leland to arrive. What follows is Durant's account of the Cadillac purchase:

"The usual greetings, with my statement, 'You understand the object of this meeting, Mr. Leland, but before discussing the price and terms, I would like to ask one question. Can you produce at a fair profit the new four-cylinder Cadillac car which you are offering to the public at $1,475 and give a proper discount to your retail dealers and distributors?'

"To which Mr. Leland replied, 'It can and is being done.'

"I handed him a few sheets of hotel stationery and asked him if he would be good enough to give me the figures. In a few moments, he returned the paper with the cost of the essential items with the overhead, as he figured it, showing a satisfactory profit, and we proceeded."

According to Durant the initial selling price was $2.25 million, although Leland has written that the first price was $3.5 million. "I told him that in view of the confused state of the industry it seemed like a rather large figure and I would like to talk the matter over with my associates and would call a meeting in New York on the following Monday. Mr. Leland said that he had come with a cash proposition—not an option—and had nothing different to offer."

Durant replied that he did not want an option, that he would wire Leland within a few days if his associates—meaning the General Motors board—approved the purchase, which Durant would recommend, and that in the meantime Leland was free to negotiate a sale with any other interest or to withdraw the proposition.

The meeting was called in the New York office of General Motors, 101 Park Avenue. Attending besides Durant were Fred and Angus Smith of Oldsmobile, Curtis R. Hatheway, and William M. Eaton, president of General Motors. Durant told of his interview with Leland, offered his views on the advantages to General Motors if Cadillac could be purchased, and explained that the money was to be obtained by issuing GM obligations. Wrote Durant: "Expecting that the deal, so far as General Motors was concerned, was as good as closed, I was somewhat surprised when Mr. Fred Smith[*] entered a mild protest. He

[*] Fred Smith was a strong admirer of Durant. In his recollections, "Motor-

referred to the fact that there was an indebtedness to his father—which I had guaranteed—of $1.8 million.

"This small matter I had entirely overlooked and, realizing that he was absolutely right, without further comment I wired Leland that our people were not in favor of the purchase and that my proposition, much to my regret, must be withdrawn.

"A few months later, when I had paid Mr. Smith his $1.8 million, I again took up the matter of the Cadillac acquisition. I called Mr. W. C. Leland and asked if he cared to reopen the negotiation. He informed me that he was willing to discuss the proposition, but on an entirely different basis. I made an appointment and arranged to meet him at the [old] Pon-chartrain Hotel in Detroit.

"Getting down to business immediately, I was informed that the price was $4.75 million cash—that $500,000 had to be deposited as a forfeit—the balance to be paid in 30 days. I asked him if there were any other conditions, to which he replied, 'For every three days that the balance is delayed, the price is to be increased one per cent.' He estimated the profits at 10 per cent per month, or one per cent every three days.

"I asked him how much General Motors preferred stock he would take and while he was not in favor of preferred stock of any kind, after some hesitation he said that his father would take $50,000 and he would take $25,000—the consideration being $4,675,000 cash and $75,000 in preferred stock. . . ."

As Leland wrote out the figures for the record, Durant picked up the telephone, called the president of the Peninsular State Bank, and told him he had just bought Cadillac and

---

ing Down a Quarter of a Century" (*Detroit Saturday Night*, 1928), he wrote: "Durant saw the possibilities of a strong combination earlier and more clearly than anyone else in or out of the industry, and he put it over; a feat more staggering at the time than can be easily appreciated today. In spite of frequent and earnest scraps with W. C., I had at least the intelligence to see in him the strongest and most courageous individual then in the business and the master salesman of all time. No man ever lived who could sell such a variety of commodities in so short a space of time, cigars, buggies, automobiles, ideas and himself, believing wholeheartedly in his wares and in the last item especially. . . . It would be a poorly-posted analyst who failed to list W. C. Durant as the most picturesque, spectacular and aggressive figure in the chronicles of American automobiledom. He certainly made some capital mistakes . . . but the man who makes no mistakes rarely makes anything at all on a large scale."

needed $500,000 at once to bind the bargain. He then asked the banker to finance a serial note issue of $2 million secured by the entire capital stock of Cadillac. If more collateral were needed he would provide notes of the Buick Motor Company owned by Durant and Dort. The carriage company, according to Durant, was the largest holder of Buick common stock which had not yet been transferred to General Motors. The banker prepared an offering of eighty notes of $25,000 each. Durant said that the entire issue was subscribed in ten days, thus releasing the $500,000 forfeit deposit. He wrote:

"A management contract with the Lelands, giving each a handsome salary and a percentage of the net profits, was arranged, making any change in the personnel unnecessary.

"It was several months before I had occasion to inspect my purchase, although I received many invitations from the Lelands to do so, giving as my reason 'pressure of important business.'

"The real reason was that I was negotiating for the purchase of many other concerns, some of whom were fearful that a connection with General Motors might mean a change of policy and management. To meet this situation, it was only necessary to refer them to the Cadillac management, who could truthfully say that Durant had never been in the Cadillac plant. In passing, I might add that the Cadillac earnings in 14 months returned the entire purchase price, $4,750,000."

The amount of cash involved was $4.67 million, generally referred to as the largest cash transaction negotiated in Detroit up to that time.

While these talks were going on, Benjamin Briscoe, Jr., was also trying to develop a combination—or, preferably, to join Durant's new General Motors. Durant and Briscoe discussed the possibility of selling Maxwell-Briscoe to GM for $3.5 million, but the Morgan investors said they would agree only if Durant would pay a substantial portion—about $2 million—in cash. Briscoe fumed about the Morgans' shortsightedness. He then tried to finance the purchase of Cadillac for Maxwell-Briscoe. At one point Briscoe had an option to buy, but his backers dragged their feet, the option expired, and Durant got Cadillac for General Motors. Briscoe was determined to have a combination. Ignoring his setbacks, he soon got his backers to approve the creation of his own version of General Motors—the United States Motor Company.[5]

As for Durant, he had acquired a bargain in Cadillac. Though it cost him more than $4.5 million, it was earning $2 million a year in net profits. Other men, including the financial backers of Cadillac and the big financiers of Wall Street, were frightened by the speculative nature of the automobile business. Only Durant—and perhaps Briscoe—had the vision and courage to make that kind of a deal.

With the exception of the Cadillac purchase, Durant didn't need much cash to acquire companies. With General Motors as his holding company, he could exchange GM stock for the stock of the company he was buying. The individual auto companies didn't need a lot of money in those days either. They could buy their supplies on credit and finance expansions with profits.[6] It was a time made to order for Durant's abilities.

In the first two years of General Motors' existence, Durant purchased all of, or a substantial interest in, the following firms and plants: Buick Motor Company, Flint; W. F. Stewart Company's Plant 4, Flint; Olds Motor Works, Lansing; Seagar Engine Works, Lansing; Oakland Motor Car Company, Pontiac; Marquette Motor Company, Saginaw; Cadillac Motor Company, Detroit; Michigan Motor Castings Company, Flint; Randolph Truck Company, Flint; Champion Ignition Company (later AC Spark Plug Division), Flint; Reliance Motor Truck Company, Owosso; Ranier Motor Company, Saginaw; Welch Motor Car Company, Pontiac; Welch-Detroit Company, Detroit; Jackson-Church-Wilcox Company, Jackson; Michigan Auto Parts Company, Detroit; Rapid Motor Vehicle Company, Pontiac; Cartercar Company, Pontiac; Ewing Automobile Company, Geneva, Ohio; Elmore Manufacturing Company, Clyde, Ohio; Dow Rim Company, New York City; Northway Motor & Manufacturing Company, Detroit; Bedford Motors Company, London, Ontario; National Motor Cab Company; Novelty Incandescent Lamp Company; Heany Lamp Companies (Heany Company, Heany Lamp Company, Heany Electric Company and Tipless Lamp Company); McLaughlin Motor Car Company, Ltd., Oshawa, Ontario; Brown-Lipe-Chapin Company, Syracuse, New York; and Oak Park Power Company, Flint.

Of these, twenty-two were gathered in by the end of 1909, less than sixteen months after General Motors' incorporation. Durant wanted to be the leader of the motor vehicle industry, but he had no clear idea what kind of vehicle would emerge as the most popular. So he grabbed all kinds of companies—some whose only real assets were patents on dubious inventions. Carter-car had friction drive, Elmore had a two-cycle engine. He bought car companies in various price ranges, truck companies, parts manufacturers. Many proved worthless, but hadn't cost much. A few were severe liabilities. Some were solid gold—Buick, Cadillac, Oakland (Pontiac), Oldsmobile, AC, McLaughlin.

Durant's burst of empire-building in this period was incredible. He worked late into the night, and people waiting to see him were amazed when he made appointments with them at midnight, or 1 a.m., or even later.

"One-thirty a.m.? Don't you mean p.m.?" asked one man.

"No, 1:30 a.m.," Durant answered. "We'll get this in yet today."

Durant was pushing himself hard. W. W. Murphy, his long-time personal secretary, recalls one particularly revealing episode. He and Durant were headed by car for Detroit to catch a train, and Durant was driving. Along the road they were slowed by a tractor pulling a huge load of hay. It obstructed the entire road. Durant gunned the car around the haywagon and veered through a ditch. There was a loud snap as a spring leaf broke.

"What was that?" Murphy shouted.

"Never mind," yelled Durant, pulling out of the ditch in front of the wagon. "We're still running."

Murphy never forgot the remark. It caught the spirit of the whole of Durant's life.[7]

Durant was getting a lot of newspaper notice as his business activity increased at a frenzied pace. In 1909 Louis E. Rowley presented this profile of Durant in *Detroit Saturday Night:*

> There is nothing very striking about the personal appearance of Mr. Durant. He is slightly under the medium height* and his weight cannot be more than 140 pounds. But his

---

* Durant was just under 5 feet, 8 inches tall.

trim, lithe body suggests illimitable static force. His manners are refined and cordial, and he is usually as easy of approach as an information bureau. He has a zestful conciseness of expression that is refreshing. His voice is soft and he invariably speaks in a low tone. If he had to turn in a fire alarm, the chances are that he would whisper it.

There are no harsh lines in his face, no note of autocrat in his speech or act. In fact, he is a man of extreme reticence. He has that modesty which frequently accompanies tenacity of purpose. Yet there is something about him that makes you feel that here is an extraordinarily virile personality. The strongest impression he makes on one who meets him for the first time is of intense but perfectly controlled energy.

It is often remarked that he is calmest in the time of stress and cheeriest under the heaviest burdens. It is at such times that he invariably smiles—and his smile is very attractive. It is as innocent as a child's and as philosophic as a sage's.

Probably his eyes are Mr. Durant's most distinctive feature. They are brown, frank eyes, shrewd, but not the shrewdness of the eye that tries to read you just to find out what is in the back of your head . . . bright and gleaming eyes and yet with a feminine softness. The face is the face of an idealist, the planner, the dreamer—but the dreamer of realizable dreams.

To sum up his characteristics, Mr. Durant is a most interesting man; a perpetually fresh, sensible and likeable man; a man of heart and very attractive human failings. . . .

There is not the slightest taint of money-madness about him. For money itself he cares nothing, except so far as it means power. He works from a pure love of accomplishment. . . . In a word, he is a typical American benefactor, a creator who confers inestimable benefits upon society.

Durant's almost offhand way of making decisions requiring great outlays of cash amazed his contemporaries. Lee Dunlap, general manager at Oakland after Murphy's death, recalled that Durant paid a visit to the Oakland factory and was expected to stay for several days. Instead, after a few hours of conferences he announced, "Well, we're off to Flint." Dunlap pleaded that he needed to expand his plants. Would Durant please take a

Famous photo of Durant, believed taken during a Glidden Tour in the East, in 1908, the same year he founded General Motors.

look? Durant took a quick tour, agreed that expansion was necessary, and asked Dunlap to bring his expansion plan to Flint the following day.

Dunlap gulped. There was no plan. Dunlap and a few draftsmen worked through the night, drawing up a map and making a toy factory layout.

> I took this layout to Flint and rather fearfully placed it before the chief. . . . He was pleased pink. We placed those new buildings first here, then there, debating the situation. When we agreed as to where they should go, he said, "Glue them down and call W. E. Wood [a contractor]." Mr. Wood came in after a few minutes and received an order for their construction. Wood had men, materials, and machines moving toward Pontiac within 24 hours and we were installing machinery in part of the structures within three weeks.[8]

On another occasion, as he entertained a friend in his room at the Pontchartrain, Durant received a call from a contractor. He offered to give the caller ten minutes right then. The contractor arrived and Durant sat down with him. "Now I want you to begin on these buildings," Durant said, drawing a line sketch on a pad.

> I want this building 150 feet long by 80 wide, and three stories high, concrete and brick just like the others. Then off here at the right a wing 200 feet long, 60 feet wide and three stories high. Over here, two buildings just alike, 400 by 90 feet, three stories high. This street is to be cut through here. See that knoll—you remember it—see that it is leveled down and the street opened. Do you understand? I'll see you in Flint next Friday. Have everything worked out and we'll attend to any details that have to be considered. Goodbye.[9]

It was just another example of the way Durant attended to details that could have been delegated—when it was his whim. When General Motors later became a corporation worth hundreds of millions of dollars, Durant was still passing personal judgment on such details as the wiring diagrams at one of his factories.

As Louis Rowley wrote in Detroit:

> He has literally a consuming passion for work. His endurance and indefatigability are the marvel of all who know him. Besides the capacity for intense and incessant application, he has that power of initiative which goes by the name of genius for organization. He has the Napoleonic faculty of thinking out details beforehand. These things mean power. There is almost nothing he cannot do except rest.
>
> He was always in advance of his time, and time always vindicated the soundness of his judgment. He will pardon almost anything except stupidity and disloyalty.[10]

Durant almost bought the Ford Motor Company and the E. R. Thomas Company for General Motors. Thomas was a big name in 1909, for a year earlier one of its Thomas Flyers had won the famous New York-to-Paris race, covering three-quarters of the world's circumference and traversing the wretched roads of Siberia. The sale to General Motors failed to materialize, however, probably because cash, not stock, was required.

There are several versions of the negotiations between Durant and Ford. Here is Durant's account:

"When the International Motor Car consolidation—the Briscoe-Morgan plan—failed to materialize, it was generally understood that the Ford Motor Company could be purchased, but the price during the many conferences held in New York and Detroit had never been disclosed.

"I waited a reasonable time, having plenty to do getting the General Motors organization in shape, before I approached Mr. Couzens [Ford Business Manager James C. Couzens]. I spent the entire day with him one Sunday, going carefully over the Detroit plant and told him frankly that the General Motors would like to acquire the Ford Motor Company, and asked him if he would talk the matter over with Mr. Ford.

" 'If he is agreeable, bring him to New York prepared to close the deal.' Couzens said okay and expressed himself as favoring the sale.

"I had reason to believe that if we were successful, General Motors would not require any more motor car companies. Our time and energy from that time on should be devoted to building up or acquiring manufacturing plants to supply General Motors with the important items it would require in ever-increasing numbers, such as forgings, bodies, castings, wheels, tires, axles, transmissions, steering gears, ignition systems and small parts of all kinds.

"Controlling this enormous volume would make it possible for these accessory plants to materially reduce costs because of the volume of business from General Motors which they could depend upon if motor cars and trucks, as I was firmly convinced, were to become important factors in the industrial life of America.

"On the day appointed it so happened that Mr. Ford had eaten something on the train the evening before that did not agree with him [other reports say Ford, suffering from lumbago, was lying on the floor in his room in New York's Belmont Hotel because he could get no comfort in bed]. But he authorized Mr. Couzens to submit his proposition, which he did:

" 'Mr. Ford is very much concerned about the Selden patent suit and its outcome. . . . Mr. Ford will sell the Ford Motor Company for $8 million, giving me [Couzens] the privilege of purchasing 25 per cent of the company's stock as part compensation for my many years of services . . . the balance of the purchase price, $6 million, to be paid as follows: $2 million cash at time of sale, the remaining $4 million at 5 per cent interest due on or before three years.' "

Durant wrote that he asked Couzens if the sale carried the Ford name in connection with all automotive interests and if he would agree not to become interested in any other automobile company for ten years. Couzens replied that Ford wished to retain the right to manufacture motorized farm implements, but that the other conditions stated by Durant would be included in the contract.

Durant continued, "Mr. Couzens having delivered the message, I told him to say to Mr. Ford that I was in hopes that a deal could be worked out as suggested by him and that he would hear from me within ten days, that I regretted he was indisposed and hoped for him a speedy recovery."

The next day Durant met with officials of the National City Bank of New York to ask for a loan of $2 million to make the

Vast industrial development of Flint's North Side is shown in this 1909 view. The buildings in the foreground include the W. F. Stewart Body Works, Armstrong Manufacturing Company, Flint Varnish Works, Flint Axle Works, Imperial Wheel, and a Drop Forge Plant. The larger buildings behind them are dominated by Buick and Weston-Mott. Michigan Motor Castings Company is in extreme background at right center.

deal with Ford. According to his notes, the bankers were most encouraging, though they said that the loan would have to be authorized by the bank's board of directors and loan committee.

On October 26, 1909, the General Motors board gave Durant authority to purchase Ford if financing could be arranged. A few days later, at the Buick factory in Flint, Durant received a phone call from an officer of the bank. In Durant's words, "The answer, by long distance telephone, not favorable, with the explanation that the business was new, that the bank had just recently been severely criticized for a sizable transaction with a copper company, and the committee felt that it would be unwise to have it understood that they were sponsoring an automobile venture. It must be remembered that the banks, as a rule, were not at that time in favor of the automobile industry, as a matter of fact, they were extremely antagonistic. I made no further attempt to secure the $2 million and notified Mr. Ford that the purchase could not be financed at the present time."

A few years later, Durant wrote, he met Couzens on a train, and Couzens told him that Ford's earnings were then up to $35 million a year. Durant said that his banker friends never forgave themselves for failing to approve the loan. He himself, however, appeared to feel no regrets. "I never would have built up that business the way Ford did," he remarked decades later. "The Ford business would never have been what it is without Henry Ford, who has done more for America than any other man—more for the world. I made that statement years ago to the American Club in Paris. I make it again."

By the end of 1909, dark clouds were gathering over the Durant empire, though they were hardly noticed, even by many stock market analysts. In the middle of November one stock market letter did note that there was some discussion about the health of General Motors. Judging from its financial statements, the letter said, "the General Motors Company is well named, for they deal largely in generalities with the public." Nevertheless,

> that the management of the company is in capable hands is not questioned by anyone. The prominent figure is Mr. W. C. Durant, and while actual information is hard to get, the unbounded confidence in Mr. Durant displayed by those in close touch with him goes far towards maintaining a value

131

for the stock, which would not be possible in many other corporations with the same dearth of definite information.

The analyst concluded: "It looks good."

On March 16, 1910, Durant sent a brief letter to stockholders noting that the authorized capital of GM was $40 million in common stock and $20 million in preferred stock (with $15 million common and $8.5 million preferred outstanding). He reported that "valuable properties have recently been acquired," that net assets were three times the issue of preferred stock, and that the earnings of the company were twenty times the fixed charges. "General Motors securities are valuable to hold as a permanent investment," he concluded.

Also in March a million-dollar stock issue was floated for a new Buick engine plant. Flint employees were said to have subscribed to $122,000 of it by March 18 and the rest was allegedly sold within the next three days—half in Flint, the rest in Detroit, New York, and Cincinnati.

That same week GM common stock rose from 80 to 97 in Detroit (GM was still not listed on the New York exchange). Buick had produced 14,606 cars in 1909. For 1910 that figure would be more than doubled. If Durant smelled trouble ahead, he gave no sign of worry. After all, he had cashed in on the panic of 1907. Confidence and optimism were the order of the day.

Chapter Seven

The Bankers Take Over

Looking back, Durant figured that his troubles of 1910 began at an annual convention of bankers late in 1909, only about a month after the bankers in New York had knocked down his plan to buy Ford for $8 million:

"A member of the group—never in sympathy with the automobile—delivered a fiery speech saying that the people were spending money recklessly, that many concerns engaged in the manufacture of automobiles were not properly financed, that the bankers were responsible for a situation which, if not carefully watched, might result in an industrial and financial panic. The speaker claimed that the demand for automobile money was so great that many of their customers in other lines were being deprived of credit to which they were reasonably entitled.

"The picture painted was anything but rosy, and when it appeared in print and was nationally publicized, caused much comment. I sensed the effect immediately and tried to strengthen my position. My bankers—up to that time—had been more than generous but there is nothing more sensitive, more sought after, more godlike, if I can use the term, in the minds of the great majority of men, than money."

Some of the remarks at the bankers' meeting seemed pointed directly at Durant—and perhaps with some reason. Buick and Cadillac were profitable operations, Oakland was making some money, and Olds was showing signs of recovery. But it was

133

almost impossible to put together more than twenty companies of varying profitability and uneven management in two years and be entirely certain of what was going on. Durant had little faith in a large central staff, so he didn't have one. There was no uniform bookkeeping procedure, no clear control over inventories. The various GM subsidiaries still operated, for the most part, independently. Durant was operating largely on Buick's success, on his own confidence and salesmanship, and on his infectious optimism.

The wide publicity given to the anti-automobile talk at the bankers' convention threatened to cut into his ability to sell that optimism. And he reacted to the prospect of tight money days ahead as he always did when under attack—he went on the offensive. Just as he had battled the trusts which had once threatened the Durant-Dort Carriage Company, he now challenged the bankers by preaching optimism and acting accordingly.

On November 14, 1909, a GM stock dividend of 150 percent was declared. Durant wrote an article in a GM publication, emphasizing that "the automobile is here to stay." He reported that the appraised value of Buick alone was $17.4 million. Buick took 5,000 of the 12,000 shares when McLaughlin Motor Car Company, Ltd., of Oshawa, Ontario, was incorporated with $1.2 million capitalization. He sent a circular to holders of GM preferred stock, asking them to cooperate in a plan to establish a holding pool to control the stock for fifteen months. He explained that the stock was selling at too low a price "for the reason that the market is now controlled by brokers acting entirely in their own interest and for their own personal gain."[1]

In the spring of 1910 Durant was censured by the Association of Licensed Automobile Manufacturers for having sent out a circular showing the number of automobiles produced and the amount of royalties paid to the Selden patent interests by each member of the association.* The association had concluded that

---

* Although Henry Ford led the fight against joining the Association of Licensed Automobile Manufacturers (ALAM) and paying royalties to the Selden patent interests, Durant also had no love for the ALAM. According to William Greenleaf in *Monopoly on Wheels*, Durant had brought Buick into the organization by acquiring the license of the Pope-Robinson

GM was the guilty party "from the fact that Buick Motor Company and Cadillac Motor Company, both General Motors concerns, led in this list, and the further fact that the names of all General Motors concerns were printed in the list in heavy type." The association sternly emphasized that its members considered the information confidential.[2]

Durant did not deny the charge. He said he wished to dispose of wild rumors set afloat about enormous production by companies for "whose factories the first brick has yet to be laid." By this time he realized that GM was in serious financial trouble, and he wanted desperately to build faith in his organization. Between 1908 and 1910 Durant had pulled into General Motors some of its most productive divisions. But Cadillac had cost more than $4.5 million in cash, an obvious bargain but also a drain on vital liquid capital. And some of the other subsidiaries were disasters from the start.

The biggest blunder was the purchase of the Heany Lamp group of companies. Durant's enthusiasm for the electrical revolution was well founded, but he had bet the wrong horse. John Albert Heany had acquired a patent on a tungsten-filament electric lamp bulb, but his patent rights were cloudy, to say the least. GM paid $1.1 million in GM preferred stock, $5.9 million in common stock, and $112,759 in cash for these companies. As Lawrence H. Seltzer, in *A Financial History of the American Automobile Industry*, pointed out, this was more than Durant had paid for Buick and Olds together. Seltzer suspected a stock-watering deal to sweeten the consideration to be paid for the Maxwell-Briscoe Company, which Durant also tried to buy in 1909. Whatever the reason for the Heany purchase, it was a mistake. The Heany patent rights were voided, and published estimates of the eventual loss to GM as a

---

Company shortly after taking over Buick in 1904. However, when his attorney concluded in 1908 that the Selden patent did not mean anything, he stopped paying royalties on each car sold. When the Association brought suit against Buick, Durant fought back with countersuits, claiming conspiracy in restraint of trade, a predictable action for a man who had earlier fought the carriage trusts. But when a lower court (later overruled) upheld the Selden patent in 1909, Durant gave in and paid an estimated $1 million in back royalties. Greenleaf writes that a portion of this was apparently returned to General Motors in the form of dividends paid by the ALAM.

result reached as high as $12 million, not including the dividends paid annually to holders of the stock involved in the exchange. Yet, even after Heany was a confirmed disaster and Durant admitted he had lost confidence in John Heany, he still insisted that Heany had a more "elastic" and more efficient tungsten filament than did General Electric.[3]

GM's sales volume increased from $29 million in 1909 to $49.4 million in 1910, but net profits rose only by $1.1 million to $10.2 million in 1910. There was not enough money to finance expansions and purchase supplies. GM was forced to borrow heavily from its suppliers and commercial banks.[4]

The automobile market had started strong in 1910. Buick production jumped from 14,606 cars in 1909 to 30,525 in 1910. But quite abruptly the money needed to continue production dried up. Workers were laid off and for months the Buick plant in Flint was almost deserted. Conditions were also bad in Pontiac and Lansing and other places where GM plants were leading industries. GM shares fell from about $100 to $25.

The panic of 1910 was on, and Durant finally realized he could no longer operate on sheer optimism. He dropped plans

Buicks lined up for shipment in 1909. By the summer of 1910, operating capital had virtually dried up and production came to a halt. Despite the financial problems, however, official records show that Buick production hit 30,000—about equal with Ford—that year.

to try to buy into two major tire companies and to take over Willys-Overland, and tried to hold on to what he already had. He also announced a plan to increase GM's capitalization and to declare a stock dividend of 400 percent.

Before he could carry this out, however, his creditors decided it was time to get together and see what was what. They met in New York in August, 1910, toted up the company's debts, and discovered that Buick alone owed between $6.7 million and $7.7 million. The creditors made arrangements to provide temporary financial relief. They also named a general committee of creditors to try to "effect a reorganization of management and a restriction of enthusiasm."[5]

Durant recorded his version of his trials of 1910:

"I am placing this recital ahead of at least 20 stories of lesser

Louis Chevrolet (left) and Wild Bob Burman in their almost identical Buick "Bugs." The two Bugs were built in two weeks in 1910 and were said to be the fastest cars made to that time in an American shop by American workmen. Burman was clocked at an astonishing 105.8 miles per hour in his Bug at Indianapolis in 1910—the year before the Indy 500 race was inaugurated. The Bugs were perhaps the best, and also the last, major contribution by Buick to early auto racing. At the time Buick was tearing up the Indianapolis Speedway, the Buick company and Durant were in deep financial trouble. Soon Durant would be out, the racing program would be drastically curtailed, and Louis Chevrolet would be designing his own car. One of the two Bugs—perhaps Burman's—is still in existence, on display at the Sloan Museum. It is still in operating condition.

importance because I want this story preserved before it is too late. If the other 20 are never written, it will make no material difference.

"We all know our limitations, and at my age, while able to work 15 hours a day and like it, I do not have to be told that 'the sands of time are running low,' with the knowledge that I am just an ordinary human being.

"Now for the story:

"You will recall that General Motors from 1908 to 1910 was expanding very rapidly. To handle this business, in addition to the earnings of more than $10 million a year, additional working capital of approximately $15 million was required. This $15 million, under my direction, was obtained as follows:

"Seven million dollars from bankers evidenced by General Motors's notes endorsed by W. C. Durant (it required 204 different banks to provide this line of credit).

"Eight million dollars from suppliers of material. The credits in every instance guaranteed by W. C. Durant. (No other stockholder of General Motors was asked to endorse or guarantee these obligations.) Note: General Motors for many years was called a one-man institution. With respect to these endorsements and guarantees, it might be so considered.

"Why did I assume these obligations? Did you ever hear of such an unbusinesslike and senseless procedure? Let me tell you why.

"My early associates for the most part were my personal friends with limited capital. Many were willing to and did risk every dollar they possessed, believing as I did in the future of the automobile industry. I confess that I erred in not providing for 'an anchor to windward.' We sometimes pay dearly for overconfidence and in this case I did pay plenty. Had I taken the time and been inclined in that direction, I might have arranged with a responsible financial group to provide the necessary capital by surrendering a portion of the profits as an insurance against a severe loss or a temporary stoppage of business in 'squally times.'

"It is easy to offer suggestions or speculate as to what 'might have been,' but if you knew, as I did, the opposition and skepticism of the bankers and financiers generally, you can understand that in those early days of the industry, money in the amount required was not readily available."

Durant discussed the negative publicity out of the bankers' convention in the fall of 1909 and wrote that as a result of this publicity, "inquiries started to come from many of our bankers asking if our loans could not be reduced, indicating that the panic was on.

"And—listen to this—by May 1 [1910], our bank loans were all called and we were deprived of every dollar of working capital—the life-blood of our institution—which brought about the complete stoppage of our business with a loss to us of more than $60,000 a day."

One day, two Detroit banks loaned GM $500,000 so it could meet a Cadillac payroll. In the East, Harry K. Noyes, manager of Buick's Boston district, was sending money to Flint in suitcases for fear the banks would seize the cash if sent through regular channels. Durant combed the Western states, seeking bank loans, finding none.[6] "I tried the large financial institutions" he wrote. "I tried the life insurance companies. I tried the men who were known to possess large fortunes—but while I was considered an excellent salesman and had a wonderful proposition to offer, my efforts in that direction were to no avail. I admit that it was discouraging, but as I never had what might be called a 'soft job' in my life, and my experience had taught me that 'the tougher the job the harder you must work,' I kept right on looking for the money."

A bank in Chicago almost saved the day. It was ready to lend $7.5 million, but the request was upped to $9.5 million. The loan offer was rescinded.[7]

As the crisis of 1910 deepened, Durant appeared to be lost in thought. Some Flint men still recall his walking the streets alone at night, or standing aloof from the crowd waiting for the train to Detroit. Laverne Marshall, who chauffeured him around Flint in this period, remembers a cold autumn morning at the station: "Mr. Durant wore a long straight overcoat with a fur collar which gave him a military appearance. He paced up and down the platform, his arms folded snugly in front of him. His head, covered by his fur collar, was drawn down closely to his shoulders. To me he was the image of Napoleon heading his staff."

The lights in his office at Buick burned late into many nights as he pondered his options for saving the company. Finally, on his way home, he would tell the chauffeur to stop at a small restaurant in downtown Flint for a last cup of coffee. Art Sarvis, an enterprising young reporter for *The Flint Journal*, knew this and often would be waiting when "The Man" walked in. There they would sit, Durant talking quietly, Sarvis listening with fascination, some of the drama of the time being learned first hand.

One day in the fall, Sarvis was visiting Durant at his office when they were interrupted by a telephone call from an Eastern banker. Sarvis listened as Durant and the caller talked about a multimillion-dollar loan, and it appeared that Durant was getting a cold reception on the other end of the line. Finally, Durant replied to some question from the banker: "No, sir, there is no such thing as a saturation point—not until every man, woman and eligible child in the country has an automobile."

Cut off from the supply of money needed to continue production, GM was on the brink of collapse. Some of Durant's associates had already given up hope of saving the company. But Durant pressed on. Finally, J. H. McClement, a GM stockholder, advised Durant that there was hope. He had explored the financing problem with Lee, Higginson & Company of Boston, which he believed could get together a group to come up with enough money to save GM.

The negotiations continued for several weeks, with Wilfred C. Leland of Cadillac playing a key role. He impressed the bankers with Cadillac's money-making ability and sound business practices, talked of GM's great profit potential, and helped convince them that GM—not just Buick—was worth saving. Finally the Boston firm and J. & W. Seligman & Company, New York, agreed to underwrite up to $20 million worth of 6 percent notes, although only $15 million worth was actually issued. In effect, they were offering a loan of $15 million.

But the terms were severe. In return for the loan, GM had to give the bankers a commission of $4.1 million in preferred stock and $2 million in common stock, at par value. The bankers also required a blanket mortgage of GM's Michigan properties. And instead of getting $15 million, GM received $12.75 million. GM would have to repay $2.25 million it did not receive. (Durant's figures are somewhat higher than those generally reported—he wrote that the worth of GM stock given to the bankers was $21.6 million and that GM received only $12.25 million, giving the bankers a total compensation of $9.3 million.) There was another condition. The bankers also demanded control of the company, a voting trust, at least for the five-year term of the loan. Durant could remain vice-president and a member of the Finance Committee, but he would no longer be in control of the company he had founded.

Durant had no choice but to accept. General Motors consented to the loan on September 26, 1910. The contract was dated November 11.

The Flint Journal carried the story under the headline: SYNDICATE NOW IN CONTROL OF GENERAL MOTORS. GM publicly reported:

> The arrangement entered into some weeks ago with the New York banking syndicate . . . has been consummated and as a result thereof, the company has received sufficient funds to enable it immediately to pay its entire debt and the debt of all its subsidiary companies. . . .
>
> To provide for the repayment of these advances, the company has issued $15 million of 6 per cent five-year sinking fund notes of a total authorized issue of $20 million, secured by a first lien upon the manufacturing plants of the subsidized companies to the Central Trust Company of New York as trustee.

And in a statement Durant said, "The management believes that the financial arrangements which they have made place the company in excellent shape for the successful prosecution of its business."

Automotive historians have generally described the terms as exorbitant. And Durant, in his memoirs, fumed:

"The $15 million loan finally offered had outrageous terms which I was forced to accept to save my 'baby,' born and raised by me, the result of hectic years of night and day work and diligent applications.

"Under the terms, I received $12,250,000 cash (not $15 million), for which I gave $21,600,000 of the best securities ever created—the enormous interest of $9,350,000. (I also paid Mr. J. H. McClement, for his services in the Lee, Higginson & Company matter, 1,100 shares of General Motors common stock.)

"And listen to this—it took seven months to secure the money at the frightful price paid for it to start the wheels in motion and put thousands of men back to work. This having been accomplished, we notified our dealers that we were again doing business as usual, and the first week we received orders for 13,886 Buick cars having a money value of $13,886,000.

"I refer to this situation because of the fact that [later] the bankers reported that at the time they became interested, General Motors was a 'scrap heap,' which statement I have always resented."

On November 15, eleven directors retired, including Eaton, the president; Curtis Hatheway; Dr. Campbell; Wilfred Leland; and R. Samuel McLaughlin. Members of the new board were Anthony N. Brady, J. H. McClement, Albert Strauss, Nicholas L. Tilney, and James N. Wallace, all of New York; James J. Storrow, Boston; Emory W. Clark, A. H. Green, Jr., M. J. Murphy, and Thomas Neal, all of Detroit; and Durant. The majority of the preferred and common stock of the company, under the voting-trust agreement, was deposited with a five-member board: Wallace, Strauss, Storrow, Brady, and Durant. Storrow was named interim president of General Motors, followed by Neal, a Detroit paint manufacturer. The new board created confidence in the financial world. Stocks rose in private trading and the Buick plant soon got back into full production.

The bankers moved quickly to cut loose some of Durant's subsidiaries, consolidate others, and to straighten out the tangled financial affairs of Durant's loose-knit organization. One of the casualties was Buick's fast-selling Model 10, GM's answer to the Ford. James H. Whiting said he fought in one all-night meeting to save the car, but reportedly some of the new leadership did not care for the comparison with the low-priced

Ford—the "carriage trade" often preferred to build expensive, prestigious automobiles.

Durant was dismayed with what he saw. The banking board, it seemed to him, appreciated nothing of what he had accomplished. Whatever limbs it felt were unprofitable it simply amputated from the company in cold blood. And he was powerless to stop it. Despite his vice-presidency, he was on the outside. He knew it, and so did the bankers. How could he work with men he did not respect, and who did not respect him? In his notes he wrote that "the very thing that counts for progress and success—quick decisions and leadership"—was lacking.

"Many of the new men, friends of the parties in control (splendid men, no doubt, in lines in which they were familiar) never having had experience in, or with, automobile design and production, with ideas of their own as to how business should be run, trained in banking rather than practical lines, made my position a difficult one, and I realized that I was up against a real problem.

"I discovered also that some of my own organization 'weak sisters,' so to speak, men who felt that they could lift themselves up by catering to the 'powers that be,' were not quite 100 per cent. (Have you ever found a large organization where you could absolutely count on every man in it?). Although I wished to please and be cooperative, I felt that I could not adapt myself to the situation which I alone had created and that I was wasting my time.

"I had been given a title and a position, but the support, the cooperation, the spirit, the unselfishness that is needed in every successful undertaking, was not there. In a way, it was the same old story, 'too many cooks'; a board of directors comprised of bankers, action by committees, and the lack of knowledge that comes only with experience. I saw some of my cherished ideas laid aside for future action, never to be revived. Opportunities that should have been taken care of with quickness and decision were not considered. The things that counted so much in the past, which gave General Motors its unique and powerful position, were subordinated to 'liquidate and pay.' Pay whom and for what? The people that took control of the business and received $9,350,000 in cash and securities as a commission for a five-year loan of $12,250,000.

"With no idea of being disloyal, it seemed to me that it would be better to let the new group handle the business to suit themselves and if I ever expected to regain control of General Motors, which I certainly intended to do, I should have a company of my own, run in my own way. In other words, another one-man institution, but taking a leaf out of Henry Ford's book—No bankers."

Durant plainly felt that banking interests had created the situation which forced him out of control, and then had profited outrageously with their loan and taken away his company.

Some financial publications argued that he should have financed the Cadillac purchase rather than pay $4.5 million in cash. But financing was hard to get in 1909, and Cadillac had made $3 million profits in fiscal 1910 alone. Orders had been taken for 12,000 of its 1911 models. Buick closed the year with $4 million net profit. Olds netted $700,000 for the year, with estimates that it could double its sales in 1911. In many ways General Motors had a good year in 1910.

"They say I shouldn't have bought the Carter-car," Durant later told A. B. C. Hardy. "Well, how was anyone to know the Carter-car wasn't the thing? It had friction drive and no other car had it. How could I tell what these engineers would say next?"[8]

Apparently investors thought GM had a future. The five-year notes offered by the banking syndicate were disposed of before there could be any public sale.

As for Durant, he was far from through yet. Hardly had he been forced from absolute control of General Motors than he began to talk seriously with one of Buick's former racing stars.

"I need a car," he told Louis Chevrolet.

Chapter Eight

Durant's "New Baby" – Chevrolet

By the time he reached his forty-ninth birthday on December 8, 1910, Durant might have seemed a rather spectacular failure. Some writers in fact compared him with Halley's Comet, which had streaked through the sky earlier that year, displaying magnificent fireworks but disappearing quickly into the night.

Durant could not be so lightly dismissed. He was still a wealthy man and he always rose to a challenge. Some of his old business associates have noted that he seemed most happy when the odds against him were the longest.

He was hardly impressed, then, with the difficult task ahead—that even in 1910 it was no simple matter to start a new automobile company. He was able to ignore the odds because he still had some resources, the most important of which were his reputation among Flint auto men and his magnetic personality. When he decided to create a new organization, without relinquishing his vice-presidency of General Motors, many old associates dropped what they were doing to join the new parade.

He first put some money behind Louis Chevrolet. Louis had retired as a race driver for Buick and had wanted to design and build his own car for a long time. Ecstatic about Durant's support, he immediately set up shop on the second floor of a building on Grand River Avenue in Detroit and by early 1911 was at work with several associates designing a car. As Chevrolet himself remembered his arrangement with

Durant: "He was planning a comeback and told me, 'We're going to need a car.' So I built it."

Next Durant began making moves in Flint. It was an opportune time. James Whiting and the Flint Wagon Works on the city's West Side—the original backers of Buick's move to Flint—were still building some horse vehicles, and also a little car named the Whiting. But the bottom was dropping out of the wagon business as the gasoline engine muscled past the horse, and the Whiting car, though quite attractive, was not very profitable. The Wagon Works was in debt, Whiting was getting old, and he wanted out. Durant needed a factory, and Whiting's associates, Charles M. Begole and William S. Ballenger, were only too happy to be able to join up with Durant again. Begole had succeeded Whiting as Buick president when Durant had taken control in 1904, and Ballenger had been Buick's treasurer. So an arrangement was made in which Durant would take over the Wagon Works—buildings, land, unfinished Whiting cars, wagons, axles, wheels, and all—for $200,000 on a promissory note.[*]

The Wagon Works wasn't nearly as impressive as the Buick complex Durant had built on Flint's North Side, but it was a factory, and it was in Flint. Durant was beginning to enjoy life again. Perhaps from the start, as he claimed in his autobiographical notes, he had plans to try to regain control of General Motors at the end of the five-year bankers' voting trust. Or maybe his thoughts were not that well defined. But no sooner had he acquired the Flint Wagon Works than he started to create a whole string of companies, groping for the right car, the right manufacturing setup.

Durant was working from memory, following step-by-step the path he had followed in building Buick. He obtained the services of Arthur C. Mason, who had built Buick engines from the start in Flint, and told him to organize a company to build engines. He could set up operations in a corner of the Wagon Works. The Mason Motor Company was incorporated on July 31, 1911, with Mason, Charles F. S. Byrne, and Charles E. Wetherald as incorporators.

[*]Whiting's son-in-law, Hubert K. Dalton, tried building a Dalton car elsewhere in Flint. It looked very much like the Whiting, but only three were ever built.

Durant had other plans for Begole and Ballenger. They would join William H. Little, who had been Durant's general manager at Buick, to organize the Little Motor Car Company. It would also be housed at the Wagon Works. The Little was to be a small, inexpensive car, using Mason motors, to fill the void created when Buick dropped the Model 10 as a competitor to Henry Ford's Model T. Little, Begole, and Ballenger were the incorporators, and the papers were filed October 30, 1911.

Four days later, on November 3, the Chevrolet Motor Company of Michigan was incorporated, with headquarters in Detroit and with Louis Chevrolet, Bill Little, and Dr. Edwin R. Campbell, Durant's son-in-law, as incorporators.

Within a week after Chevrolet was organized, there were

The Whiting car, considered a Chevrolet predecessor, was built by James Whiting and the Flint Wagon Works until the Little automobile got into production in that factory.

147

rumors in the newspapers that Durant would soon announce larger plans. *The Flint Journal* reported:

> Profiting by his experience as a student of automobile construction, Mr. Durant, it is stated, will enter several fields, in the types and styles of cars produced, and will seek to anticipate needs not yet supplied. While he has declined thus far to disclose his plans, men close to him, who know his energy and talents for handling big business, predict that the Durant organization will mean a new element of competition in the automotive field, such as to put the other makers to their mettle. Whatever Mr. Durant's plans are, they appear to have been so framed as to take particularly good care of his home town of Flint.

As the year 1911 neared an end, the people of Flint were excited that Durant was operating in the city again. He had boomed Flint's carriage industry, salvaged Buick and promoted it into a giant, and brought in thriving AC Spark Plug (then Champion Ignition) and Weston-Mott. Now he was backing the Mason Motor Company and the Little Motor Car Company, and there were rumors that Flint might get Chevrolet as well. Once, Flint citizens had persuaded Durant to move Buick back to town from Jackson. Maybe they could get him to consolidate his new industries there too. Clearly it was time to honor Durant.

On November 28, 1911, less than a month after the incorporation of Little in Flint and Chevrolet in Detroit, 150 citizens packed the Masonic Temple for what was billed as "The Wizard's Banquet." Tickets for the event had been sold out. Durant was eulogized as "El Capitan de Industria," a slogan that was also printed on the labels of cigars handed out that night. It was almost a birthday party, preceding Durant's fiftieth birthday by ten days. One after another, Flint's civic leaders stood to recite their praise of Durant and to predict greater developments for the city. And when it came Durant's turn to speak, he singled out many of the men who had helped him, all the way back to Robert J. Whaley of Citizens National Bank. Durant told his friends, "Do not think that I have left Flint and am coming back. I never have been away from this city or from you. You cannot come into contact with persons for thirty-eight years and ever go away from it."[1]

A few days later, Chevrolet's capitalization was increased from the original $100,000 to $2.5 million; the officers were Little, president; Durant, vice-president; Curtis R. Hatheway (who had filed the GM incorporation papers in 1908), secretary; and Ballenger, treasurer. Louis Chevrolet was not an officer. Still, he worked in Detroit on his experimental cars. By the end of 1911 he had produced several prototypes of a large luxury vehicle, the Classic Six, which also had a large price—$2,150 at the factory door.

Durant began to juggle his team. He sent Bill Little to Detroit to help start Chevrolet production. And in January, 1912, he brought in A. B. C. Hardy and placed him in charge of the Little Company in Flint. Hardy took over the old Flint Wagon Works plant, was given $26,500 in working capital, and was told to start building the Little. He also had to fill outstanding orders for wagons and sell off the wheels, axles, and other remains of the wagon business.

If any man could handle such a formidable job, it was Hardy. He had been an officer in the Durant-Dort Carriage Company before 1900, he had been Flint's first automobile manufacturer in 1902-03, and after the Selden patent interests had forced him out of that business he had become manager of a carriage company in Waterloo, Iowa. Durant had brought him back to Flint in 1909 to assist in the early management of General Motors, and he had continued with GM for a time under the banker management, winding up the operations of some of the subsidiaries that were being lopped off.

Although the Little was underpowered, it was attractively styled—and it was inexpensive. "Our plan was simple to the point of innocence," Hardy said later. "We took a small motor, had it revamped and improved by Mason, and put it into a small racer for sale at $650, which was somewhere near Ford's latest price. . . ."[2] The cars sold respectably—3,500 in 1912—and provided Durant's new operations with a small amount of capital.

In Detroit, the Chevrolet was not doing as well. Durant did not think too much of Louis Chevrolet's large and expensive creation. At its fancy selling price it was hardly geared for the

Earliest Chevrolet known to exist, a 1912 or 1913 Classic Six. This was the car designed by Louis Chevrolet which Durant decided was too large and expensive. He wanted a small, inexpensive car to compete with Ford. This antique is in the Sloan Museum, Flint, and may be the most valuable vintage Chevy of them all.

mass market, and the job of starting production dragged. It is doubtful that production in Detroit came anywhere near the 2,999 figure that is often cited. But Durant did like the Chevrolet name. It was unusual, as was Buick. And Louis had made it famous. A man would be more likely to buy a car named Chevrolet than one named Little. (Hardy himself urged Durant to drop the Little name.) Yet neither the Chevrolet nor the Little was quite what Durant wanted. "I had found a name for my company—the Chevrolet," he wrote. "My next job was to find a car worthy of the name, a car for power, speed, stability, appearance and price that would outclass any other car in the country. Some job. The first built in Detroit, from the standpoint of appearance, not satisfactory. The second built in Detroit, from the standpoint of cost, impossible. The third built in Flint [the Little], a disappointment. It did not stand the grueling test to which it was subjected, driven to its death in less than 25,000 miles."

Durant was still groping. He moved Chevrolet operations from the shop on Grand River into a fine-looking former lamp factory on W. Grand Boulevard in Detroit, and used the plant's plush offices as his headquarters. He created a good deal of speculation when he erected a sign on some vacant property he had bought adjacent to the Ford factory in the Detroit suburb of Highland Park, announcing that a modern automobile plant would be built there. (That might have been his plan, or perhaps only a publicity move. A few years later, the property was sold to Ford.) More new plans were announced. *The Flint Journal* reported on July 11, 1912:

DURANT IN BIG DEAL

William C. Durant, who is actively interested in the Chevrolet Motor Company . . . is one of the leading members of the new corporation just formed in New York with $65 million capital to manufacture automobiles in New York City.

The company will establish factories in 11 other cities of the country and so reach the public direct. The name of the company is the Republic Motor Company, but whether the Chevrolet Motor Company of Detroit and the

Little Motor Company of Flint, both Durant properties, will be included . . . could not be learned.

In regard to locating right in the center of cities on valuable property, Mr. Durant said in New York:

"The motor car is rapidly nearing perfection. The problem today is not that of production, but of distribution. The enormous waste and extravagance in the marketing of automobiles, if continued, must result in the undoing of the industry. Regardless of high commissions, the majority of dealers are unable to make a profit. Under the plan outlined by us, the cost of distribution is materially reduced and each district is given the type and style of car best suited to its local requirements. Our trademark will be, 'Built on the Spot'."

Durant leased a small factory in New York City fronting on Eleventh Avenue between 56th and 57th streets. His friends, he noted, thought he was crazy because of the high cost of property and labor in New York. But as usual Durant had a purpose that was not immediately obvious to his associates. He wanted to assemble Chevrolets where the operation would be highly visible to the masses of people, and to the country's financial and opinion leaders. He wrote in his autobiographical notes: "We intended, for example, to have dealers in every city in New England, and when the dealers brought their customers to the factory in Flint (grown-up people are very much like children in many respects, they like to see the wheels go 'round), it was a long and expensive trip. But a very short one from New England, New Jersey and Pennsylvania points to New York City."

But while Durant made moves in the East, the main thrust of his manufacturing plans centered in Flint. On August 9, 1912, it was announced that Chevrolet had bought the Imperial Wheel plant of the Durant-Dort Carriage Company, near Buick, and was going to move its entire Chevrolet production from Detroit to Flint. "No doubt," said *The Flint Journal*, "it will develop into one of Flint's most substantial institutions."

As the summer of 1912 wore on, Durant's plans became clearer. The Republic Motors Company of Delaware was to be a holding company—sort of a new General Motors—for Chevrolet, Little, Mason, and other companies still to be organized. Dallas

Dort and other Durant-Dort officers were allied with Durant in Republic. The carriage company, which had earlier invested heavily in Buick, subscribed for half of Chevrolet's $2.5 million stock issue.

Before the summer was over, still another company, Sterling Motor, was formed, with Durant, Dort, Dr. Campbell, Little, and Hatheway as directors. For the first time, Durant stepped out of the background to accept a presidency, that of Sterling. Dort was vice-president and Fred Aldrich was assistant secretary-treasurer. In December Durant took on another presidency, that of Chevrolet. But he served only a few months.[*]

As Durant promoted new companies right and left, one of his old associates ran into trouble. The United States Motor Company, formed by Ben Briscoe after the International Motor talks collapsed, went into receivership in 1912.

By 1912 the Flint of "Vehicle City" carriage days was taking a marked turn into automobile-making. Flint Wagon Works was no more, its properties occupied by Little and Mason. The big Imperial Wheel plant was earmarked for Chevrolet. The Durant-Dort Carriage Company, heavy financial backer of Buick and Chevrolet, would soon get into motors itself by building delivery trucks. W. F. Stewart Company, producer of bodies for carriages, was also building bodies for Buick and Little. William A. Paterson, whose carriage company had helped Durant and Dort build their first road carts back in 1886, was now assembling Paterson automobiles. Albert Champion was manufacturing spark plugs. Charles Stewart Mott was building axles (and also holding office as mayor of Flint). W. C. Durant was planning the move of Chevrolet from Detroit to Flint.

And then there was Buick, operating in the huge plant Durant had built, and headed now by none other than Durant's old associate in the carriage company, Charles W. Nash. When James J. Storrow, interim president of General Motors under the new bankers' board, was looking for a new man to take control of Buick late in 1910, Durant recommended Nash.

---

[*]He later served a shorter term. During a reorganization of Buick in September, 1917, Durant, then president of General Motors, was named president of Buick for one hour. Walter P. Chrysler, who had been elected Buick president in 1916, was re-elected at the end of the hour.

Durant and Dort had nurtured Nash, had recognized his ability to work with men and to manage a large manufacturing operation, and had promoted him to general superintendent of the Durant-Dort Carriage Company. Nash had once thought Durant "crazy" for turning from carriages to Buick; but in the fall of 1910 he accepted Storrow's offer to become acting president of Buick.

Nash felt comfortable with the conservative outlook of the bankers. And the new board was so impressed with his rebuilding and reorganizing of Buick that before the end of 1912 Nash was elected president of General Motors. One reason for Nash's success was that he had taken on a works manager of unusual competence, Walter P. Chrysler.

Chrysler, born in Wamego, Kansas, son of an engineer on the old Kansas Pacific Railroad, was so intent on becoming a machinist that as a youth he made his own machine apprentice tools. When the automobile came along, he bought a Locomobile and spent months tearing it apart and putting it back together before ever learning how to drive.

By 1911 he had become assistant works manager at the American Locomotive Company plant in Pittsburgh, transforming the plant into a money-maker for the first time in years. James Storrow, a director of American Locomotive as well as interim president of GM, summoned Chrysler to New York for a meeting. Chrysler had never heard of Storrow and furthermore had never been to New York. But his boss advised him to go.

Storrow's pitch to Chrysler was that Buick was the most important of the General Motors companies, that Nash was well chosen to head Buick, but that Nash was also new to the automobile world and needed someone with a lot of experience in machinery to run the manufacturing end.

Nash and Chrysler met at lunch one day in the Fort Pitt Hotel in Pittsburgh. Nash was cool at first, sizing up his man carefully. Later, over cigars, the two became better acquainted, and Nash invited Chrysler to visit Flint. Chrysler went. "What I saw astonished me," he wrote later in his book *Life of an American Workman.*

Of course I was a machinist, and I was looking at workmen trained to handle wood. The bodies were being built of wood. In a big carpenter shop, long poplar boards were being bent and shaped in steam kilns. With wood they were admirably skillful, but wherever they were handling metal it seemed to me there was an opportunity for big improvement. I saw a hundred such opportunities, so that I became excitedly eager, saying to myself, "What a job I could do here, if I were boss."

Nash, still somewhat cautious, said he could pay Chrysler no more than $6,000 a year. Chrysler, who was then making $12,000 at American Locomotive, accepted nevertheless. He wanted to get into the automobile business.[3]

Meanwhile, for some unrecorded reason, the alliance between Durant and Dort fell apart. Within the span of a few months

Durant (standing just left of the windshield) and some of his "boys" at the introduction of the first Chevrolet—the Classic Six—in Detroit. The man in the white coat is Louis Chevrolet. Standing to the left of him, wearing a cap, is Big Bill Little, after whom the Little car was named. A. B. C. Hardy is looking over Durant's shoulder, just to his right. Durant's son, Cliff, is at the wheel.

early in 1913, the whole grand plan for the $65 million Republic Motors was dropped cold. Chevrolet was reoriented away from Durant-Dort and toward the old Flint Wagon Works, where the Little car was being built, and Durant resigned as treasurer of Durant-Dort, ending a twenty-seven-year partnership. He was paid a high tribute by Dort, who called him "easily the firm's leading force and genius."

At about the same time, Dort and Aldrich withdrew from their posts at Chevrolet. Charles M. Begole of the Wagon Works succeeded to the Chevrolet presidency. Durant dropped back to his more customary post of vice-president. A. B. C. Hardy of the Little Motor Car Company became a vice-president of Chevrolet and its general manager.

Instead of using the Imperial Wheel Works to manufacture Chevrolets, it was decided to center Chevrolet production at the Wagon Works. On June 4, 1913, came an announcement that Chevrolet had purchased the Little Company. Chevrolet then also bought the Sterling Motor Company and set it up in the factory in Detroit that was being vacated by Chevrolet. Bill Little was placed in charge of Sterling. All Republic affiliates were taken over by Chevrolet.

In the summer of 1913, Durant was starting to put it all together. With the acquisition of the Little, Chevrolet had acquired for the first time an automobile factory in major production. The Chevrolet of today is much more an outgrowth of the Little Company in Flint than of the brief and unproductive Chevrolet operation in Detroit.[*] Chevrolet increased its hold on Mason Motor (which remained a division of Chevrolet until absorbed as the Chevrolet Flint Motor Plant in 1917), and Hardy became a vice-president of Mason as well as general manager of Chevrolet.

The last of the Little automobiles were built in the summer of 1913. In the fall the Royal Mail roadster and the Baby Grand touring car, the first Chevrolets with valve-in-head engines, were introduced as 1914 models. These models and the Light Six—all

---

[*] William S. Ballenger later recalled that Chevrolet's credit was so poor in the first several years that it had to pay cash for most of its materials. The Little Motor Car Company had better credit, and for a time Chevrolet material was purchased in the Little company's name.

built only in Flint for a short time—were the first to use the famous Chevrolet "bow-tie" emblem.

According to Mrs. Durant, that emblem was first spotted by Durant in an illustrated Sunday newspaper when they were vacationing in Hot Springs, Virginia, disputing an old yarn that he first noticed the design on wallpaper in Paris.

"I was with him," she said. "We were in a suite, reading the papers, and he saw this design and said, 'I think this would be a very good emblem for the Chevrolet.' I'm not sure he said Chevrolet, because I don't think he had even settled on a name yet."

Late in 1913 Louis Chevrolet and Durant parted company. The real reason, perhaps, was that Durant had decided not to continue the large, luxurious car of Louis Chevrolet's dreams. Instead he wanted to compete more directly with the low-priced Ford. But a more immediate reason was an ongoing, and petty, dispute over Chevrolet's cigarette-smoking habits. Louis Chevrolet's version is that Durant told him he wouldn't make any money until he became a gentleman, that he should smoke cigars, not cigarettes. Every time they talked, Durant would mention this. Finally Chevrolet could contain his irritation no longer: "I sold you my car and I sold you my name, but I'm not going to sell myself to you. I'm going to smoke my cigarettes as much as I want. And I'm getting out."[4] And very shortly he did.

Mrs. Durant recalls: "I don't think it was so much that he was smoking, but the way he did it. Louis would have a cigarette hanging on his lower lip and it used to annoy Willie to tears. So it wasn't just the smoking. Willie smoked cigars, but never cigarettes."

Louis Chevrolet went back to racing. Among his proudest achievements were designing and building racers which won the Indianapolis 500 in two successive years—1920 and 1921. The 1920 winner, a Monroe-Frontenac, was driven by his brother Gaston. Six months later Gaston was killed at the Los Angeles Speedway. Louis Chevrolet's later business plans collapsed, but he lived until 1941, long enough to see the car bearing his name become the number-one seller.

In 1913 the Mason Motor Company moved out of the main

Durant (right) and his long-time associate, Arthur C. Mason.

Wagon Works building and into the nearby factory which was built originally for Buick in 1903. Buick had long since moved out to concentrate in the huge complex Durant had built on Flint's North Side. After Buick, the original plant was occupied for a time by Randolph Truck assembly. When Randolph moved out, Mason moved in. Arthur Mason was back where he had started building motors for Buick in Flint—but now he was building them for Chevrolet.

It is an example of the striking similarities in the early histories of Buick and Chevrolet. Both companies started in Detroit, but neither got into significant production until they moved to Flint. Both were financed with the help of the Durant-Dort Carriage Company. Both grew after W. C. Durant took over operations of James Whiting. Both David Buick and Louis Chevrolet left early, yet their names remain famous today because Durant kept them on the cars he promoted into great successes.

The parting of ways between Durant and Dort has never been adequately explained and may have been no more than a mutual decision to pursue different avenues of business. Their long friendship continued until Dort's death in 1925. Not long after they split in 1913, they met by coincidence in the office of George C. Willson, Durant's cousin, in the Flint P. Smith Building (now the Sill Building) in downtown Flint. They hugged each other, and Dort walked Durant to a window where they could look down on bustling Saginaw Street.

"Everyone here owes everything to you," Dort said to Durant.

"That's not true, Dallas," Durant replied. "They owe it all to you."[5]

They were both partly right. Dort had remained in Flint, operating the carriage company, supporting Durant's ventures in Buick, General Motors, and, briefly, Chevrolet, and later heading the Dort Motor Company (1915-25). The city's most beloved citizen, Dort was called the father of Flint's city planning, including its park system, and was a founder of the city's Industrial Mutual Association, its community music association, and its golf club. Durant had been the spark plug for Flint's great automotive industries, and he was far from through yet.

With his manufacturing operations centered in Flint, Durant was ready to burst forward with the production of 25,000 Chevrolets in 1914. Hardy said that was impossible. If it is true that most of Durant's associates were yes-men, Hardy was an exception. He could say no to Durant and make it stick. In 1914 Chevrolet built and sold only 5,005 cars. Yet Chevrolets were in great demand, and Durant knew he could sell as many as he could build. While the Chevrolets were more expensive than the Model T Ford, they were lighter and much less expensive than the first Chevrolets and much more powerful than the old Littles. And Ford couldn't build enough cars to satisfy the entire demand for a low-priced automobile.

Durant needed more working capital to increase production. He wanted to get his New York City plant into full production and to purchase the old Maxwell Motor Car plant in Tarrytown, New York. To get the money, he had to violate his own rule of banning bankers from his organization. He found an ally in Louis J. Kaufman, president of the Chatham & Phenix Bank of New York City. In his autobiographical notes, he explained how he made this connection.

"In a short time, we were building 20 Chevrolet cars daily, but we needed 40. I discussed the proposition with Mr. Nathan

Hofheimer, who at the time did not have much money (later, as the result of his association with me, he left an estate of practically $30 million). He had a number of influential friends, one in particular L. J. Kaufman, president of the Chatham & Phenix group of national banks. Hofheimer asked how much I could pay for the additional capital. I told him $5 per car for every car built in excess of our present production, 20 cars a day. As the result of this offer, he arranged a meeting with Mr. Kaufman at his apartment in the Ritz-Carleton Hotel.

"Because I had never met Mr. Kaufman and wished to have a friend in the event of our discussing a production proposal, I took with me Mr. A. B. C. Hardy, who was familiar with my

The first Chevrolet valve-in-head engine and the Chevrolet trademark were part of this 1913 Baby Grand touring car.

many operations and proved a great help to me in many of the deals which I put through at the time.

"During the conversation, Mr. Kaufman asked me: 'How much money can you use?' To which I replied that I could use the entire amount controlled by all of the Chatham & Phenix banks. The discussion that followed led to the deal in which Mr. Kaufman's institution became interested in the enterprise and the leading financial influence in the development of the Chevrolet."

Durant wrote that Kaufman agreed to take up the matter with Hornblower & Weeks, well-known Boston and New York brokers, who underwrote a stock issue of 50,000 shares (par value $100) at $55 a share, with Chevrolet receiving $2,750,000. This, according to Durant, provided enough capital to develop production to full capacity in the New York City plant, to purchase the Tarrytown plant, and to start Chevrolet's "magnificent growth which has not stopped since."

Chevrolet's growth was magnificent indeed. Sales offices were established in Chicago, Philadelphia, Boston, Atlanta, and Kansas City. Russell E. Gardner in St. Louis and R. S. and G. W. McLaughlin in Canada began to manufacture Chevrolets under profit-sharing contracts. Both had been associates of Durant's from the carriage days. A wholesale sales organization, and then an assembly plant, were begun in Oakland, California, with Durant's son Cliff as an officer in the West Coast operation. Chevrolet operations were established in several other cities as well, mostly with local money. In August, 1914, the Monroe Motor Company was organized to build a $450 runabout, purchasing the Imperial Wheel plant in Flint that had once been slated for Chevrolet. R. F. Monroe was president and general manager, Durant was vice-president, Curtis Hatheway was secretary, and Arthur G. Bishop, treasurer.

About 7,000 Monroes were built in 1914-15. In 1916 there was talk of consolidating Monroe with Chevrolet, since the Monroe had been sold through the Chevrolet sales organization. But the negotiations failed and Monroe moved its operations to Pontiac after R. F. Monroe traded his Chevrolet shares for Durant's Monroe shares. Imperial Wheel, vacant again, was soon sold to Buick.

Durant decided to compete more directly with Ford. In 1915 the Baby Grand and Royal Mail were joined in the Chevrolet lineup by a new model, the Four-Ninety (or "490"). This, Durant said, was his masterpiece. It was a "good-looking, easy-riding, well-made, powerful car" that could reach speeds of fifty miles an hour with ease "if you care to drive that fast." The Four-Ninety was introduced at the New York Auto Show in January, 1915, at a price of $550, complete with electric lights and starter. Durant announced that the name "meant something" and that when production justified it, the price of the car should be $490. It was not until August, 1916, however, that Durant could announce that the price had indeed dropped to $490. He wrote in a brochure:

> To build a satisfactory car to sell for $1,000 is not a difficult task. To build a satisfactory car to sell for $490 is quite an undertaking. Cars ordinarily sold for $490 are not satisfactory because they are built in enormous quantities and under great pressure, lacking refinements of detail, which, regardless of price, is now required in every automobile.

The Four-Ninety was designed by Alfred T. Sturt, another example of how well Durant was served by Flint men. Alfred's grandfather, George Sturt, descendant of seven generations of English wheelwrights, had built wagons, cutters and sleighs in Flint from about 1860. Alfred, a born mechanical genius, had test-driven some of the first Buicks at Jackson and was later, successively, chief electrician of the Flint Wagon Works, chief of Buick's experimental department and chief engineer of the Paterson Motor Car Company. Then he was persuaded by Arthur C. Mason to design some of the new models for Durant's Chevrolet operations. Sturt did most of the design work on the Four-Ninety at his home on Lippincott Boulevard in Flint.

Just how well the Four-Ninety began is indicated in a letter from Durant to Arthur G. Bishop, which was published on the front page of *The Flint Journal* on July 13, 1915:

> I am pleased to report as follows:
> On June 1, 1915, the "Four-Ninety" was placed on sale. At the close of business June 19, the Chevrolet Motor

Company had accepted orders from dealers and distributors—with every contract secured by a cash deposit—for 46,611 [cars], valued at $23,329,390—a fairly good record for 17 working days. Since June 19, we have orders for more than 1,000 cars per day.

Durant concluded his letter with his latest slogan—"A Little Child Can Sell it." Frank Rodolf points out that some of these "cash secured" sales must have been for delivery in 1916, for according to official records, sales in 1915 totaled only 13,292. In 1916 Chevrolet sales soared to 70,701, a total which included the first 41 Chevrolet trucks and about 7,000 Canadian-built cars.

In 1914 Durant had moved the headquarters of Chevrolet from Detroit to New York, taking an office over a saloon and restaurant across the street from his New York City plant. The last four years he had been busy with the details of starting a new empire. Now he was ready to get back to the important matter that had probably always been in the back of his mind—wresting control of General Motors back from the hands of the bankers.

Chevrolet 'Four-Ninety' was a major factor in the firm's early success.

163

Chapter Nine

"I Took General Motors
Back from the Bankers Today"

By 1915, after nearly five years of experimenting and promoting, Durant had created a respectable Chevrolet organization. Two years after the move to Flint, the company had produced about 16,000 cars, with net sales of $11.7 million and net profits of $1.3 million.[1]

General Motors, however, had not been asleep during the years of banker control. With conservative, hard-headed management led by Charles W. Nash and James J. Storrow, some order had been brought to the loose-knit organization Durant had created. The number of passenger car divisions had been reduced to Buick, Cadillac, Oldsmobile, and Oakland. Truck units had been merged into the General Motors Truck Company. Compared with General Motors, which produced net profits of nearly $15 million in fiscal 1915 alone, Chevrolet was still a pigmy. With Walter Chrysler's help, Nash had pulled Buick, the Company's most important division, through a period of retrenchment and then into one of steadily advancing sales. Buick sales rose from 19,812 in 1912 to 124,834 in 1916.

But despite its accomplishments the banker management was not without its critics. This was a period when the market was wide open. Henry Ford had aimed his Model T at the mass market. And while Ford and Buick each sold about 30,000 cars in 1910, Ford sales soared to 735,000 a year by 1916. General

Motors produced 21 percent of the country's automobiles in 1910, the year Durant left, but only about 8.5 percent in 1915.[2]

Lawrence H. Seltzer, in *A Financial History of the American Automobile Industry*, quotes an unnamed General Motors vice-president:

> The bankers were too skeptical about the future of the automobile industry. They were chiefly interested in trying to realize savings, so they closed down some plants, concentrating in others. They didn't take advantage of the opportunities. Under Durant, the company might have had a little financial difficulty now and then, but it would have grown much faster and its earnings would have been much greater.

The bankers of General Motors, concerned about protecting their $15 million mortgage and collecting their interest, seemed unable to envision the company's potential. They paid no interest on common stock and its market price languished. Voting-trust certificates for GM stock, which had been listed on the New York Stock Exchange since the summer of 1911, had fluctuated between $25 and $99 from 1911 through 1914. The price stood at $82 at the start of 1915, the year in which the last of the $15 million loan was to be paid off and the voting trust to expire.[3]

Early in the year, however, the price began to rise rather dramatically. Someone was buying GM—and buying in great quantities. The man bulling the market was Durant, still a vice-president of General Motors but inactive in management through most of the banker regime. The stock-buying signalled the beginning of Durant's fight for control.

Durant was aided by new alliances. One was with Louis J. Kaufman, president of the Chatham & Phenix Bank of New York, who was backing his Chevrolet expansion and who was his close financial adviser. The other was with Pierre S. du Pont, president of E. I. du Pont de Nemours & Company, Wilmington, Delaware. John J. Raskob, treasurer of the Du Pont Company, had bought 500 shares of GM stock in 1914 and convinced Pierre du Pont to invest in 2,000 shares.[4] Both Durant and

Kaufman have claimed credit for getting Pierre du Pont interested in Durant's effort to regain control of General Motors.[5]
One story is that Durant learned of Raskob's initial investment,
took him on a tour of GM factories, and convinced him of the
company's bright future. Durant and Kaufman had formed a
syndicate to buy GM shares and during the summer of 1915
recruited Pierre and some other members of the du Pont family
into their tight circle of friends loading up on the stock.

Frank Rodolf, who discussed the situation with Durant,
wrote:

> Late in the summer of 1915, Mr. Durant arranged a meet-
> ing with Mr. Raskob and Pierre S. du Pont. John Thomas
> Smith, a New York attorney [later general counsel of
> GM], and Dr. Edwin R. Campbell, Mr. Durant's son-in-law,
> attended with him. Other conferences followed. Arthur G.
> Bishop, president of Genesee Bank in Flint, recalled a
> session at the Du Pont office in Wilmington. The deal was
> closed and the Flint men elated. Then they were invited to
> the Du Pont estate for dinner. "Let's not go," Dr. Camp-
> bell whispered to Mr. Bishop. "They might change their
> minds." The doctor was afraid the small-town delegation
> would be too far out of its element and make a poor
> impression.

According to that account, it was agreed that the du Ponts
would join on a fifty-fifty basis in Durant's program of regaining control of GM provided they could acquire enough stock at
the right price. At the time of the du Pont negotiations, according to Rodolf, GM certificates stood at about $125 on the
market, but Durant assured the du Ponts that he could get
certificates for them at anywhere from $20 to $120. He was
able to do this, he explained, because he and several other
holders of large blocks, who were his friends, were willing to
part with some of their shares at an apparent sacrifice in order
to bring the powerful du Ponts into General Motors and thereby
enhance the value of their remaining shares.

Like most of the stories that surround Durant, however,
there is more than one version. Pierre du Pont once wrote that
he could not recall ever having met Durant before the GM board

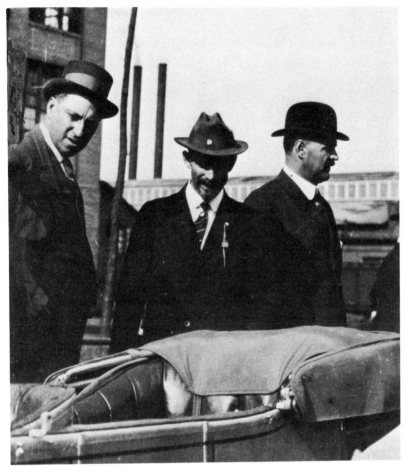

Walter P. Chrysler (left) and Charles W. Nash (right) in their Buick days examine a "Cyclecar" designed by Walter Marr (center). All three men played major roles in Durant's career. The one-of-a-kind Cyclecar is today in the Sloan Museum, Flint.

of directors meeting of September 16, 1915. Du Pont was apparently dealing largely with Kaufman in the critical months preceding that meeting.[6]

Durant had chosen the September 16 meeting—on the seventh anniversary of his founding of the company—as a target date for regaining control. The reasons were practical, not sentimental. He knew that the last $2.5 million of the $15 million loan was to be paid October 1, that the voting trust would then expire, and that a new board of directors would be nominated to be presented at the stockholders' meeting in November.

As the date approached, Durant worked frantically to pull enough voting stock together to regain control. He reportedly operated in a suite of three rooms in New York's Belmont Hotel, using wall phones in each room to buy stock from brokers across the country. A. B. C. Hardy is the source for the often quoted story of how A. M. Bentley of Owosso, near Flint, brought in large briefcases of GM certificates and turned them over to Durant without asking for a receipt.[7] Bentley still had the stock GM had paid for Reliance Motor Truck Company, only to dissolve it. The story is an example of the loyalty that existed between Durant and so many of his associates, particularly in Michigan.

Some of the drama of Durant's drive for control can be seen in cryptic messages he sent from New York to his cousin, George C. Willson, in Flint:

August 22, 1915—"Don't sell any part of your holdings. I will protect if necessary."

September 1, 1915—"Hold every share you have regardless of price changes."

GM stock was rising rapidly. Between January and December, 1915, it would climb from $82 to $558.

Sometime before the meeting of September 16, Durant went to see his former carriage superintendent, GM President Nash, and revealed his plans.[8] He explained his position that General Motors belonged to the stockholders, that the company had paid the bankers a huge commission for their loan. What more, he asked Nash, did the bankers want? He urged Nash to retain the presidency, assuring him that he himself would be satisfied with the vice-presidency.

Nash was not so sure. At a Flint civic tribute in 1912 honoring him on reaching the GM presidency, Nash had recalled how Dort had been almost a father to him and how Durant had shown more confidence in him than any other man in the world. He owed much to Durant, he knew.[9] But he had also become president of General Motors, and he knew that with Durant again active, only one man would run the company.

Charles W. Nash. Durant had hired him as a laborer in the Flint Road Cart Company, and saw his rise to general superintendent of the Durant-Dort Carriage Company. Durant later recommended Nash to become chief at Buick. But in 1916 the two parted ways, Durant succeeding Nash as president of General Motors.

Durant was a genius and he was a man of great charm. But Durant was also a dictator—he ran a one-man show. Nash had a great respect for money, an indelible characteristic rooted deeply in his impoverished childhood. Durant had no regard for money, except as a plaything, as a tool for empire-building.

In the first two weeks of September, 1915, after Durant had revealed his intentions to Nash, there were a number of informal meetings between the Durant-Kaufman interests and the banker interests. On September 13 Albert Strauss of the bankers' board told the GM Finance Committee that there was diversity of opinion among certain board members as to com-

169

pany policy. He made a motion that Durant, and any other board member for that matter, be given a chance to express views at the September 16 directors' meeting and to offer statements to be considered for the annual report. Durant supported the motion, and the Finance Committee adopted it unanimously.

It has been variously reported that Durant either bought more stock to tip the scales or decided to try to bluff the other directors into thinking he had gained control of a majority of the voting stock though actually he was still short of his goal. Quite possibly no one was sure who held the power in those last days before the meeting. At any rate, by then Durant was claiming he held control. James J. Storrow reportedly met with Durant the morning of September 16 and asked that there be no quarrel at the meeting, to which Durant replied that there would be no quarrel, that "I'm in control of General Motors today."

Some accounts have it that Durant and three associates had spent the previous night passing stock certificates from hand to hand, carefully counting each share, and that Durant showed up at the board of directors meeting followed by aides carrying bushel baskets filled with certificates. Others say that this happened the following spring, or that it didn't happen at all—that some writers of the time took dramatic license. But there was more than a little real drama to the meeting.

It opened at 2 p.m. on September 16, 1915, in Room 282 of the Belmont Hotel in New York, with everyone realizing there would be a clash between the bankers and Durant—everyone except Pierre du Pont, who had been invited to attend by Kaufman and who had expected that Kaufman and Durant would be in complete control. He was therefore somewhat surprised to find that Durant and the bankers were in a dead-lock over the naming of new directors. Durant was described as cool and smiling—the calmest man in the room. But for six hours the two sides wrangled over the nominations. Each side had nominated six men, of which du Pont was on the Durant-Kaufman side. Finally, at a moment when du Pont was outside the directors' room talking with Kaufman, Storrow approached him and said that the bankers would like du Pont to name three directors not connected with either faction. Kaufman agreed and du Pont quickly nominated John J. Raskob, J. Amory Haskell of the Du Pont Company, and his own brother-in-law, Lammot Belin. That broke the deadlock. Raskob had attended the meeting with Pierre du Pont, but the other two were notified they had been nominated as GM directors after the fact.[10] A proxy committee of Durant, du Pont, Kaufman, Nash, and Storrow was named to vote the majority of shares for the nominees at the November stockholders' meeting.

Agreement on the new board was not the only big event of the day. The directors also agreed on a cash dividend of 50 percent on the common stock—$50 a share on stock which had sold for as little as $25 a share two years earlier because no dividend had ever been paid. Nash made the motion for the dividend; Durant seconded it. Later in the meeting Durant stated that he now believed the board was justified in paying the large dividend, a move he said he had previously felt would be unwise.

By early evening, the threat of a schism among the directors averted, both sides were in a conciliatory mood. Nash said that the harmonious agreement resulted from the "broad view" taken by Durant, and Durant replied that all sides had made concessions. He pointed out that Storrow and Nash were directly responsible for bringing about agreement after so many days of unsuccessful negotiations.

The next day, the newspapers were filled with accounts of the meeting. The big news was the $50 dividend, which amounted to about $10 million on about $20 million worth of common stock ($100 par value) on the market. The news pushed GM stock up $31 a share. Some brokers who had "sold short"—sold stock they did not own in anticipation of a decline—were stunned that the meeting had ended on an extremely positive note. They had to scramble to cover their losses. Financiers publicly hailed Nash as "the world's greatest manufacturer." The dispatch from New York by a staff correspondent of *The Flint Journal* noted that the last payment on the $15 million banker loan, due October 1, could be met without further obligation. "This is considered a most remarkable showing on the part of the company," the writer said, "and it is particularly appreciated in financial circles in New York City. For at the time the loan was made in 1910, it was freely predicted here that the company would never be able to meet its obligations."

The Journal significantly observed that

> while the matter of the dividend is one that vitally concerns the stockholders, a question of even more general importance was determined at yesterday's meeting of the board of directors, and that involves other Flint men in addition to Mr. Nash, for it means that William Crapo Durant has again come into his own.

The Journal said that the "spirit of Flint" seemed to have been transplanted to New York, for not only had "Mr. Durant been re-established on the pinnacle of finance," but four Flint men were nominated for the new GM board. Besides Durant and Nash there were also Charles Stewart Mott, who had originally joined the board in 1913 after Weston-Mott was fully purchased by GM, and Arthur G. Bishop, the Flint banker, who for years helped support Durant ventures.

The newspaper's correspondent, Myles Bradley, said that Kaufman had played a major role by learning that Durant was being "misunderstood" in financial circles in New York and by members of the bankers' board, and by setting about to overcome that attitude. This was achieved, he wrote, as Durant's position was "thoroughly re-established" in General Motors and that there was no longer "the slightest degree of ill feeling."

In Flint news of the big dividend and the surge in GM stock prices was met with jubilation. Durant had been sending telegrams to his friends in the city for weeks urging them not to sell—that the price was going higher. It was said that the majority of GM stock was held by Flint men and "many fortunes have been made in the last few weeks." One man reportedly bought some stock on the margin and in a few days sold it for a net profit of $70,000. A leading citizen said that if Durant were to return to Flint "there would be a mob of Flint people from the station in every direction ready to welcome him." Between September 14 and September 22, the market price of GM went up from $250 to $340.

Despite reports that all had ended in harmony at the September 16 meeting, Durant immediately intensified his drive for complete control. He had fallen a little short of that goal at the meeting. Though he may have had an edge with Pierre du Pont and his three "neutral" directors, those four were still something of a buffer between Durant and the banker faction.

He had been planning to incorporate a large new Chevrolet company to take over all of the smaller Chevrolet and subsidiary firms around the country, but had delayed taking formal action until after the September 16 meeting. Now he was ready to move. On September 23 Durant incorporated the Chevrolet Motor Company of Delaware with $20 million capitalization.

Durant was president; R. H. Higgins, chairman of the board; Kaufman, chairman of the Finance Committee, and Hardy and Dr. Campbell, vice-presidents. Among the directors was H. M. Barksdale, a du Pont representative.

Of the $20 million authorized stock of the large new Chevrolet company, $13.2 million was exchanged for the stock of the smaller Chevrolet companies in New York, Michigan, and Ohio, and for stock in Mason Motor and contracts with the Canadian and St. Louis Chevrolet firms. The rest, $6.8 million, was offered to the public with the explanation that funds were needed to increase production from 100 to 300 cars a day. [11] As usual with any Durant promotion, all of this was regarded as good news in Flint. *The Journal* bannered the news of the new Chevrolet company:

MORE MILLIONS WILL BE BROUGHT TO FLINT

And the newspaper quoted Durant:

There is not enough money in this country to buy Chevrolet or take from our little crowd control of Chevrolet. The Chevrolet is my newest, latest and best-prized baby, dedicated to and controlled by the men who built it up against great odds.

This was followed by a dispatch to the newspaper from A. B. C. Hardy:

You will be interested to know that William C. Durant of Flint and New York has just concluded a deal which will bring more millions to Flint and which will make Flint the home of two of the largest and greatest automobile concerns in America.

The Chevrolet Motor Company of Delaware, organized with a capital of $20 million, backed by some of the strongest men in New York and having for its purpose the manufacture and worldwide distribution of Chevrolet cars, with plants at Flint, New York City, Tarrytown, Toronto, St. Louis, Oakland, Calif., and other strategic distribution points, was incorporated yesterday, with its capital stock largely oversubscribed.

It has been decided that the major manufacturing plants, which will supply to the several assembly plants the more important items, such as motors, axles, etc., will be located at Flint, as well as an assembly plant to manufacture "490" cars at about 200 a day.

On October 14 Durant wrote to George C. Willson in Flint that

I had an opportunity of securing 10,000 shares of Chevrolet Motor Company underwriting at $75 a share, which I allocated to my friends and associates as follows. . . .You can send me a check for your allotment as necessary. Chevrolet will more than likely be an "active" issue with radical changes in market quotations. . . .You can accept my statement that the company has a wonderful future and is not for sale.

Among those listed as being allocated shares were Arthur G. Bishop, J. H. McClement, A. H. Goss, the McLaughlins, Arthur C. Mason, A. B. C. Hardy, W. L. P. Althouse, and Durant's wife Catherine and mother Rebecca.

Durant's name in connection with the large new Chevrolet company led to such widespread interest that the subscription books were closed before the new stock issue was formally authorized. Applications for the stock had already exceeded ten times the amount offered. The 10,000 shares of stock Durant sold to his friends at $75 were selling for $97 on the New York curb market within a few days.[12]

At the November meeting of GM stockholders, the new directors nominated on September 16 were elected, and Nash was reelected president, with Durant remaining vice-president. Pierre du Pont was elected chairman of the board, a position he retained until 1929.

Durant continued his drive for complete control. At first, as manager of the stock syndicate formed in the summer of 1915, he privately offered certain GM shareholders a chance to trade their General Motors common stock on a basis of five shares of Chevrolet for one share of General Motors. On December 21, 1915, he made the same offer to all GM shareholders. It was an attractive proposition, and the GM stock rolled in. On the same day, William S. Ballenger wrote from Flint to Curtis R. Hatheway in Boston to inform him of Durant's position:

> Mr. Durant (with the people who are closely associated with him) now controls more than 50 per cent of the outstanding General Motors stock. This is not taking into consideration the interests of the du Ponts or people in the du Pont crowd. . . . There has been a terrific fight on as to who should eventually control General Motors Company, but Mr. Durant seems to have the upper hand of it at this time. . . .

On December 23, Chevrolet stockholders voted to increase Chevrolet's capital stock from $20 million to $80 million and the shocking headlines read:

CHEVROLET COMPANY WILL ACQUIRE CONTROL
OF GENERAL MOTORS

The announcement said that the $60 million increase in capital stock was voted in order to purchase the controlling interest in General Motors, "which has already been acquired by a syndicate." *The Flint Journal*'s account of December 24 explained:

> It is generally understood in New York that the proposed merger of interests was conceived by William Crapo Durant, whose sensational return to control of General Motors at the recent annual meeting of that company caused such a stir in financial and industrial circles.
>
> With Mr. Durant in control of both companies, it was anticipated that a merger would develop sooner or later,

but the general impression was that General Motors would absorb Chevrolet rather than the opposite.

"No greater compliment could be paid me than the placing in my hands, as syndicate manager, to be handled for the account of my friends and associates with and as my own, securities valued at more than $40 million," Mr. Durant said. "It is unnecessary to say that I will not betray this great trust."

In New York City the newspapers heralded the news of Chevrolet's swallowing giant General Motors as one of the greatest achievements in the history of American finance. A New York banker was quoted as saying that Durant had not only accomplished the seemingly impossible, but had succeeded in entrenching himself and his friends so completely at the head of two of the greatest automobile companies that "a bomb wouldn't remove them."

But the announcement had its critics. Some financial writers were frankly skeptical of Chevrolet's ability to take over General Motors. One reported that Chevrolet's intentions were not being well received among New England shareholders and argued that "Chevrolet is not only a medium-sized proposition, relatively speaking, but it is not seasoned. Its proposal to absorb control of General Motors has a great many aspects of getting the cart before the horse."

A number of GM's directors resisted Durant's efforts to give GM control to Chevrolet. In January, 1916, eight directors proposed to the stockholders that a new three-year voting trust be created. In their letter they said they believed that the results achieved under President Nash had been satisfactory to the stockholders and that if a significant number of stockholders agreed, a new voting trust would be created. The letter was signed by James J. Storrow, Albert Strauss, Samuel F. Pryor, Albert H. Wiggin, Thomas Neal, Charles H. Sabin, Emory Clark, and Charles Stewart Mott.[13] That letter, and another to the same effect signed by thirteen stockholders in March, had little impact. Despite the sound and conservative management of the bankers during the five years they had control, the momentum was now with Durant. It is said that even some of his opponents finally sold or traded their stock to him.

The first half of 1916 was a time of torment for Charles W. Nash. He owed to Durant his start in the carriage business and his entry into General Motors by way of Buick. But he had aligned himself with the bankers for five years. As the fight between the Durant faction and the banker faction continued, Nash found his name drawn into the fray by stockholders favoring the bankers. Nash protested that he didn't want to serve as a member of a new voting trust "as I do not want to get mixed up in any way with this scrap."[14] Early in March, 1916, when Durant wired Nash to inquire if he had lent his name to advocates of the new voting trust, Nash replied that he did not want his name used, "as stockholders would think I was trying to insure my job. I do not want this impression to prevail as I am fast becoming discouraged and losing interest in the whole proposition."

Writing from California, Dr. Campbell advised Durant that "if you get control and can hold Chrysler, it would not make any

Walter P. Chrysler

difference about Nash going. 'Keep a stiff upper lip.' " In another letter, on April 10, 1916, he advised his father-in-law:

> I hope you have enough General Motors tied up to give you absolute control, for you must not make a failure of it this time—the promised land is in sight so don't stub your toe and when the election time comes around, just put your own friends on the board.

By then Durant was confident he was securely in control of General Motors. On April 12 he informed Raskob that subject to the approval of the Chevrolet board at its next meeting "an offer to purchase General Motors Company (conveying to the Chevrolet Motor Company all of the assets and the entire business of the General Motors Company) will be made." On the 16th he went to Flint, where the citizens had provided both a spiritual and financial base for his return to power.

"Flint is wonderful, it is unique," he told Flint's civic leaders in a speech.

> In the history of the world, there was never anyplace like it and I am always glad to call it home. The people of Flint are showing a spirit that, I believe, has never been equalled anywhere. It is a spirit of mutual help and cooperation. Everybody here seems to have it. Everybody is ready to help and work with everybody else for the good of Flint and for the good of the people of Flint. The whole world is talking about Flint today and with good reason. Let them keep talking about us.[15]

In the middle of May, Durant announced to the directors that he was in control of a majority of the General Motors voting stock—that Chevrolet owned 450,000 of the 825,589 shares outstanding.[16] Apparently he was still trying to retain Nash as president. But by then Nash had made his decision. On June 1, 1916, he resigned as president of General Motors. Durant then became president for the first time of the company he had founded.

"When Durant regained control, his policies and mine were so at variance that I resigned and started my own company," Nash said, years later. "I hate to tell the salary that was offered to me by Durant if I would stay. It was more than any man's worth. But I had wanted for years to build my own car."[17]

In July, 1916, Nash bought all the assets of a going concern, the Thomas B. Jeffery Company in Kenosha, Wisconsin, and changed the name to the Nash Motors Company. By 1917 the Nash nameplate was on some models, and within ten years Nash was producing more than 130,000 cars a year. Nash Motors was eventually to become part of what is now the American Motors Corporation.

Storrow, realizing that Durant had won, did not attend the June 1 meeting at the Guaranty Trust Company office in New York at which Durant was elected president of General Motors. He and several other bankers retired from the board, and for a short time he backed a plan to purchase the Packard Motor Car Company, a plan which was to include both Nash and Chrysler. But the plan fell through and Storrow then backed Nash with the Jeffery company. Wilfred C. Leland of Cadillac returned to the GM board in late June, succeeding Albert Strauss, one of those who had retired at about the same time as Storrow.

Pierre S. du Pont had watched the internal struggle from the sideline, deciding that he and the three "neutral" directors—Raskob, Haskell and Belin—would not side with either faction. When it became clear that Durant had regained full control without their help, du Pont offered to give up his place on the board.[18] But Durant urged him and his associates to remain in their positions. Their stature and financial resources would be helpful in developing his new plans.

The change in presidencies was most keenly felt in Flint, which had seen both Durant and Nash rise to fame. On learning that Nash had resigned and Durant was again president, *The Journal* editorialized:

> There is widespread regret over the severance of Mr. Nash's relations with the company and its affairs compensated only in the man who has been selected to succeed him. Both of these men are idols in Flint. Each made his start here and each climbed to the pinnacle of success in Flint enterprises which have developed into world enterprises.

Durant's clear and dramatic victory might well have been

followed by a great celebration. Instead—and entirely in character—he took his wife out to dinner at a fast-food chain restaurant in New York City. In the course of the meal, he casually mentioned, "Well, I took General Motors back from the bankers today."

Catherine replied, "Oh, Willie. At least we could have gone to the restaurant in the Plaza."[19]

Chapter Ten

Durant's Rule –
and Another Collapse

Durant's coup in reestablishing personal control of General Motors had astounded the world of business and industry. The bankers had been routed. Chevrolet held the controlling interest in General Motors and Durant and his friends controlled Chevrolet. Writers of the time likened the situation to Jonah swallowing the whale.

Typically, Durant was juggling more than one big business scheme in the first half of 1916. In May, after he was firmly in control of GM but not yet its president, he formed United Motors Company with the help of Louis Kaufman. United Motors was at first a holding company to control some of the leading automotive parts suppliers, including the Hyatt and New Departure roller bearing companies, Dayton Engineering Laboratories (Delco), Remy Electric, Jaxon Steel Products and Perlman Rim.

The president of Hyatt was Alfred P. Sloan, who had reorganized the company in 1898 with an investment of $5,000. In 1916 he sold it to Durant for $13.5 million. Durant then named Sloan president of United Motors, which in 1918 became a division of General Motors. Sloan was eventually to rise to president and later to chairman of General Motors. He was to become the great leader of GM's post-Durant era.

The first order of business for Durant after succeeding Nash as GM president on June 1, 1916, was to woo Buick's tough, brilliant general manager, Walter P. Chrysler. "When the results of the election were known and the bankers were no longer, much to their chagrin, active in General Motors, the situation internally was very intense," Durant wrote in his memoirs. "The first thing of importance that occurred was a letter of resignation from Chrysler. He was tied up very closely with the bankers and felt their defeat very keenly."

Durant said he received Chrysler's letter in New York and took the first train to Flint. He went to Chrysler's office at Buick, turned on his charm, and opened the purse strings. "I was frank to say that he occupied a position of great responsibility . . . that I trusted him implicitly and had planned to make the Buick the pivotal part of a very large institution, and that I needed his organization without interruption.

"I talked with him about the responsibility toward the men who believed in him and who had come with him because of their belief in him; that I had made the acquaintance of some of his men, mentioning the name of K. T. Keller [later president of Chrysler Corporation], who was devoted to him, and whom I would like to see in my organization. I used every argument that I was possessed of, having to do with the future of the good men whom he had secured as part of his organization. When I had exhausted every argument, in his usual direct manner came the following:

" 'What is your proposition? What have you to offer?' "

"In reply, quite as promptly, I made the following proposition:

" 'I will execute a three-year contract with you dated today, giving you $10,000 a month in cash and at the end of each year $500,000 in cash or, if you prefer, $500,000 in General Motors stock, based on the price of the stock today. In other words, if you take the stock, you are to have whatever value General Motors has obtained as the result of the organization which you are to create to handle the business, which organization is to be of your selection without interference.'

"When I had finished, Chrysler asked me if I would repeat the statement, which I did. He said: 'I accept. Billy, I didn't think you could win. You have beaten the bankers and have upset their plans.'

Chrysler remembered that he made one strong point at the meeting:

> "I can accept only if I'm to have full authority. I don't want any other boss but you. Just have one channel between Flint and Detroit: From me to you."
>
> Durant was beaming at me then. I saw him touch his fingers lightly to the table top for emphasis. "It's a deal," he said.[1]

Durant continued:

"From that time on, the situation was different. We proceeded to line up work for the near future and found plenty to talk about. As everybody knows, the Buick took the lead under Mr. Chrysler's management, and while we did not always agree ... the contract was finished under the terms agreed upon."

Durant had offered fantastic salaries to two of the most competent automotive leaders in the country. He had lost Nash, but was able to retain Chrysler, who was named president as well as general manager of Buick. Now he began to turn General Motors away from the conservatism of the banker years and to complete his creation of the General Motors empire.

In the fall of 1916, Durant reorganized the General Motors Company into the General Motors Corporation, which bought the assets of the company and its subsidiaries, turning them into divisions. As the last of the bankers retired from the board, Durant replaced them with the general managers of his car and truck divisions. Among the board members who remained from the banker era was Durant's old associate, Charles Stewart Mott of Flint, who was first elected in 1913—and who was a member of GM's board for sixty years until his death in 1973.*

Despite the legal change from company to corporation, Durant continued to allow his divisions to operate with a free hand—though he operated at the top largely as a benevolent dictator. He believed that the individual factories should be

---

*Although Mott had sided with the bankers in proposing a new three-year voting trust, and he was personally closer to Nash than to Durant, he also appreciated Durant's abilities and Durant's contributions to his success. He later said that he always tried to support policies he felt were best for the corporation as opposed to siding with any faction.

operated at the local level without contending with a large centralized bureaucracy. Throughout his years as president of General Motors, he resisted the notion of a large central staff. He had learned that he was much more successful when he made the big decisions than when a committee made them. Nothing in his career had shown him that he was wrong to think that way.

Durant's return to control was good news in other Michigan cities as well as in Flint. Six weeks after he was named president, eighty businessmen in Pontiac paid tribute to Durant at the Bloomfield Hills Country Club. They presented him with a plaque "in grateful recognition of the unprecedented courage, foresight, energy, enterprise and personal effort in the transformation of our defunct carriage factories into the busy, thriving, growing automobile plants of today."

Durant's optimism about the future of the automobile was as

Alfred P. Sloan, Charles Stewart Mott, and Charles W. Nash on a visit to Nash's plant in Kenosha, Wisconsin, after Nash left General Motors.

great as ever. Late in 1916, when a reporter asked him what would happen when the production of automobiles reached the saturation point, Durant replied:

"Saturation point? There is no such thing as a saturation point. The term is not well chosen." He admitted that there might be temporary overproduction, "but people will ride and the vehicle must be supplied." The reporter wrote that "one hundred men who have made $100,000 to $6 million owe it all to this dreamer and practical man. I wonder how great a part of this success is due to the Durant smile, for it is one of the most pleasing I have ever seen."

In the summer of 1915, while Durant was marshalling his forces to regain control of General Motors, two men working in a back yard in Fort Wayne, Indiana, were on the verge of another kind of success. In July Alfred Mellowes and Reuben Bechtold succeeded in completing their first experimental electric refrigerator. After rejecting a series of possible names for the device—including Keep-O, Cold-Wave, Jack-Frost, December Morn, Kleen-Kold, and Northern Light—they agreed on the name Guardian, suggested by patent attorney Walter A. Knight.[2] Knight also suggested the word "Frigerator," explaining: "There is no such word as 'Frigerator' in the dictionary. 'Refrigerator' comes from 're' (again) and 'frigerare' (to cool). Now, we are not going to cool again, but we are going to make an initial cooling. . . . It seems to me that a special word like this, as part of the company name, would serve to help in advertising. . . ."

Guardian Frigerator was incorporated March 28, 1916, in Michigan with Mellowes, Wesley J. Claxton, and Edward H. Lapham as incorporators. It moved into the old Farrand organ factory on Twelfth Street in Detroit. On August 17 the first Detroit-made "frigerator" was completed, and on August 21 it was installed in the home of Charles R. Talbot at Farmington, Michigan.

But Guardian had many problems, the greatest of which was lack of money. Only thirty-four Guardians were sold between March, 1916, and early 1918, and the company had lost $19,000. About that time, however, J. W. Murray of the Murray Manufacturing Company became personally and financially interested in the company and announced that his goal was to build fifty Guardians by June 1.

Durant, in his autobiographical notes, recalled that shortly after J. W. Murray became involved in Guardian, one of Murray's sons showed up at Durant's office. He was concerned that his father—a personal friend of Durant's—was spending too much time and money in the venture. Would Durant please talk to his father and try to discourage him? Durant said he would try.

They talked, and Murray explained the great future of the Guardian. The current method of protecting food was very crude; something better than the old ice box was needed; a

Durant with his wife Catherine and A. B. C. Hardy at a state fair in New Jersey, 1919.

great many people would gladly pay for the device if only it could be perfected. "He was very enthusiastic and regardless of his son's statement, I was in no position to discourage him," Durant wrote. "As a matter of fact, I was becoming quite interested myself."

Durant agreed to visit the refrigerator shop, climbing several flights of stairs in the old organ factory to a room filled with a clutter of insulation, motors, radiators, fittings, and other items. "From what I had seen and been told, the situation at the moment looked hopeless," Durant wrote. "An absolutely new deal, in my opinion, was required. I told Mr. Murray: Let me organize a new company with paid capital of $100,000. You can turn over everything that you have relating to the refrigeration unit . . . and your crowd take for the business one-quarter interest in the new company, represented by $25,000 worth of fully paid nonassessable stock. General Motors will take the balance of the stock, paying $75,000 cash for same. This will provide ample working capital for the new company. . . ."

Murray set about to acquire full ownership and bought all of the outstanding stock except the shares held by Mellowes. Durant, looking for something for GM to build and dealers to sell at a time civilian car production and sales were being curtailed by World War I, then bought the stock from Murray. It was a personal purchase by Durant, not by General Motors. Corporate wheels sometimes moved slowly and to Durant time was the most precious of all things. He would offer the refrigerator company to the GM board of directors when he found time.

Durant named A. B. C. Hardy, his troubleshooter from way back, to create an organization. Hardy, said Durant, "was a student, a good judge and director of men, particularly suited for this kind of work. I am pleased to say that he was very largely responsible for laying the foundation for what later proved to be one of America's great humanitarian institutions." The Guardian operations were moved in June, 1918, from the old organ factory to larger quarters at 725 Scotten Avenue in Detroit.

Mellowes later recalled that Durant showed great interest in the business. It was his special project, and he seemed to favor it over the automobile divisions. On his train trips from New York to Detroit on the Michigan Central, Durant would alight at the station and head immediately for the refrigerator plant, only a few steps away. If Guardian officials knew he was coming, they would be at the plant at 6:30 a.m. to open the doors for the fast-moving boss.

"As we progressed, we needed a name for the company," Durant wrote. "This was a matter of some concern as many people were interested, and it was suggested that a cash prize be offered for the best name submitted, if accepted. While the competition was in progress, as I was riding to the office one morning, it occurred to me that our main effort, for a considerable time, had been the creation and use of . . . frigid-cold air. Upon my arrival at the office, I applied for registration the name FRIGIDAIRE, and announced to the contestants for the prize that the name had been selected—an excellent name, I must admit."*

The GM board finally got around to acquiring Frigidaire on March 31, 1919, at the price of $56,366.50, reimbursing Durant for his expenses in acquiring the company's stock. Sloan later commented:

> Mr. Durant had put his own funds into the development . . . before he sold it to General Motors. You might think he had reckoned on making a big profit for himself. Not Durant. I'd bet my life he did not make a dollar for himself in that or any other similar deal. He was not that kind. In Frigidaire, he gave the corporation the nucleus of a great industry. . . . W. C. Durant habitually behaved unselfishly.[3]

Durant, thinking big as always, ignored Mellowes' plea that the company go slowly at first, and announced plans for 3,000 refrigerators. He tactfully suggested that Mellowes was not used to doing things on a big scale, but that this was the only way to get results. And, typically, Durant's vision was on target but his

---

*Mellowes himself remembered that one day Durant called him into the office, wrote a word on a piece of paper, and showed it to him. The word was "Frigidaire." "What do you think?" asked Durant. Mellowes was as enthusiastic as Durant—the name was a natural. Mellowes disputed reports of any contest, but he agreed that the name was the creation of Durant's own imagination.

impatience with detail costly. The first big production run of about 1,500 refrigerators contained so many 'bugs' that most of them had to be scrapped.

By this time Mellowes was gone. Like A. B. C. Hardy in 1900 and David Buick in 1908, and probably many others, he found that carrying out the details to meet Durant's schedule was too much for him. He told Durant he had to leave or his health would break. On the night of the "false armistice" in 1918, the two men conferred in Durant's room in the Detroit Athletic Club from 4 p.m. until after midnight. Durant tried to talk Mellowes into staying and said he had plans to make General Motors a billion-dollar corporation, with Frigidaire playing an important role. Mellowes later remarked that had Durant also suggested a three- or four-week vacation in the north woods he probably would have stayed.

By 1972 the Frigidaire Division of General Motors could boast that it had built 80 million refrigerators, freezers, washers, dryers, electric ranges, dishwashers, air conditioners, trash compactors, and other products, and that its plants in the Dayton, Ohio, area comprised more than 6.6 million square feet. Durant was not dreaming that night in 1918 when he talked to Alfred Mellowes about the future of Frigidaire.

Perhaps it was inevitable with Pierre S. du Pont the board chairman of General Motors, and John J. Raskob among the directors, the Du Pont Company would become more deeply involved in GM affairs. Pierre was somewhat disturbed about being ignored by Durant, who developed and acted on his own plans without bothering to consult with the chairman. But du Pont was also extremely busy—the Du Pont Company was piling up enormous profits selling smokeless powder to Great Britain, France and Russia, and Pierre devoted most of his time to that company's expansion. Raskob, one of the three neutral GM directors elected in 1915, was consequently the major Du Pont spokesman within General Motors. Short, energetic and brilliant, Raskob was taking a keen interest in GM affairs and by the end of 1916 was urging the consolidation of General Motors and Chevrolet.[4] At the time they were separate firms, with Chevrolet holding the controlling interest in GM—450,000 of the 825,000 GM shares outstanding.

But it was not until late in 1917 that events led to a large Du Pont Company investment in GM. The opportunity was apparently the result of a sharp drop in GM stock prices after the United States entered the war. The stock fell from about $200 in the early summer to $75 in the late fall.[5] Durant, as a major GM stockholder probably holding large blocks of stock by paying only the 10 per cent margin required in those days, was in personal financial trouble. He complained to Raskob that "viciously untrue and scurrilous articles designed to create a panic in General Motors" were being widely circulated and proposed that Raskob, du Pont and himself start a new syndicate to buy GM stock "to prevent our valuable property from being made a football for the 'gamblers of the street.' "[6] Instead, Raskob and Kaufman persuaded the GM board that Durant needed the money because his efforts to protect the market price of the stock were absorbing his attention to the detriment of the company's interests. After some debate, the board authorized Durant a salary of $500,000 a year with immediate payment for two years, a sum later written off as "extraordinary expense."

But more money was needed, and Raskob then proposed that the Du Pont Company and its stockholders invest $25 million in GM common. He could point out to the Du Pont Company's board that it had vast wartime surpluses to invest and that GM was a solid investment—since Durant's return to power, GM earnings had more than doubled and Chevrolet was also strong. It seemed certain that auto sales would grow rapidly after the war. Also, General Motors would be an important customer for Du Pont-developed products, such as paints and artificial leather.[7] In agreeing, Pierre du Pont added his view that GM could benefit from the Du Pont Company's experience in financial and business management and that large GM dividends would help finance Du Pont's development of new products, which would still be in the development stage, and therefore not profitable, for several years after the war ended.

On December 20, 1917, the Du Pont Company decided to make the investment. In January, 1918, a Du Pont-created holding company was established and bought 23.8 percent of the combined GM-Chevrolet stock for $25.1 million. In return for this investment, Durant agreed to bring both Chevrolet and United Motors under the General Motors corporate structure. Also, the GM Finance Committee would be strengthened and controlled by Du Pont people, headed by John J. Raskob. Durant would still be in charge of operations as chairman of a revived Executive Committee.[8]

The Du Pont Company's heavy investment was announced by Pierre du Pont at an elaborate dinner at the Metropolitan Club of New York on February 21, 1918, attended by fifteen leading bankers. Recalling that dinner, Durant wrote:

"It was a swell affair. As an observer, I learned the following lesson: When you do anything in which the public is interested, for your own satisfaction and for other reasons, do it well.

"At that dinner, which lasted beyond the midnight hour because we had so much to talk about, I was asked to give a brief history of General Motors, which I did. I concluded my remarks with the statement that the corporation was 11 years old, that the automobile was fairly well covered, that the corporation was becoming interested in other lines, that it had recently given time and thought to an unusual and novel household fixture, a self-contained electric refrigerator—a model of which I did not believe a single gentleman present had ever seen. It was about ready to be placed on the market. It was the 'baby of the General Motors flock,' called Frigidaire.

"I was confident and did not hesitate to make the statement that when the public recognized its importance and value as a household unit, the earnings of that division alone would be sufficient to pay the dividends on the entire issue of General Motors preferred stock."

In its annual report for 1918, the Du Pont Company said:

> We feel fortunate in our partnership with Mr. William C. Durant, president of General Motors Corporation and the father and leader of the motor industry not only in the United States, but in the world. The alliance leaves the management and general conduct of the General Motors Corporation as heretofore except that the responsibility for financial management is now shared by the officers of our company.

The Durant-Du Pont partnership was a major change. Durant was no longer fully in control, though as president and chairman of the Executive Committee he continued to wield great power and often seemed as independent as ever. But the partnership brought Raskob into a position of major importance. He headed the Finance Committee, comprised largely of representatives of the Du Pont interests, and so was in charge of raising and distributing the money.

One might suppose that Raskob and the Du Ponts would bring financial order to Durant's empire. Pierre du Pont himself certainly expected GM management to become less haphazard.

John J. Raskob

But Raskob was an optimistic fellow, hardly more interested than Durant in conservative fiscal policies. In fact, Raskob admired the way Durant operated, and seemed to enjoy cooking up plans to get more money for more expansions. The Finance Committee avoided making unpopular decisions by giving all factions within the corporation all the money they wanted.[9] There was nobody around to apply the brakes and so GM took off on a massive expansion program.

In May, 1918, Chevrolet assets were sold to General Motors for 282,684 shares of the GM common stock. With Chevrolet joining Buick, Oldsmobile, Cadillac, and Oakland (later Pontiac)—all brought into GM by Durant—the modern lineup of General Motors car divisions was completed. Yet Chevrolet continued to exist for a few years as a separate holding company, its function being to hold the controlling block of General Motors stock.

By the end of December, 1918, United Motors was also added to the corporation. The price—$46 million in debentures and stock. Its president, Alfred P. Sloan, became a GM director, vice-president in charge of accessory operations, and a member of Durant's Executive Committee. In the same month, GM bought the last minority interests in three McLaughlin affiliates in Canada, and General Motors of Canada was born.

Following the lead of Ford, Durant decided that GM should get into the tractor business. A factor in this decision, as in the case of Frigidaire, was that there were government restrictions on the use of steel in car production during the war. He persuaded the GM board to purchase the Samson Sieve-Grip Tractor Company of Stockton, California, and to buy the Janesville (Wisconsin) Machine Company and 122 acres for a tractor plant.

The idea of selling tractors spurred Durant's imagination. He had ideas of revolutionizing the business of selling farm implements. To help offset the problem of a weak sales organization in the farm-implement business, GM designed elaborate traveling tractor displays in large prefabricated buildings to be set up at county fairs across the country. Arthur C. Mason, who had built Buick and Chevrolet engines for Durant, was placed in charge of designing the tractor for GM's new Samson Division.

No sooner was Samson's Model M tractor ready for production than Durant became captivated by a new contraption called the Iron Horse. It was a special tractor—driven by reins just as a team of horses is driven—and it was supposed to do for the farmer almost any task that horses could do. General Motors branched into portable electric lighting systems and appliances for the farm. Two models of Samson trucks were produced, the first 128 of which were built in Flint before production was moved to new plants built at Janesville. Later a Samson nine-passenger family car was displayed—but quickly forgotten.[10]

There was perhaps nothing wrong with the idea of building farm tractors. With the right management, engineering, and timing, it might have been as successful as Frigidaire later became. But the Iron Horse was an engineering failure. A

Durant personally demonstrated the controversial Samson 'Iron Horse' at a state fair in Trenton, New Jersey, in about 1919.

postwar recession was coming, and with it a shortage of money for development and a slump in farm prices. It finally turned out that the Samson tractor could not be sold profitably at a competitive price. After several years of trying, GM got out of the tractor business, and Pierre du Pont later estimated the loss at $33 million.[11] The Janesville factories were not a loss, however, as Chevrolet got them for an assembly operation and they are in use by the corporation to this day.

The big setback in tractors was still in the future when World War I ended in November, 1918. Durant and Raskob quickly developed a $52.8 million postwar expansion program. GM needed to modernize old factories and build new ones for the expected boom in automobile sales. To help finance the expansion, the Du Pont Company almost doubled its holdings of GM stock in 1919.

As the expansion accelerated, Durant became more deeply enmeshed in a thousand details—but always there was time for a visit to Flint, and another display of his lighthearted flamboyance, which always flowered best there. On January 31, 1919, he was again honored by the community leaders of Flint, with 550 persons attending a banquet in his honor. *The Flint Journal* editorialized:

> Seldom does a community have an honored son who is held in such general high esteem. And seldom do the people of a community have the opportunity to pay such a tribute to an honored son as was paid to Mr. Durant Friday night in Dryden Hall. It was an event that was unique in many respects· and it was an occasion that will not soon be forgotten by any of those who participated in the tribute, nor is it likely to be forgotten soon by the guest of the evening.

The Journal pointed out that Durant, as founder and except for five years active head of GM from its birth to 1919,

> has favored Flint with a large share of the fruits of its marvelous growth, through the location here of some of its larger and many of its smaller plants. Through his constant consideration for his home town, the growth of Flint from a village of 10,000 persons to a city of 85,000 has resulted. . . .

The hall was elaborately decorated with flags and bunting, and with flowers on the tables. Fred A. Aldrich was toastmaster. Durant was joined at the head table by Raskob.

In a long speech, reported in full by the newspaper, Durant reminisced about his early days in Flint. He looked around the room, referring to old associates by their first names—John J. Carton, William S. Ballenger, Arthur G. Bishop, Charles M. Begole, and many others—and said that while he got the credit for General Motors, some of them had been as responsible for the success of the vast enterprise. He told his audience:

> Competition is the life of trade. I stand for competition. I am opposed to monopoly or control on the principle that it destroys initiative, curtails freedom of action, and frequently leads to abuse of power. In a controlled situation, the people take what they can get. In a competitive situation, the people get what they want.
>
> If I controlled the motor car business, the public would very likely get what I cared to build. With open competition, as we now have it, the people will get what they want. If I do not supply it, my competitors will. Supply and demand are the best and only regulator of production and price. We may adopt other measures with temporary success, but supply and demand are the only permanent determining factors.

Discussing the record of Flint's factories in producing war materials, Durant read aloud a letter he had just received from Winston Churchill, then minister of munitions for Great Britain. It was a gracious note of thanks for GM's war contributions. Durant said that with the permission of those present, he would send a cable of reply on behalf of those at the banquet, offering Churchill good wishes and sincere thanks from Flint, "the birthplace of the General Motors Corp., the pride of every Flint citizen, everyone without exception interested in the development, progress, ideals and standards of that organization." (This incident is somewhat ironic because Durant opposed U.S. entry into World War I. He was a man of peace. He also strongly opposed involvement in World War II, at least before Pearl Harbor. Yet most General Motors plants became heavily involved in World War I production.)

Of the alliance with the Du Pont Company, Durant said:

> About two years ago, I became acquainted with some people whose name you well know, who stand the highest in the list, and because of the great growth of the General Motors and the thought that we would have some time a great company, I took it upon myself to know these people. The name is du Pont, and let me say that wherever the name Pierre du Pont is mentioned, the people know that it is one of the best and safest, one of the fairest and most considerate, one of the most generous in the country.

Other speakers that night were Raskob, Walter P. Chrysler, and the Rev. T. J. Murphy, who said:

> I hope that the memory of this event will be in my mind as long as I live. I feel that I am at home among the friends of W. C. Durant. He deserves that welcome from the bottom of our hearts. If all those who employ labor were wielding the influence that he wields and were as considerate of his employees as he is, there would be no anarchists. It is a blessing for Flint and for all of the United States that he is president of General Motors.

One final tribute came in a telegram from Dallas Dort, who regretted missing the "great love feast in honor of my dear old partner, W. C. Durant, the superb architect and builder of Flint." Dort continued: "Our appreciation of him grows with each succeeding year as rings to an oak, and may those mighty rings ... bind him stronger and stronger to us during the many years of accomplishment which are still before him."

For General Motors 1919 was a year of great prosperity and great expansion. Vehicle production increased by nearly 60 per cent over the previous year. Net profits jumped from $15 million in 1918 to $60 million in 1919.

The corporation plunged boldly ahead in many directions. General Motors Acceptance Corporation, designed to finance sales of GM products, was incorporated in New York. Housing construction companies, to build homes for GM workers, were formed in Flint, Detroit, Lansing, and other cities, leading to corporate investments of millions of dollars. There were large investments in tire, die casting, and other manufacturing companies.

GM purchased a 60 percent interest in the Fisher Body Corporation, the world's largest producer of automobile bodies, for $5.8 million in cash and $21.8 million in notes, and a big cost-plus contract. It was to be one of GM's most important acquisitions.

The corporation completed purchase of Charles F. Kettering's companies, including the Dayton Wright Airplane Company, in Dayton, Ohio, bringing the inventor of the automobile self-starter fully into the GM fold. The General Motors Export Company was established to develop overseas sales.

William Crapo Durant—a telephone always close at hand.

Negotiations were begun to buy other firms, including Interstate Motor of Muncie, Indiana, where the Sheridan car was produced in 1920-21.

Also in 1919 the Durant Building Corporation was established to build in Detroit the $20 million Durant Building (renamed the General Motors Building, its present name, in 1921). It was to be the world's largest office building, fifteen stories tall, faced with Bedford limestone, with four wings and 1,700 offices—a total floor space of 30 acres. Durant always insisted that he opposed the project, that it was Raskob's idea. And although Durant sent Sloan to buy the land for the building, his general opposition is documented by the testimony of other GM executives. He wanted to use the corporation's money for working capital, not for office buildings. He saw no need for a building to house a huge bureaucracy he did not want.

While the great expansion program continued, Durant was coming under increasing criticism from within by those who were unhappy with his insistence on running the corporation as a one-man show. Pierre du Pont pushed for Durant to develop more orderly administrative methods such as were used by the Du Pont Company. He even sent one of his assistants to study GM management. The man's report criticized the absence of a central staff or a central engineering department. Procedures for authorizing the construction and maintenance of GM factories were haphazard, he said. There was little or no bidding for contracts. Durant involved himself unnecessarily in details. [12] When du Pont told Durant all this, Durant nodded, smiled, and agreed. But his style was to continue to run things by himself. When he needed a little bureaucracy, he would borrow it from the Du Pont Company.

Alfred P. Sloan also pushed strongly for improved managerial methods. He wrote three reports on the weaknesses of the internal management and offered solutions. Durant praised the reports—and ignored them. Sloan thought he might quit.

General Motors was changing. In 1919 it was a huge network of divisions and subsidiaries, employing 86,000 men and women. But Durant was still operating as he had in the old days, on a personal basis. He believed more in his own hunches than in the considered opinions of a staff of experts. But the auto business was getting far too complicated for one man to make all the major decisions.

Durant's interests were not entirely in company operations either. He had a large battery of telephones on his desk and kept in touch with stockbrokers around the country. At times of unusual price changes, Durant became so involved with his brokers that it was almost impossible for his small cadre of top assistants to get into his office.[13]

On occasion he kept his top executives waiting for hours to start a conference. Or a meeting would start, and Durant would be called out of the room to the telephone, not to return for hours. His assistants could hardly continue their discussions without him, so they sat, and quietly fumed.

But there was one man who could not remain quiet for long—Walter Chrysler. Durant had treated Chrysler well since their agreement in 1916. He was being paid a very large salary, particularly with his stock bonuses, and in April, 1919, was named vice-president in charge of all GM operations and assistant to president Durant. He retained his position as president of Buick, though Harry H. Bassett, once manager of Weston-Mott, succeeded to general manager. But no lofty position or huge salary could keep the strong, direct Chrysler happy when he was dissatisfied with policies.

And Chrysler was. He was concerned about the expansion program—Durant had paid too much for the Janesville plant, he complained—and irritated at being called to Detroit or New York only to cool his heels while Durant attended to something else. There was a further problem. One of the conditions Chrysler had extracted from Durant when he agreed to stay in 1916 was that he, Chrysler, would run Buick without interference, and would report directly to Durant. But Durant liked to deal directly with the general managers of his car divisions. It was frustrating for Chrysler to be president of Buick and in charge of all operations and find that Durant was dealing directly with his subordinates. The two executives were both strong-minded men and their arguments became more frequent, sometimes flaring at meetings of the Executive Committee. Finally Chrysler demanded that Durant just tell him his policies. As Chrysler recalled:

> Billy laughed at me. "Walt, I believe in changing the policies just as often as my door opens and closes."
> I wagged my head and said, "You and I can never get along." That's the kind of fellow he was, though; we'd fight, and then he'd want to raise my salary.[14]

Perhaps the most famous incident between the two was actually won by Chrysler. He had told Durant he was about to make an attractive deal with the A. O. Smith Company in Wisconsin to supply frames for Buicks. A short time later, Chrysler was attending a civic luncheon in Flint when Dallas Dort announced, "Boys, I've got great news for you. Here's a telegram from William C. Durant. He says he has just authorized the spending of $6 million to build a GM frame plant in Flint."

Chrysler was outraged. He knew about Flint's serious housing shortage and could not see the need for another plant to bring in still more workers. He could not understand Durant's strange loyalty to Flint, which had already turned the city into one of the country's largest manufacturing centers. Chrysler confronted Durant, who argued, then backed away from the decision. Chrysler said he then made a very attractive deal with the Smith company.

Late in 1919, however, not long after his three-year agreement with Durant had expired, Chrysler felt it was time to go. He had had enough of the Durant style, though the two men remained friends for a lifetime. Durant said he bought Chrysler's stock from him for $10 million, a well-earned but certainly substantial fortune for the man who had started with Buick seven years earlier at $6,000 a year. Chrysler's departure from GM eventually led to the creation of the Chrysler Corporation.

Durant had created an enormous organization. But he was so self-confident, so dominant a figure that many of his best men either quit him, or wanted to. Men such as Nash, Chrysler, and Sloan had minds of their own. They were not built to be "yes" men. And yet, years after their business associations with Durant, all three wrote quite kindly about the man with whom they had so strongly disagreed.

Chrysler, in his autobiography, described Durant as a genius and wrote that "the automobile industry owes more to Durant than it has yet acknowledged. In some ways, he has been its greatest man. Sometimes we found ourselves in arguments but we also had a lot of fun."

Nash once wrote to an old Durant-Dort Carriage Company salesman, Alva Davis, that

> I think you and I agree that Mr. Durant has been a great man. [We] . . . never were in very close accord on a good many subjects, although we were great friends up to the time I was put into the Buick Motor Company. His policies and mine, of course, were absolutely opposed to each other, but I like Mr. Durant, I meet him usually about once a year, and he certainly carries my very best wishes with him at all times.[15]

And Sloan, in his *Adventures of a White-Collar Man*, wrote:

> I was constantly amazed by his daring ways of making a decision. Mr. Durant would proceed on a course of action guided solely, as far as I could tell, by some intuitive flash of brilliance. He never felt obliged to make an engineering hunt for facts. Yet at times he was astoundingly correct in his judgments. . . . Durant's integrity? Unblemished. Work? He was a prodigious worker. Devotion to General Motors? Why it was his baby! He would have made any sacrifice for it and ultimately he did make for it almost the ultimate sacrifice.

But Sloan also felt that General Motors had gotten too big and too complicated to be a one-man show: "In any company, I would be the first to say that William C. Durant was a genius. But General Motors justified the most competent executive group that could possibly be brought together."

It was seemingly impossible for most of his associates to be of one mind about Durant. They were awed by his vision and daring way of doing business, they admired him, and many of them loved him. At the same time, their feelings were sometimes mixed with impatience and anger. The man seemed to operate in a different dimension. His motives were misunderstood, his impulses unpredictable.

Some of his highest-paid assistants resented being called to his office on Sunday mornings to discuss business while Durant presided from a portable barber chair as his barber shaved him.[16] Others complained that he took advantage of three-day holidays by organizing a factory-inspecting junket and they would have to go along. But though they grumbled that they never had time for their families, they admitted they were also fascinated to be in his entourage because the trips were interesting and unpredictable.[17] His associates often found it difficult to get his attention for some project; yet, when he finally did get to it, they railed about his close attention to the merest detail. He could be cold and severe in his criticism, they said, while acknowledging that he could also be the most charming man they had ever met.

It is almost true that work was Durant's only form of recreation. He seldom attended parties, though he enjoyed them. The reason, according to his widow, was that he saw that she did not particularly enjoy them, being much younger than his contemporaries. "But all of the ladies thought Willie was grand—they kept telling me how charming he was."

Nor was Durant very enthusiastic about sports. He played some golf and a little tennis, but was not much good at either of them. W. W. Murphy recalls that Durant's golf game had one strong point. He was a superb putter.

At the office Durant would, however, often take a break from his intense concentration on business and the stock market for a game of checkers. "You couldn't beat him at checkers," Murphy said. "He had a miniature set in his desk and if someone would be visiting with him, the person might get through talking and Durant would say, 'You want to play a game of checkers?' One of his opponents was the elevator starter. Along about 5 or 5:30, the fellow would go in there and they would play checkers until Mr. Durant wanted to go home."[18] He also played poker for high stakes, at least in the early days, and was an excellent bridge player.

Though once a cigar salesman, Durant gave up cigars on the advice of Dr. Campbell. He asked people not to smoke in his office, but for years he carried a cigar in his pocket and would take it out and smell it when he felt the urge to smoke. Though he became a strong advocate of prohibition, he did drink occasionally, though moderately.

What Durant seems to have enjoyed as much as anything were his visits with his mother at her summer home in Pentwater, Michigan. Murphy would often make the trip with him. Durant adored his mother and found the sand and pine setting at once invigorating and relaxing. Here his childlike exuberance returned. He once invited Murphy to walk with him to the top of a nearby sand dune. There, they took off their coats, sat down, and slid the length of the dune down to the water's edge.

From Durant's return to control through the end of 1919, General Motors had grown into a vast enterprise. Both Durant and Raskob were expansionists. They did not always agree on direction, perhaps, but through 1918 and much of 1919 they appeared to agree in philosophy—always ready to push forward with new ideas and new programs. Raskob acknowledged Durant's contributions in a letter in January, 1920:

> Enclosed please find comparative statements of the General Motors Corporation for 1915-16-17-18-19.
>
> This comparison is exceedingly interesting because it shows that in 1915, the year in which the voting trust matured and the properties turned back to you, the company was employing about $58 million, whereas, according to our latest balance sheet, October 31st, 1919, four years later, the total assets employed aggregate $452,000,000. In other words, the General Motors Corporation of today is eight times as large as the company which the bankers were managing.
>
> This is indeed a fine tribute to your foresight.[19]

It was almost a final tribute. Shortly after Raskob wrote that letter, the economy in general and General Motors in particular ran into trouble. In 1920 the boom that had followed the end of World War I came to a rather abrupt halt, and the United States slumped into a sharp recession. In the early summer, the price of GM stock began to decline steadily. So did car sales. General Motors sold nearly 47,000 cars and trucks in June, 1920. By November, monthly sales were down to 12,700—which was one-third the volume of the previous November.[20]

The decline in sales presented all sorts of problems. Dealers became overstocked with new cars, and the corporation had to take whole shipments back and store them. Despite corporate efforts in the spring to hold down inventories at GM factories, the inventories soared to dangerous levels. Neither Durant nor Raskob had strong control over the individual operating divisions—GM was still very much a decentralized organization despite Durant's reputation as a dictator. As a result, the division managers spent far more for inventory and expansions than the central administration permitted, and by September had exceeded their limit by nearly $60 million. It was a case, said Sloan, of "decentralization with a vengeance."

Durant, however, had been concerned for some time about the sort of problem the corporation was facing in the summer and fall of 1920. As early as October 31, 1919, he had expressed his alarm about some aspects of the expansion program and the means of financing it. On that day he wrote to Raskob:

> I do not wish to annoy you, but I feel that I should call your attention to the enormous expenditures and capital commitments which are being authorized by the Finance Committee against prospective earnings—a method of financing which I do not think is either safe or sound and which, in the event of industrial disturbance or paralysis, might seriously impair our position. Frankly, I am very much worried and I know that many members of our organization in the managerial and operating divisions are much concerned.[21]

That same day, at a meeting of the Executive Committee, he stepped down from the chair to recommend rejection of spending requests of $7.2 million for additional costs on the Durant Building in Detroit (a Raskob project) and $7.1 million for plant extensions at the New Departure Manufacturing Company. Durant may have been deeply concerned about the spending, but he was also probably reacting to a decision by the Finance Committee on October 17 to turn down his request for more tractor appropriations. The Executive Committee voted with Durant to reject the Durant Building and New Departure expenditures, though five days later, on Raskob's recommendation, it reversed itself and approved them.[22] On the same day, the Finance Committee approved Durant's request for money for the tractor program and proposed the sale of $50 million to $100 million in new debentures to help finance the expansions. All sides would thus get everything they wanted.

Durant was apparently as concerned as was Sloan about this horse-trading way of running the business and in November and December, 1919, made recommendations for a tough program of retrenchment and for improved procedures for investigating and reporting expansion requests. Durant cannot be absolved of all responsibility for the plight of General Motors in 1920, but the evidence at least suggests modification of his reputation as a man rushing blindly ahead on expansion programs in the face of growing financial difficulties. Richard P. Scharchburg, an associ-

Early photo of the General Motors Building in Detroit—at first named the Durant Building, though Durant opposed its construction.

ate professor at General Motors Institute who has thoroughly studied early corporate records, wrote in a 1973 manuscript:

> as one reads the minutes of the Executive and Finance committees of this period, in late 1919, it can be clearly seen that the Executive Committee, dominated by Durant, developed a conservative posture, whereas the Finance Committee, dominated by Raskob, maintained its aggressive expansive posture throughout. There is no evidence of an open break of relations, but certainly they must have been strained.

"Had Durant had his way," Scharchburg told the writer, "perhaps the corporation wouldn't have been in the fix it was in the fall of 1920."

In January, 1920, the GM stockholders authorized a ten for one split of GM shares, ten shares of no par common for each share of $100 common. They also authorized the plan developed by Raskob to issue new debentures in a move Raskob expected would raise $85 million in new cash to help pay the costs of the postwar expansion program.[23] In the worsening general economic situation, the plan was a partial failure, raising only $7 million by late February and only about $12 million by May. Durant's concern about "enormous expenditures and capital commitments" was beginning to look prophetic.

Despite the debenture failure, Raskob felt that the corporation had to come up with $64 million to complete the expansion program, and also for working capital. In a new effort to get the money, GM decided to issue 3.2 million new shares to existing stockholders at $20 a share. Durant and the du Ponts would turn over their rights to about 60 percent of the new shares to investors, who would then become new partners in the corporation. Explosives Trades Ltd. of England—sort of a British counterpart of the Du Pont Company—agreed to take $30 million worth of the new shares, and to pay for this in installments until December. Canadian Explosives Ltd., a joint subsidiary of the Du Pont Company and Explosives Trades, agreed to take $6 million worth. Then Raskob and Pierre du Pont persuaded J. P. Morgan and Company to become another new partner by forming a syndicate to distribute 1.4 million of the new shares, which would raise $28 million more. Durant was concerned about the Morgan partnership—he had never really trusted bankers after his experience of 1910, and he still remembered the difficulties with some of the Morgan partners in 1908. The Morgans, for their part, were wary of Durant, considering him a speculator. But Durant realized GM needed money; the Morgans saw that the du Ponts were in command of the GM Finance Committee.[24] The agreement was made.

As part of the agreement, the Morgan Company was to appoint one representative to the GM board of directors and companies in the Morgan-organized syndicate were to select five new GM board members. The Morgan Company was offered the 1.4 million shares at $20 at a time GM common was selling for about $27 on the open market, having drifted from $37 several months earlier. However, as compensation for itself and the underwriting syndicate, the Morgan Company also demanded the right to purchase 200,000 GM shares at the "inside" price of $10 a share. The DuPonts felt that the total commission of about $2 million in shares for a net return of $26 million in cash was reasonable, given the fact that the stock market prices were declining rapidly; Durant, however, objected strenuously before finally agreeing to permit borrowing the shares from the Chevrolet treasury.[25]

In July, 1920, after the Morgans had distributed the new shares, Durant was involved in several syndicates in an effort to support the market price of GM stock. One of the syndicates was managed by Edward Stettinius, a Morgan partner who had just become the Morgan representative on the GM board. The purpose of the syndicate was to stabilize the price of GM while the last of the new shares were being distributed. But Durant was also involved in other syndicates; he was deeply committed to supporting the price.

Still it declined. The market price of GM stood at $27 on July 10. By July 20 it was down to $25. On July 27 it broke to $21. Durant was called at his home in Deal. A block of 75,000 shares of GM had just been sold. Durant said he investigated and learned that Morgan and Company had sold, within a few days, 125,000 shares. In a statement in Durant's personal papers, "dictated by Mr. W. C. Durant in the presence of Mr. Stettinius," Durant (referring to himself in the third person) wrote:

> When Mr. Durant learned where the selling came from, he called in Mr. Stettinius to his office and in the presence of Mr. Pierre S. du Pont and Mr. John J. Raskob made it known to Mr. Stettinius that the selling had been traced and asked for an explanation. Mr. Stettinius' excuse was that he believed the stock could be repurchased at a lower price but agreed that the syndicate would support the price at $20 a share. This Mr. Stettinius failed to do, as evidenced by purchase slips at a meeting two or three days later, showing the purchase by Mr. Durant and his friends at less than $20 a share.

According to Durant, Stettinius told him he thought the stock would go still lower and that they should sell 200,000 shares short. Durant opposed the idea. He was always against short selling, and he told Stettinius they should be on the constructive and upbuilding side.[26] Durant told Stettinius later that he felt the stock sale was "almost a betrayal of trust" and that it led directly to his personal disaster, his loss of more than $90 million. Catherine Durant remembers that her husband felt he was the victim of "a well-conceived plan to take over his holdings."

But there are at least two sides to the story. Stettinius later said he sold the shares "for the account of the syndicate" and that the bankers made no money on the transaction.[27] GM stock was already falling as a result of the national economic slump (and partly because market "bears" were driving down the price). In the face of a falling market, Stettinius may well have felt that the wise move was to sell some of the syndicate's stock to protect its investment and to repurchase later at a lower price. And Pierre du Pont said it was his understanding that when the syndicate was formed by Morgan and Company, Durant would not operate in the stock market in any way "as it is impossible for two parties to act independently in a satisfactory way."[28] Certainly Durant had not been required to buy stock outside of the Morgan syndicate. Had he not been buying in large volumes outside of that syndicate, he could not have been so severely hurt by the dip in market prices.

Why was Durant buying so heavily to support the market price of GM? The answer to that is not entirely certain. Durant himself said he was trying to support the price so that the British-Canadian money that had been pledged would come in.[29] As it turned out, Explosives Trades finally decided it could not raise $30 million after all, but only $15 million.[30] To cushion the blow, the Canadians were persuaded to increase their participation and short-term loans were made. Catherine Durant told the writer:

> When either the Canadian or British firms felt unable to subscribe the amount pledged . . . Mr. Durant offered to assume this burden. At this time he wrote a form letter to several of his friends inviting them to participate in the acquisition of the new General Motors stock issue. He stated that the investment was sound and implied that he would support the stock at $20. Now, it must be remembered that at the time the margin requirement was 10 per cent and as the stock skidded continually during the ensuing months, brokers began to call. Willie stood alone in the support of the stock to protect his friends who (I remember well) called and wrote seeking his assistance. Meanwhile the . . . [other participants in the banker-managed stock syndicate] did not lift a finger.

Another possible reason he was buying so heavily is directly related to an incident in March, 1920, in which Durant engineered a "corner" of the old $100 par GM stock on the market, enlisting a number of old associates to help in the buying. It was a briefly sensational episode. Durant had laid the groundwork in February, when he sent telegrams to GM stockholders, asking some to buy stock, others to hold their shares and still others to give him options on their shares at the market. In March the price of the stock became very active, soaring as much as 37 points in one day. When the price hit $409, speculators who had "sold short" were at the point of financial disaster. Officials of the New York Stock Exchange quickly broke the corner by ruling that 10 shares of the new no-par GM common could be delivered against one of the old—which was not permitted before the ruling—and there was plenty of the new stock around.

Durant mentioned the stock-cornering incident in his autobiographical notes only in the title of a planned chapter: "When General Motors Stock Was Cornered—A Startling Incident in the History of the New York Stock Exchange." He didn't get around to writing the chapter. Yet he did mention the incident to W. A. P. John, who gave this version of the story in *Motor* magazine in January 1923:

> W. C. Durant's great mistake has been that he has allowed the public to believe he is a plunger, a manipulator. . . . (But) he has never speculated in the market for personal profit. He has, however, frequently gone into the market to protect the stocks of his enterprises from ruthless attacks on the part of manipulators. Once, he caught his enemies off guard when they were endeavoring to depress the market. They had, by concerted attack, sold more General Motors than was in existence. He "cornered the market." He could have crushed them mercilessly. But in so doing he would have ruined thousands of men, dozens of banks, and scores of brokers; and so after conferring with the officers of the New York Stock Exchange he placed a nominal value on the stock—the average price which he had paid in purchasing it. And the guilty were allowed to escape because the innocent were being ruined.

John L. Pratt, a former Du Pont man who had become an assistant to Durant late in 1919 after undertaking numerous assignments while on loan to the GM president, recalled that Durant opposed short selling. "He didn't think it was right for anyone to sell something he didn't have," Pratt said. The question of whether Durant was speculating, or was acting to fight speculators, is one of interpretation. Alfred P. Sloan wrote, in *My Years with General Motors:*

> I think Mr. Durant's personal stock market operations were motivated essentially by his great pride in General Motors and everything relating to it, and by his unbounded confidence in its future. . . .

Whether Durant had himself become dangerously overextended in the stock-cornering effort is unknown. With the ability to buy stock on 10 percent margin, he may have become carried away by the battle to crush short-sellers. From the moment the corner was broken, the price of the stock declined through most of the rest of 1920. It is certain, however, that some of Durant's friends had bought more stock than they could handle in the declining market, and it was not in his character to abandon them.

Loyalty between Durant and his business associates had always been an important factor in his success. There were men he could count on, and who could count on him. So when some of these associates who had bought GM stock on his advice said they were facing ruin as the price declined, Durant offered to take up their stock, though he was in trouble himself. John L. Pratt recalled several such occasions. In each case, he said, Durant took the stock off the hands of old friends who came to him and said they were in financial trouble.[31]

At one point during 1920 Durant was so concerned about GM's financial situation that he decided to liquidate one of his favorite projects, Frigidaire, because it was not yet profitable and all available cash was needed for the car divisions. He sent Pratt to Detroit to administer the coup de grace. Instead, Pratt found the Frigidaire owners so loyal to the product, despite its shortcomings, that he persuaded Durant to retain it.[32]

As the economic decline worsened and the price of GM stock continued to fall, Durant worked feverishly at the battery of telephones in his New York office, buying stock from brokers all over the country. Everyone seemed to be selling; only Durant bought. In late September, 1920, he wrote to Raskob asking if any of the partners were selling stock, and seeking Raskob's help in persuading the banker syndicate to step in and start buying. Raskob replied on October 4 that he was trying to get the syndicate to give some support to the market, but the bankers "felt that the stock was acting well in the market as compared with what other stocks were doing and under the circumstances thought our full buying power ought to be held in reserve to be used in the event of a more serious general situation developing." Raskob wrote that he told the bankers he did not agree, that he felt "some little support could be given."[33] But to no avail. Durant was not going to get any help. He stood alone.

It was not Durant's nature to quit. He continued his buying in a single-handed attempt to hold up the market price. "I felt he had about as much chance for success," wrote Sloan, "as if he had tried to stand at the top of Niagara Falls and stop it with his hat."[34]

By this time, Durant's alienation from some of the other GM executives was becoming more apparent. He had warned against some aspects of financing the expansion program and against part of the program itself, particularly the Raskob-backed $20 million Durant Building in Detroit, which was looking more like an extravagance every day. Nor had he been in sympathy with the new stock issue and with the price that had to be paid for some of the new partners.[35]

On the other side, there was criticism of the unsuccessful tractor program administered by Durant. There was disenchantment over the loss of Walter Chrysler, who had left because of his arguments with the president. Factory inventories had gotten out of hand. Durant was constantly on the phone with his brokers as his fortune poured down the drain. The car divisions, with the exception of Buick and Cadillac, were said to be in poor shape because of inadequate engineering and testing.[36] And when other auto manufacturers slashed their prices to try to boost sales in the recession, Durant fought to hold the price line before finally agreeing to reductions. If Durant could complain of Raskob's expansions, others could criticize Durant's management.

Sloan, distressed that his ideas for improved management had been ignored, and concerned about a number of policies, went to Europe for a month to consider whether he should resign. He had almost decided that he would, but when he returned from his trip, in August, 1920, he detected that things were coming to a head.[37]

Durant, in what must have been some of his most desperate days, still found time for a personal touch. Three retiring Flint mail carriers opened letters one day in the fall of 1920 to find ten shares of GM stock each and personal letters from Durant. He offered congratulations on their retirements and said the stock was a "souvenir" and a reminder of "old times."

By October Durant had bought so much stock on the margin

that he was in grave financial trouble. He borrowed 1.3 million shares of GM common from the Du Pont Company, a loan approved by Pierre du Pont, and apparently used it as margin for more stock purchases. He formed the Durant Corporation, publicly offering to sell blocks of stock to GM investors on the installment plan.[38] That may have been the ultimate clue to his plight. Nobody could remember Durant's ever selling GM shares before. On October 27, GM stock was at $17. A week later it was $16. On November 10 it went to $14. A few days later the price was $13. . . .

Now the Morgans expressed concern. Dwight W. Morrow, one of the Morgan partners, asked Raskob and Pierre du Pont about Durant's personal financial situation. The two were unsure, so a meeting was arranged in early November of Morrow, Durant, du Pont, and Raskob. Durant insisted under questioning that he knew of no "weak accounts" in the market.[39] But in a matter of a few days Durant invited du Pont and Raskob to lunch. There he told the chairman that "the bankers" had asked for his resignation and he would "have to play the game."

Du Pont and Raskob, perhaps still uncertain that this would be necessary, met in Durant's office a short time later to try to find out the extent of Durant's indebtedness. Durant was so busy answering the telephone, seeing visitors, rushing in and out of his office, that it was several hours before they could start adding up his troubles. The indebtedness was in the millions of dollars, he admitted, but he was not certain of the figures since he had no records. It would take several days to get reports from all his brokers.

After that things reached a head rather quickly. On November 18 the Morgan partners, who said they were concerned that Durant's "failure" could be disastrous to several banking houses, met with Durant, Raskob, and du Pont. The meeting lasted all night. By 5:30 a.m. an understanding had been reached. The Morgans and Du Ponts would raise enough money to make a cash offer for all of Durant's indebtedness. That would take at least $20 million. Durant would be left with something. Durant would also resign as president of General Motors. When the dust had settled, Durant figured that he had lost $90 million.

The following week Pierre du Pont, describing the sequence of events in a letter to his brother Irénée, then president of the DuPont Company, praised the Morgans for their assistance. "Throughout the whole transaction the Morgan partners have appeared to the greatest advantage," he wrote. "They threw themselves into the situation wholeheartedly, stating at the start that they asked no compensation."

Durant took it all "very complacently," Pierre du Pont recalled in testimony in a government antitrust suit against the Du Pont Company more than three decades later.*

> You wouldn't think anything had ever happened to him. He was quite as agreeable and unconcerned as he was before anything did happen, and he told me [at the all-night meeting] that he would resign, as he felt that the bankers would insist on it, or had insisted on it, and he said he wanted me to take his place. I told him it was not my intention at all for him to leave, much less to take his place, but we ended that part of the conversation. He brought it up, told me he was going to resign. He felt it was compulsory.

Those of his legion of loyalists who got wind of what was happening tried to stop him from resigning. From Flint, William S. Ballenger of Chevrolet wired: "Your friends have great confidence in you and your ability. You owe it to them to remain with General Motors to the last ditch."[40] He was already in the last ditch.

Sloan related:

> A man of genius, of courage, of vision and great wealth, is seen sacrificing practically all he had in a fruitless effort to protect, according to his way of thinking, his creation, General Motors—loyal to the very end. You knew he was grief-stricken [at his final board meeting November 30, 1920], but no grief showed on his face. He was smiling pleasantly, as if it were a routine matter, when he told us he was resigning as president of General Motors.[41]

Durant and his personal secretary, W. W. Murphy, went to his

---

*The antitrust suit eventually led to a ruling that the du Pont interests would have to divest themselves of their General Motors holdings.

W. W. Murphy, Durant's personal secretary for more than twenty years.

office to pick up portfolios of personal papers. Durant turned to those watching and said lightly, "May 1st is usually moving day, but we're moving December 1st."[42] Then, followed by Murphy, he walked out of the building. That day, it is said, tears were shed in a number of offices at GM headquarters. The Durant era at General Motors had ended.

Margery Durant recalled that she saw her father immediately after his disaster. "He came home and, for the first time, gave way for a few moments to his emotions. He put his arms around me and I could feel his body tremble slightly and all the tears running down his cheeks."[43]

John L. Pratt has related that a day or so before Durant's resignation, Durant invited a number of his close associates—he called them his "boys"—to his home for dinner. As Pratt recalled:

Well, we had a nice dinner. After we were through, Mr. Durant got up and told the boys he wanted to tell them directly what had happened. He said, "I was trying to support General Motors stock in the market and I became over-extended. I am telling you this because you will hear rumors that the Du Pont Company took advantage of me and forced me out, and you will find possibly some people will show resentment in General Motors because I am out. But I want you to know that the Du Pont Company treated me as fine as anybody could treat me. If they hadn't gone out and borrowed to the extent of"—I think he said—"$35 million to take over the brokerage holdings, General Motors stock would have gone to practically nothing. I would have been broke and you boys who have your money in General Motors would have been broke. I don't want any resentment toward the Du Pont people because I am getting out. I want you to remain with General Motors and support the Du Pont people. Mr. P. S. du Pont is coming in as president, and I want you to support him just like you did me."[44]

Catherine Durant remembers no such dinner at the house, and is positive that she could not have forgotten an event of such significance. Her husband, she says, "was depressed and in no mood for dinner company for several weeks. He was quiet and as usual when things went wrong, hid his feelings. There was never any doubt in his mind that he was the victim of a plot. The record is clear that his 2,500,000-plus GM shares passed to the DuPonts at $9.50 a share and shortly thereafter the stock regained its value."

And that is another example of conflicting accounts by informed sources which make objective judgments almost impossible.

In Flint the resignation of Durant was felt so keenly that Mayor Edwin W. Atwood felt called upon to make a statement. He said that Flint citizens

are proud of Mr. Durant and, more than that, they know that primarily through his regard for his home city, great industrial developments have occurred. . . . Naturally, it is something of a shock and a regret to Mr. Durant's fellow townsmen to learn that he has laid down the reins, but they should be thankful that he had interested in the company such men of constructive ideas and ability as Mr. Pierre S. du Pont and his associates.

To keep Durant's 2.5 million shares of GM stock from being dumped on a jittery market, the Du Ponts, aided by the Morgans, established the Du Pont Securities Company to hold his shares. They paid $23.7 million cash to his brokers. For his interest in the shares Durant received 40 percent of the stock of the Du Pont Securities Company. A short time later Durant turned over his stock in that company to the Du Ponts in exchange for 230,000 shares of GM stock, then selling for about $13. Although this gave him stock worth $2.9 million, Durant said that when he had cleared up all his debts, he had nothing left.[45]

Negotiations continued for more than two years between Durant and GM over his compensation for services and over claims involving the corporation. He said he had received $500,000 for 1916 and 1917 (which was the $1 million he received in connection with the 1917 stock-supporting syndicate), but no salary or commission for the final three years of his presidency. According to memorandums in Durant's personal papers, there was a corporate suggestion that GM would pay him $1.5 million if he would make a claim the corporation could recognize. He then made a claim in connection with certain shares of United Motors and Scripps-Booth Company stock which he had turned over to Chevrolet in 1916, but the claim was not recognized. There was, according to the memorandums, another tentative offer to sell him the net assets of Chevrolet for about 60 percent of book value, but this involved about $60 million—more than he could handle. He offered to buy the Chevrolet plant at Tarrytown, the Oakland plant at Pontiac, and the Sheridan plant at Muncie for 75 percent of book value, but GM officials said they might be criticized if these were sold. Finally, in December, 1922, both sides agreed that Durant would turn over some property he owned in Janesville and would receive as final settlement $328,325 in cash and 55,159 shares of GM stock—a total of $1.1 million.

In the immediate aftermath of his departure, Durant tried to set the record straight on several matters. In February, 1921, he sent letters to members of the GM Executive Committee, asking if they recalled whether he had advocated or endorsed construction of the Durant Building, or whether they had ever heard him question the wisdom of the project. In general the answers were that they remembered he had not favored the project, that he was disappointed and surprised at the increased cost over original estimates, that he felt the money could have been used to better advantage in the business. Some recalled that they had agreed with him. Several felt that Durant had questioned the building, but had yielded to Raskob's judgment. Sloan replied that "I had always presumed that you advocated it in the beginning, but later on I feel quite certain that you commenced to question the wisdom of the project either from the standpoint of its magnitude or our financial condition, or perhaps for some other reason."[46]

In March, 1921, Durant wrote to Irénée du Pont, president of the Du Pont Company, protesting a remark in Du Pont's annual report that Durant "desired to resign and sell his interest in the corporation to liquidate his personal indebtedness. . . ."

The facts were, Durant said,

> that on the evening of Nov. 15, a personal friend of mine, representing the Du Pont interests, called at my apartment and informed me that my resignation as president of the General Motors Corporation was desired and would be accepted—the reason given, that I was not in sympathy with the policies of the controlling interests and would not cooperate. I must and do plead guilty to the charge.
>
> Two days later, when I came to discuss the matter with Mr. P. S. du Pont and Mr. Raskob, I told them (and up to that time they knew nothing of the situation) of the burdens which I had assumed in attempting to correct the mistakes and errors which had been made, for which I was in no way responsible, and FROM THAT POINT we started to work out a plan which would relieve me of my embarrassment and which resulted in the Du Pont Securities Company taking over my General Motors holdings. In our attempt to adjust to the new conditions, I trust nothing will occur to destroy our friendship.[47]

The question of whether Durant was solely a victim of his own efforts to support the price of GM stock, or whether he was also the victim of a plan to remove him from control, was raised in 1949 by U.S. government lawyers in a pre-trial brief of the antitrust suit against the Du Pont Company. In the brief the lawyers said that "it is clear . . . that from the very beginning of this [Durant-Du Pont] relationship, the Du Pont group was planning on ousting Durant when the opportunity was ripe and of taking over sole and complete control of General Motors." [48]

The lawyers based their contention, at least in part, on a statement written by Raskob to the Du Pont Company in 1917 in support of his recommendation for the initial GM investment:

> Mr. Durant should be continued as president of the company, Mr. P. S. du Pont will be continued as chairman of the board, the Finance Committee will be ours and we will have such representation on the Executive Committee as we desire, and it is the writer's [Raskob's] belief that ultimately the Du Pont Company will absolutely control and dominate the whole General Motors situation with the entire approval of Mr. Durant, who, I think, will eventually place his holdings with us, taking his payment therefor in some securities mutually satisfactory. [49]

When Pierre du Pont was called as a witness on May 24, 1951, he said there was no truth to any suggestion that there was some kind of prearranged plan to freeze Durant out of GM, nor was the purchase of his shares in 1920 made in order to throw Durant out. "I am sure nothing of the kind would have happened if Durant had not fallen into that unfortunate position," du Pont said. "In fact, I believe if he had come to us in time, that the whole matter could have been straightened out, possibly, without his losing out."

Alfred D. Chandler, Jr., co-author with Stephen Salsbury of *Pierre S. du Pont and the Making of the Modern Corporation*, has told the writer that he has found no evidence that the Du Pont group had in 1917 long-term plans to oust Durant. "Indeed all the evidence (and there is a massive amount of it) shows that Pierre and his associates expected to continue to rely on Durant to run the corporation and did so until the middle of

Durant in an undated photo, his face showing signs of stress from his many financial crises.

November, 1920, when they learned of Durant's financial difficulties."

In their book, Chandler and Salsbury blame the Finance Committee for bringing the corporation "to the edge of financial disaster" yet point out that the new money brought in during 1920, which was soon needed for working capital instead of expansions, kept GM solvent late in 1920 and into 1921. This was a period in which $84 million in inventories was written off as a loss.

Durant himself did not get around to writing about his leave-taking in his autobiographical notes, though he had intended to do so until ill health overtook him. However, he once told an interviewer that he had General Motors in good condition but that Raskob, instead of furnishing money for expansions, exhausted the corporation's capital.[50] And Catherine Durant remembers "that there was never any doubt in my husband's mind that the collapse of GM stock was artificially created." She said she does not intend her statements to exonerate her husband completely for his downfall, but merely to state her recollections of his feelings.

All that can be said for certain about Durant's last days at General Motors is that his activities in the stock market placed him in an extremely vulnerable situation. Whether he was nudged over the brink solely by an unusually severe quiver in the business cycle, or with a little help from his friends, probably cannot be determined at this late date. It seems likely, however, that had Durant ever recognized his weaknesses and given men such as Chrysler and Sloan their heads, and had he been able to resist the stock market, he could have remained in command of an ever growing empire. Louis Kaufman said in 1927 that had Durant not become involved in the market, he would have then been worth $500 million and still in charge of the corporation. But Durant had not created this empire by being prudent, or practical, or by listening to others. He had been daring, impulsive, erratic. He won big, and he lost big. But, on balance, he created what has become the largest industrial corporation in history.

At General Motors, Pierre S. du Pont was prevailed upon to take the office of president, retaining his post as board chairman. Alfred P. Sloan became his first assistant—executive vice-president—and new management approaches were begun. Sloan succeeded to the presidency on May 10, 1923.

As for Durant, he wasted little time mourning his fate. Within six weeks he was back in the automobile manufacturing business in a sensational manner—and offering assurances to the worried Pierre du Pont that "I shall make no attempt to obtain control of General Motors, through exchange of securities or otherwise."[51]

Chapter Eleven

A Last Empire Created and Lost

Durant was fifty-nine years old and unemployed. For the second time he had lost control of the company he had founded, and this time the ties were severed. How much money he had left is questionable. Perhaps several million dollars, perhaps nothing. His mother, and probably his wife, still held considerable GM stock, however, and his settlement with the corporation was still outstanding. He also retained his great estate in Deal, New Jersey, the magnificent white palace "Raymere," once owned by Joseph Rothschild, with its twelve bedrooms, seventeenth-century French and English furniture, rare oriental carpets, and rare books and art. Walter Chrysler had visited the place, and later declared, "I never experienced luxury to compare with Billy Durant's house."

Durant wasted little time getting started again. Six weeks after resigning as GM president, he began one last fling in automobiles that started so sensationally the leaders of General Motors had genuine fears that he would take it all back again.

Durant returned to New York from a short vacation and wrote to sixty-seven of his highly placed friends, explaining that he was about to form a new automobile manufacturing company to build "just a real good car," and inviting their participation through stock purchases. "I cannot go into details at this time," he wrote, "other than to say it will bear the name Durant Motors, Inc., with one kind of stock and every subscriber to the initial offering upon exactly the same basis as to price, with no commission, bonuses or reservations to myself or associates issued for experience, ability or past performances."

Durant Motors filed for a charter in Albany, New York, on January 12, 1921. Its capital stock was $5 million. Durant said that his letters brought an astounding response, with some $7 million worth of stock subscribed for almost immediately. He had to turn down $2 million in subscriptions.

Durant's new plans raised a great deal of excitement, but nowhere was the reaction so great as in Flint. On the day Durant Motors was announced, the Flint Chamber of Commerce said that "strenuous efforts" were being made to induce Durant to locate his new manufacturing plants in the city. Community leaders sent "a flood of telegrams and letters" to Durant, and petitions were circulated through downtown stores and offices with the hope of sending on 30,000 names of local citizens. The Chamber of Commerce pointed out in its telegram to Durant that "no city in America has such an abiding faith in your business ability, integrity and results as Flint. . . . When you contemplate your new business undertaking please allow Flint to have first place in your mind and heart." And taking no chances that Durant might not get the message, the chamber also dispatched Dallas Dort to New York for a personal conference with his old carriage partner.

Four days later, Flint had its answer. Durant's telegram to *The Flint Journal* on January 18 was reproduced on Page One:

> Flint Journal
>
> Flint Mich
>
> Dear Journal: You may say to the good people of the best little city in the country that one of the plants of Durant Motors will be located in Flint. Say to those who so thoughtfully remembered me that I am most appreciative and quite overcome by their kind messages of friendship, confidence and affection. Sincerely yours
>
> W C Durant

The newspaper and Dallas Dort arrived at a luncheon meeting of the Chamber of Commerce simultaneously, to a burst of applause. Dort strode to the podium in the Durant Hotel and announced:

Mr. and Mrs. Durant—a picture of elegance in the '20s.

The Durants' summer home—Raymere—in Deal, New Jersey.

W. C. Durant (left) and his old carriage partner, J. Dallas Dort, lunching at Thompson's 59th Street Restaurant in New York City in the early 1920s. Together they had founded the country's largest carriage company, and they worked together in the early days of Buick, Chevrolet, and General Motors. At this time, Durant was in charge of Durant Motors and Dort was president of the Dort Motor Car Company. Dort died in 1925.

They say Billy is coming back home, back to Flint—he never left Flint. Just before I left New York, I went up to the offices of Mr. Durant, two little rooms in a great big building. The first was crowded with people who had heard the announcement that he was forming a new corporation. I finally got into the second room and found seated around a table Billy Durant, Bert Pomeroy, Win Murphy and Sid Stewart. Before saying hello, I shouted out, "Line up here, Billy, line up Bert and Sid and Win. Now—all who are in favor of locating the Durant factories back home— back in dear old Flint—say aye." And those shouts of aye! aye! aye! rang all over New York.

Stock-market newsletters reported that Durant's new company and its inevitable subsidiaries were being financed "on personality." Stock-selling offices were opened in Flint, Detroit, Lansing, and elsewhere. The first public offering was at $15 a share, but quickly moved up to $24 and eventually shot up over $80. Stock was being sold on the installment plan—$3 per share initial payment and $3 a month thereafter, with 6 percent interest on the unpaid balance. Purchasers could buy from five to twenty shares, and had to promise not to sell or transfer the stock for one year from date of delivery. Brochures quoted a shop worker by the name of Bill Matthews explaining his investment in Durant Motors to his wife: "I tell you, mother, this thing is going to be just like having an extra job with wages coming in that I don't have to work for."

It is easy to understand the appeal of the stock. In less than twenty years Durant had salvaged Buick and turned it into a great success, had founded General Motors, had created Chevrolet out of almost nothing, and had returned to build General Motors into a colossus. His followers ignored the fact that he had also lost control of General Motors twice. Not only the men and women who had profited in his earlier ventures, but those who were kicking themselves because they had not, joined the bandwagon. The little people were getting in now—the shop workers, the school mistresses, the widows. Durant said his stock program was inducing thousands of families who had never saved a dollar to start paying for securities "bit by bit out of weekly earnings." This, he said, was one of the most important thrift campaigns ever undertaken.

The Durant Corporation, which Durant had established in the late stages of his General Motors presidency to sell GM and other stocks to a large number of people on the installment plan, provided much of the money for his new operations. As former associate Jacob H. Newmark described it:

> He little dreamed what a tremendous thing it would turn out to be. It was colossal. It became a money collecting machine of huge proportions. . . . The Durant Corporation was created to raise money, by popular subscription, in tremendous sums. The United States never saw anything like it; Durant, himself, did not realize or believe that the plan would attain the success it did.[1]

In the depression year of 1921, factories were being turned loose here and there. Durant, with his new capital, began to buy them up. First he acquired a plant at Long Island City, New York. He then engaged Alfred T. Sturt of Chevrolet as design engineer, and in two months began production of his new car. On August 4, 1921, the first Durant Four was exhibited in New York. It looked like a lot of car for its price of $890. Within a few days there were applications for franchises from more than 100 dealers in New York and some 30,000 cars worth $31 million were on order.

Flush with this success, Durant quickly decided to add another line. The Star was conceived to compete directly with Ford at the price of $348. When it was introduced in Washington, D.C. early in 1922, some 30,000 people showed up the first day and 10,000 dealers asked for agencies. A wave of enthusiasm swept across the country. Tens of thousands of people jammed into showrooms to see the new car as it was introduced in major cities. When stock in the Star Motor Company was placed on sale through Durant Corporation salesmen—one million shares at $15 a share—it was quickly oversold. A second stock issue also quickly sold out, $30 million raised for the Star alone.

To get production capacity to match the immediate popularity of his new cars, Durant outbid Walter Chrysler for a mammoth new plant at Elizabeth, New Jersey, which had been turned loose by Willys Corporation as it went into receivership. More than a third of a mile long and covering thirty-five acres, the factory was said to be the largest single building in the country at the time. It had cost $13.5 million to build; Durant got it at the bargain price of $5.2 million. With alterations it could produce 400 Stars and 150 Durant cars a day. Fred W. Hohensee, a Flint native who had started with Durant as a foreman at the Flint Road Cart Company in 1889 and who was later his works manager at Chevrolet, was placed in charge. The plant was opened January 10, 1923, with a great testimonial luncheon by Hohensee for Durant, and among the 300 guests were money barons of Wall Street and leaders of the parts and material industry. On the day of the luncheon, Durant stock hit a peak of $84 in New York. Within a year, some 63,000 Stars had been delivered and production was up to 19,000 a month.

A year after its start, Durant Motors reportedly had 146,000 stockholders—more than any other company except American

500 Durants on Rockville Bridge

TRAINLOAD OF AUTOS SPELLS OUT 'COURAGE'

During Period of Depression in Motor Car Industry One Man Had the Nerve to Go Ahead

Less than a year ago the stock market "ticker," which...

Big Freight Train, Sign of Prosperity, Stops in Omaha

Steel Caravan, Laden With Automobiles, Arrived Here Last Night With Rail Officials Aboard.

"Prosperity special," ... last night, 's r...

DURANT SHIPS

AUTO S AHEA

Arrives Last Altoona To dre

Scheduled out yards of the Pen perity Special," train load shipm arrived in Harris nearly two hours train, consisting cars, carries 500 billed to Earle C fornia, and is the livery of motor c retail dealer, in ad gest shipment dity ever carri nt.

nearly a mile l ed to Harrisbu The weight is 1,165,000 ht charges es in the s dels, if r would ca populatic rt. Dura nt at $3 rain lef g at 8. de at otion re m nia nc, 's

PROSPERITY SPECIAL GOES THROUGH HERE

Stretched for nearly a mile, the "Prosperity Special," a freight train composed of 100 cars and containing nothing but Durant motor cars, left Omaha today at 11:15 a. m. over the Chicago, Milwaukee & St. Paul railroad. It started from New York, headquarters of Durant Mo-

DURANT TRAIN SETS RECORD.

Half Million Dollars in a Single Shipment.

Five Hundred Cars Are Now Rushing to Coast.

Substantial Upward Trend is Seen in Industry.

CARRIES 500 AUTOS ACROSS CONTINENT

Single Train of 100 Cars Will Pass Through Chicag Next

Newsclippings reporting a huge shipment of Durant autos to a west coast dealer.

Telephone and Telegraph, which was then thirty-five years old. Some of the foremost financial experts on Wall Street were predicting that Durant would make another comeback in General Motors. He did make a short run in that direction, developing a plan for exchanging Durant Motors for General Motors stock. And a lot of people made the exchange, because Durant Motors was selling at a higher price. But the task of regaining control of GM looked insurmountable, thanks to the quick economic recovery in 1921 and to the du Pont-Sloan management, and so he decided to concentrate on building up Durant Motors.

Durant still had the vision which had always been among his most remarkable assets. On October 5, 1922, he was quoted in *Automotive Industries:*

> The next twenty years will witness an expansion of the business of automobile making more marvelous by far than that of the two decades through which we have passed. . . . Most of us will live to see this whole country covered with a network of motor highways built from point to point as the bird flies, the hills cut down, the dales bridged over, the obstacles removed. Highway intersections will be built over or under the through lanes and the present dangers of motor travel, one after another, will be eliminated.

Things were moving fast. General Motors dumped the Sheridan factory in Muncie; Durant picked it up to manufacture the Durant Six. Soon large factories were also acquired in Lansing, Michigan, and Oakland, California. Canadian money helped finance construction of a plant just outside Toronto. Among the eventual offshoots of Durant Motors, Inc., were Star Motors of Delaware, Durant Motors of Michigan, Durant Motors of Indiana, Durant Motors of California, Flint Motors, Hayes-Hunt Body, Liberty National Bank, the Durant Acceptance Corporation, and Mason Motor Truck. Some of Durant's men in his new ventures had been with him for years. Arthur C. Mason, who had built engines for Buick, Little, and Chevrolet, and then Samson tractors, was placed in charge of the Mason Motor Truck Company, making Mason Road Kings in the old Samson building in Flint. Cliff Durant, Durant's only son, had shifted from a top executive job with Chevrolet of California to Durant of California. But many old associates had decided to stay with GM, and their loss was a big factor in the outcome of his last empire.

To the citizens of Flint who had expected a larger role in Durant Motors than manufacturing Mason trucks, Durant messaged: "Have patience. When the time arrives, I am sure that Flint will agree that the prize has been worth waiting for."

Finally, in the summer of 1922 Durant announced that, in association with Durant Motors, Flint Motor Company had been organized, with $5 million capitalization, to build the Flint Six. The announcement triggered what was described as the greatest celebration Flint had ever known, with thousands gathering at the ground-breaking ceremony at a 100-acre field just south of the city's downtown. On August 30, Durant went to Flint from New York and turned the first spadeful of earth. "It is my ambition," he declared, "to make this the finest plant ever built. The plant is being dedicated to the best little city and the best and most appreciative people in the world." By the time the factory buildings were completed, the first Flint cars were already coming off the line.

The new Flint models were displayed at the New York Motor Show in January, 1923. The Flint was designed to compete directly with the Buick, and those first Flints looked like tough competition, indeed.*

Looking for an even more luxurious model, Durant went to Bridgeport, Connecticut, and acquired the Locomobile. It had been one of the great names in the industry, with some models selling for as much as $12,000. But the company was also on the rocks financially. Durant wanted a lower-priced, higher-volume Locomobile, but still luxurious enough to compete with Cadillac, and he hired George E. Daniels, his first president at General Motors in 1908, as general manager. Another new car, the Princeton, was announced as a competitor to the Packard.

The Durant empire seemed unstoppable. Next Durant an-

---

* The Flint represented the last contribution of Alfred T. Sturt, who had also headed the designing of the Chevrolet Four-Ninety, the Durant and the Star. As a native of Flint, he relished his role of designing a car with the Flint name. But no sooner had the car been introduced when Sturt, the chief engineer of Durant Motors, took ill and died in New York in January, 1923. He was 45 years old.

The Flint automobile, named as a tribute to Durant's adopted home town, was produced in Flint in the mid 1920s.

nounced that the Liberty National Bank was being formed in New York with 300,000 shareholders. It was somewhat unique in that no individual would be permitted more than one share of stock. The price was $150 a share. In the boom years of the 1920s, the stock eventually hit a price of $500 a share and assets reached $5 million.

But the new Durant empire had only a brief moment in the sun. Financial writers began to ask questions. One of the most penetrating critics was B. C. Forbes of the *New York American*, who in 1923 sent a long list of questions to Durant about the company. Durant provided answers, a few at a time.

If Durant was stripped of his fortune and in debt when he left General Motors, Forbes asked, how could he finance the creation of the new company only six weeks later? Durant replied that it was "a case of a man thoroughly, completely and artistically stripped being helped by a good friend who made subscriptions in my name and received the stock when issued." The man paid $10 a share for 6,193 shares subscribed for in his name, he said. The friend was not identified.

Forbes wrote that Durant Motors' balance sheet in 1923 had as its largest asset $23.4 million itemized as "participating contracts." Forbes explained that Durant formed two companies, Durant Motors and Star Motors, had them make contracts with each other and "Lo, this contract immediately becomes an 'asset' worth more than $20 million. When you know how, it is thus delightfully easy to make money—on paper." Forbes burrowed deeper into the company's operations, asking Durant how he justified a curb market ranging from $60 to $84 a share for stock which originally sold for $10 or thereabouts "since the company has earned little or nothing." Durant replied:

> While I am not an expert, and my opinion may be of little value, I have observed that stock market and curb quotations do not always represent the true value of a security. The well-established rule seems to apply—that where there are more buyers than sellers, prices advance, and where there are more sellers than buyers, prices decline. Durant Motors was originally sold for $10 a share. Its advance to the prices named in a free market can be considered a

compliment to the management and proof of confidence in the organization.

Durant went on to point out that when he started General Motors, the stock had gone "from nothing to $112 a share in two years." Besides, he said, Durant Motors was then operating with 48,628 employees in seventy-seven cities and had floor space of 150 acres, a production capacity of 600,000 cars, a complete line of cars, and net sales, as of December 31, 1922, or $39.9 million.

Forbes later wrote that his criticisms of Durant brought a deluge of denunciatory letters from people who accused him of "being bribed by Morgan interests or by the du Ponts or by 'Wall Street.'" Still, he felt that Durant was being too optimistic and was concerned that the public was being carried away by his plans and promises. Yet, when he coauthored *Automotive Giants of America* in 1926, Forbes noted:

> His friends . . . tell you that no other leader has as many friends in the industry and outside. I personally know of many incidents illustrating Durant's unselfishness and generosity. He has done more for others than many men whose names are blazoned in the newspapers as wonderful philanthropists. I am convinced that Durant's chief ambition has never been to roll up scores and scores of millions of dollars for himself. His is not a mercenary ambition. He loves power; he constantly itches to accomplish big things.

Some who were his close associates in the 1920s believe that Durant Motors might well have survived to this day. Certainly in its early days it was well financed by the savings of many thousands of small stockholders. But there were too many errors in judgment—the Star could be produced at Ford prices only if there was no profit. Then Ford cut his price. The Locomobile was so far gone that it was almost impossible to revive it. The Princeton never got into production.[2]

In 1925 Durant admitted to a friend that he had made a mistake in starting so many enterprises at once after leaving General Motors. GM, he said, had a management that could not be duplicated in a generation. At Locomobile he had lost $4 million almost immediately, he acknowledged—but then with the old optimism he added that he had hopes of making that up and $6 million more within a year or two.[3]

There were also problems at Flint. Durant had wanted to show his many admirers in his old home town that he was still a wizard. His factory there was a $15 million showcase, but quickly proved much too large for the business it was doing. Soon most of its branch sales departments were closed, and in July of 1926 the Flint Motor Company plant in Flint was sold to General Motors for about $4 million. The plant became Fisher Body Plant 1, which today builds bodies for Durant's first great automobile complex, Buick, on Flint's North Side. The production of the Flint was moved to the Elizabeth plant.

But perhaps the most serious flaw in the Durant Motors foundation was that Durant himself was not completely involved in it. From the turn of the century, he had been lured by the stock market. Now, in his 60s, he abandoned himself to its charms.

As early as 1924 Durant was making big money in the market, and soon other millionaires were giving him millions to see what he could do with them. It was said that the seven Fisher brothers of Fisher Body were among those in the Durant-led consortium, described by Earl Sparling in *Mystery Men of Wall Street* as one of the most powerful operating syndicates Wall Street had ever known.

John J. Carton, Durant's old personal lawyer, once told historian Arthur Pound:

> Billy never thought that GM would become the big manufacturer it did. What he desired, most of all, were large stock issues in which he, from an inside position, could dicker and trade. After Billy left Durant-Dort for Buick there were always too many yes men around him for his own good. Dallas Dort and Charlie Nash and Fred Aldrich and the rest of them in Durant-Dort could bring Billy down to earth. Away from them he just soared, high, wide and handsome.

Pound added:

> Carton, deadpan, knew all and told nothing, except to me occasionally for the sake of history. He wanted me to

THE SPORT ROADSTER $1025

WITH RUMBLE SEAT

Both seats upholstered in genuine leather. Standard equipment includes extra wire wheel with tire and cover, front bumper, rear bumperettes, and wind-shield wings.

DURANT "65" SPECIFICATIONS

ENGINE: Six-cylinder, L-head type, detachable head; bore, 2⅞"; stroke, 4¾"; piston displacement, 185 cubic inches; S.A.E. rating, 19.84; brake horse-power, 47. Engine mounted in rubber.

CYLINDERS: Cast in block with upper half of crank-case; detachable head.

VALVES: Intake, 1-7/16"; exhaust, 1-5/16"; 5-16" lift.

CARBURETOR: One-inch, plain tube, with air and fuel adjustment. Exhaust and intake manifold with hot spot, mounted on left side of engine. Air cleaner and gasoline filter.

CRANKSHAFT: Bearings—Front, 2⅛" x 1¼"; inter-mediate, 2⅛" x 1-3/16" (2); rear, 2⅛" x 1-9/16"; Torsional vibration dampner.

CAMSHAFT BEARINGS: Front, 1⅞" x 1-5/16"; center front, 1-13/16" x 27/32"; center rear, 1¾" x 27/32"; rear, 1-9/16" x 1¾".

COOLING SYSTEM: Honeycomb-type radiator; ca-pacity, 12 quarts; 16" fan, 4 blades; pump; ther-mostatic control; electric heat indicator on dash.

MOTOR LUBRICATION: Force feed to silent timing chain and all main, connecting-rod and camshaft bearings. Oil Filtrator.

CHASSIS LUBRICATION: Alemite system.

STARTING, LIGHTING, IGNITION: Generator, start-ing motor, igniter and coil; Giolite depressible-beam headlamps with control switch on toe board; combination stop and tail light; indirect instru-ment board light with individual switch.

GASOLINE SUPPLY: Capacity of tank, 11½ gallons; placed at rear. Vacuum feed; electric gasoline gauge on dash.

CLUTCH: Single-plate, dry-disc, enclosed in fly-wheel.

TRANSMISSION: Standard selective sliding-gear type; three speeds forward and one reverse. Unit mount-ing with engine.

FRONT AXLE: Standard drop-forged "I" beam section with reverse Elliott type steering mechanism. Tapered roller wheel bearings.

REAR AXLE: Semi-floating, simple design with spiral ring-gear and pinion.

BRAKES: Four-wheel Bendix mechanical, internal ex-panding, self-energizing, 3-shoe type; 11" brake drums. Easy adjustment.

SPRINGS: Semi-elliptic; front, 36" x 1¾"; rear, 54" x 1¾".

TIRES: Balloons, 29 x 5.00.

STEERING GEAR: Semi-irreversible, worm-and-gear type; fore-and-aft steering; ball thrust bearings. 17" wheel. Horn button on wheel.

CONTROLS: Center control; accelerator pedal mounted on toe board; spark and throttle levers on top of steering wheel. Speedometer, ammeter, oil gauge, electric heat indicator, electric gasoline gauge and instrument lamp clustered on instrument board. Ignition and lighting switch and choke mounted on instrument board.

WHEELBASE: 110 inches.

EQUIPMENT: Four shock absorbers; rear-vision mir-ror; automatic windshield wiper; electric motor driven horn; tire carrier and extra rim; coincidental ignition lock; front bumper, rear bumperettes, extra tire and tire cover on special models; extra wire wheel on Sport Roadster and Brougham. Chromium-plated cowl lights, heavy cowl molding and hood hinge, at slight extra cost.

The right is reserved to make changes in design and specifications without notice.

DURANT MOTORS, INC., NEW YORK, N. Y.

realize that Billy Durant put no value on money for its own sake; that the founder of General Motors was an unconventional soul who soared high above ordinary humanity, that the one and only Billy was almost a prince among mortals, enjoying first of all power, then excitement, then the affectionate adulation of his friends.[4]

Wall Street historians have devoted whole chapters to Durant. He was one of the prime movers of the 1920s, the "bull of bulls," who in 1928 alone handled more than 11 million shares of stock representing an investment of $1.2 *billion*. "Acting as a sort of market commissioner of police, he watched for weak spots in the market and whenever he found one, plugged it with millions of dollars," Sparling wrote. "He placed other millions behind key stocks which, in rising, would drag the whole market upward in sympathy. Nothing like that had ever been tried before."

Durant, who regarded "bears" and short-sellers as the enemy, said that his organized effort to protect securities of recognized value created confidence in American securities both abroad and among small American investors. Wall Street historians thought it remarkable that his confidence was so great that he grand-marshalled the greatest market in history for four years without looking at a stock ticker for hours at a time.

Durant's personal influence on the stock market was dramatically demonstrated early in 1926. On January 10 he and his wife were vacationing in their private railroad car "Patriot" attached to a train on the Florida East Coast Railroad. The train had stopped to allow another train to pass and was resuming its journey when the Overseas Limited rounded a curve and slammed into Durant's car. Two servants in the galley of the car were killed. Mrs. Durant was shaken. Durant was thrown from his bed, his head striking a wash stand. The "Patriot" was thrust against a Pullman car just ahead, injuring about thirty persons, none critically. A fireman aboard the Limited was killed.[5]

Durant struggled to his feet as blood gushed over his face, and he and his wife got out of the car through a window. The two were rushed to New York by another train provided especially for Durant by the railroad. First reports indicated that Durant was seriously injured. So extensive were his stock opera-

His head covered with bandages, Durant is helped from the train to a taxi in New York after his close brush with death in a Florida train collision.

tions that according to early accounts the market "staggered" as stockbrokers scrambled for authentic news.

But even while the train streaked toward New York, Durant was in action. He quickly sent a message reading, "We had a bad smash-up. Escaped by a miracle. Some bruised but still in the ring." When the train reached Richmond, Virginia, he heard that some of his favorite stocks—among them, General

239

Motors—had fallen off abruptly as a result of the exaggerated rumors of his injuries. Immediately he placed a string of buy orders which both steadied the market and gave him more choice stocks at bargain prices. He said he felt bullish. When the train reached Washington, he placed more buy orders.

Upon their arrival at Pennsylvania Station in New York, the Durants—his head still swathed in bandages—were met by a squad of station porters who helped them through the crowded depot. A doctor who examined Durant said that he had suffered a long scalp wound, several body bruises, general shock, a blackening of the right eye, and possibly a concussion.

The private car was one indication that this was a time of grand style for the Durants. In addition to the estate in Deal, they maintained a fine apartment in New York and owned ten cars at a time. And they discovered Europe. Until then Durant had never traveled overseas because he had once become seasick as a youth. But his friends finally persuaded him to take his wife to Europe, and he discovered he did not become ill on the big liners. So began a love affair with Europe, particularly Paris. After that first trip, they returned again and again.[6]

His extended absences from the country may have contributed to the tailspin of his automotive operations. He may have been a giant on Wall Street, but by 1927 his actions and announcements in connection with Durant Motors were taking on a tone of desperation. That year the Durant-backed car lines were in such poor shape that he announced he was "back on the job" and working eighteen hours a day to create a new distributing organization and a new lineup of six-cylinder cars. In November he announced plans for a new auto combine to be called Consolidated Motors, reportedly to include Star, Moon, Chandler, Gardner, Hupmobile, Jordan, and Peerless motor companies. Not much more was ever heard of it.[7]

Early in 1928 he asked Durant Motors stockholders in a letter:

> Why trade your Durant stock, which has a market value, for worthless securities that have no market value? All kinds of schemes have been and are being invented to induce Durant Motors shareholders to part with their

stock. The wily and unscrupulous promoter cannot sell his worthless stock to you for cash, so he gives you the worthless security in trade and, after receiving your Durant Motors stock, promptly sells it in the New York market. As a result . . . this security is selling far below its real value.[8]

The stock that day sold for $11.25.

In January, 1929, less than two years after announcing he was back on the job, he said he was withdrawing from active management of Durant Motors and turning its affairs over to a new executive team—four retired Dodge executives. "A few years ago, when Durant Motors, Inc., first started, I conceived the idea that it would be a good plan for us to have many stockholders," he said in making the announcement.

> Later I discovered that every form of misrepresentation had been used to induce people to buy stock in Durant Motors. My plan, if I am permitted and if I have the good fortune, is to reimburse every single original stockholder who has held his stock, with the price they paid for that stock, with interest. It is my purpose in life, if I am permitted, to reimburse not only Durant Motors stockholders, but also those of every organization with which my name is connected—that means Star, Durant Motor Company of Indiana, and Flint Motor Company.[9]

Durant himself had prospered during the period his auto firms were collapsing. Not only was he playing the market with huge stakes and winning, he was also a major backer of Industrial Rayon, which he reorganized and controlled, and a number of other companies. Still, he had legitimate and genuine concerns for those who had bet their savings that Durant Motors would become a new automotive empire. He told an interviewer:

> In 1926, I had $5 million set aside to restore to the stockholders in Durant Motors. Only long afterward did I learn that the salesmen had made promises and predictions that could not be fulfilled. I wanted to make some amends. Durant Motors hadn't prospered as I expected, but I had prospered in other fields. So I set aside the $5

million. That wasn't enough to take care of everybody, but it was my idea to take care of those who needed help most. In other words, those who had invested and who had the least money, the poorest. I planned to announce this in a double-page ad in the *Saturday Evening Post*. Some advice from an attorney made me think twice. When I started thinking about my plan, I realized it was impossible. I realized I must reimburse all original stockholders. A special account was created. By February, 1929, the $5 million was up to $10 million.[10]

An advertisement Durant intended to publish in the Saturday Evening Post *to announce his plan to protect Durant Motors' original stockholders. But his own financial difficulties forced him to drop the plan, and the advertisement never ran.*

W. C. DURANT

wishes to buy certificates of

DURANT MOTORS, INC.

purchased through the Durant Corporation on the partial payment plan and submits the following offer, which is good for three months from this date.

W. C. Durant's offer:

The original owners of certificates listed below (if they care to dispose of same) may obtain under this offer the price paid the Durant Corporation for the stock represented by these certificates.

The certificates must be properly endorsed and sent, by registered mail, to the Liberty National Bank in New York,(Trust Department) 256 West 57th Street, New York City, where the funds have been deposited for the purchase herein outlined.

List of Certificates

Serial Numbers   Serial Numbers

12345 12345 12345 12345 12345 12345 12345 12345 12345 12345   12345 12345 12345 12345 12345 12345 12345 12345 12345 12345
12345 12345 12345 12345 12345 12345 12345 12345 12345 12345   12345 12345 12345 12345 12345 12245 12345 12345 12345 12345

There is little question that Durant really wanted, and expected, to reimburse the original stockholders. It would have been a grand gesture, and it was consistent with his previous efforts to protect those who had shown faith in him. Catherine Durant has seen proofs of the planned *Saturday Evening Post* advertisements, complete with Durant's photo, an announcement of his repayment plan, and lists of stock serial numbers. But the Great Depression got in the way.

Since he was a major force in the stock market, Durant, by 1929, considered himself an expert on economic affairs. Therefore, when the Federal Reserve Board decided to try to cool off stock-market speculations by restricting security credit, which had the effect in some instances of raising interest rates to 20 percent, he fought back. He attacked the Federal Reserve Board in speeches, interviews, and even in a CBS radio broadcast. The board, he said, was "an autocratic group," whose power was "beyond that of any constituted authority of the United States." In his radio speech of April 14, 1929, Durant charged that at a time when the country was enjoying the greatest prosperity ever known, the Federal Reserve Board, "by tactless handling and spectacular methods, succeeded in creating a panic costing the people of this country hundreds of millions of dollars."[11]

Durant's concern about Federal Reserve Board policy was so great that he sought and received an invitation to the White House to discuss the matter with President Hoover. The appointment was made for an evening in April of 1929. Durant arrived at 9:30 p.m.—by taxicab. Had he arrived by chauffeured limousine, he reasoned, his visit might attract attention—and it must be secret. Durant waited while the President finished dinner, and then they talked. Durant reportedly warned Hoover that if the Federal Reserve Board did not reverse its policy of clamping down on security credit, a market crash was inevitable. He argued that the financial health of the country was based on credit, that the board was killing the goose that laid the golden egg. Durant returned home despondent. He couldn't change the President's thinking, he complained to his wife.[12]

Some Wall Street histories say that after his meeting with Hoover, he withdrew from the market in the summer of 1929.

Then, believing that the market had reached bottom, he plunged back in, waiting for the rally. But the market unaccountably continued to drop. Catherine Durant, however, insists that her husband did not withdraw. She recalls Durant's arguing with Bernard Baruch and others, trying to get them to stay in the market to soften the crash. Baruch's last words, she recalls, were: "I'm sorry you can't see it my way, Willie."

"If Willie had wanted to take advantage of that [the bear market] he probably would have made more money than anyone living, like Mr. Baruch did," she said. "Willie wouldn't have anything to do with the bear market forcing down the price." Durant's last personal secretary, Aristo Scrobogna, told the writer:

> He never sold out, as did other big speculators of the time who, like himself, saw the oncoming storm. In fact, he tried to support the market all the way and attempted to secure the cooperation of other men of large holdings. He believed that if the stock of 15 to 20 sound corporations could be supported that the great panic could have been prevented and the staggering depression which followed and discredited the system in the early thirties could have been avoided or at least to some degree minimized. He was truly devoted to the companies he headed and to the friends who believed in him whom he tried to save. The records show clearly that he never enriched himself at the expense of the stockholders and his failures were absolutely free and clear of scandals. It was his destiny to rise and fall hard.

As the country plunged deeper into depression, Durant's market position proved fatal to his fortune. The stockholders in Durant Motors had lost their investments, and some of those most deeply hurt were Flint men who had strongly supported Durant and who had urged many small investors to bet their savings on the new Durant empire. But Durant and his wife were also crushed in the fall. He had set up a trust for his wife, hoping to assure that she would remain wealthy for the rest of her life. But in 1927 he borrowed 75,000 shares of GM stock from her. And in 1930 he borrowed the rest—187,000 more shares! She never saw the stock again. Had she held on to it, she would have today been one of the wealthiest women in the world. Instead she was left with nothing.

The Durants also lost their large holdings in the Whittier Corporation—a family-owned investment fund, a forerunner of today's mutual funds. Catherine Durant told the writer in 1973: "It was a tragedy that at this time in his life he pauperized us both, but he tried desperately to support the market and save the country from the depression which he predicted to President Hoover in 1929 and which engulfed the country in the 1930s."

It was not out of character for Durant to squander a fortune in an effort to save the country from depression. Much of his success—and his failure—seemed to have been motivated by efforts to improve the lives of average people. In 1928 he had announced he would give the "Durant Prize" of $25,000 "for the best and most practicable plan to make the Eighteenth Amendment [prohibition] effective." He also offered a $5,000 second prize for the best high school entry. He might have been motivated partially by childhood memories of his father's drinking problem. His own explanation is that "while I did not wish to pose as a reformer I submitted the prize in the hope that public interest might be aroused and a great national movement inaugurated that would to some extent correct the distressing and dangerous conditions existing."

The prizes were given wide publicity, and more than 23,000 plans were submitted. A blue-ribbon panel of educators, business leaders and public officials awarded the grand prize to Major Chester P. Mills, who for a long time had been prohibition administrator for New York City. Malcolm D. Almock of Union High School in Palo Alto, California, won the second prize. Durant printed the best essays in a book. The result was about the same as his effort to personally fight the depression: Prohibition was repealed in 1933.

Later Durant was active in promoting an organization to be known as the World Peace League. The idea was for the children of America to donate their pennies to "buy a brick" for the league's headquarters. The slogan was to be "A Little Child Shall Lead Them," taken from a well-known passage on peace in the book of Isaiah, and also having the ring of Durant's old Chevrolet slogan "A Little Child Can Sell It."

As the depression hit with full force, the Durant Motors facilities across the country closed down, one by one. Many were taken over by General Motors. Durant tried to interest Hiram Rivitz, president of Industrial Rayon, in the idled plant at Elizabeth. "It's a fine plant," said Rivitz, "but where's the water?" Durant had not realized that rayon manufacture involved large amounts of water.[13] In 1930 Durant resigned from Industrial Rayon.

Durant was in Europe as his fortune flew away. Desperate to try to save some of it, he held a line open between Paris and the New York Stock Exchange for four hours one day—and ran up a record $1,409 in toll charges. In 1930 several brokerage firms sued him for unpaid commissions. In counteractions, he claimed that various of his accounts had been sold out without notice. Some estimates placed his loss in the crash at $40 million.

Durant tried one more go at automobiles, replacing the Dodge executives and jumping back into Durant Motors to try to keep it alive. He also made an arrangement with the French Mathis company to manufacture the small Mathis car at Lansing. But Durant was no match for the Depression. Durant Motors was finally liquidated in 1933.

The severity of Durant's financial situation was not publicly recognized until February 8, 1936, when he filed a voluntary petition of bankruptcy in New York Federal Court, listing his debts at $914,231 and his only assets his clothing, valued at $250. "My petition is due to frequent and repeated court proceedings by a few creditors, representing less than 5 per cent of my total obligations," he said in a news statement.

> Action by the creditors referred to has prevented me from giving my best efforts to rebuilding my fortune and I no longer propose to be harassed and annoyed. I wish to state that all creditors, without exception, will be treated alike and, if fortune favors me, all will be paid in full.

He listed himself in the petition as president of the Pomeroy-Day Land Company, a small concern holding property in Flint. That year he opened a combination food market and lunch room in a building that once had served as a showroom for his automobiles in Asbury Park, New Jersey. He was asked by a photographer to pick up a dish and wash it, and he went along with the gag photo. The picture of the founder of General Motors wiping a dish made newspapers across the country. It was not really as bad as it looked. Durant was merely showing the help how to get things done. And he owned the building. His nephew, Wallace R. Willett, told reporters that Durant "is just as enthusiastic over building up the food market as he ever was over automobiles. In fact, he no longer can bear the thought of an automobile." Asked about his new business, Durant replied: "Just one of the many attractions will be a really nice lunch for a dime or 15 cents."

One of Catherine Durant's few mementos of the good days—a statuette of her created in Paris.

In 1938, he was finally forced to sell the estate in New Jersey, and its collections of valuable furniture, art, and books. The total received from the auction was $111,778. "I'm glad to be rid of the place," he said.

Some of Durant's great reputation was gone, even in Flint. He was something of a lonely figure on his frequent trips to the city which owed to him all of its industrial base. He would get the cheapest room in the Durant Hotel and plan what he could do with property owned by him and by his mother's estate. The hotel's management determined, however, that he should be placed in a suite for the price of a small room.

He still had business interests of one kind or another. One was as vice-president of CVS Manufacturing Company, which was making Flint-brand spark plugs during the '30s. Archie R. Campbell, who had formerly held positions with AC Spark Plug and Buick, was president of CVS. He knew Durant well during this period.[14] He recalled that Durant, then seventy-five years old, was becoming enthusiastic again—this time about the prospects of bowling alleys.

Often Durant would call Campbell and they would look at bowling alleys together. "One night I took him back to the hotel at 11:30 p.m. He asked if I would take a look at another bowling alley," Campbell recalled. "I said, 'W. C., don't you want to go to your room and retire?' He replied, 'Gosh, no. If I went to bed now I would be awake reading detective stories at 4:30 a.m. I seldom sleep more than five or six hours a night.' "

Durant had other duties for Campbell. Durant was opposed to the United States's becoming involved in World War II, and printed a number of handbills expressing his opposition and praising Charles Lindbergh and others who were also against it. He persuaded Campbell to deliver his handbills to churches in the Flint area. "You didn't say no to W. C.," Campbell said. Durant often told friends that the United States would get into a lot of trouble "fooling around with other countries" and that the U.S. should concern itself with its own people and "trade only with Canada."

In the spring of 1940 Durant opened North Flint Recreation, an eighteen-lane bowling center in the refurbished former headquarters of a trucking firm. He had personally supervised the redecorating, measured the position of spectator seats, worked with hammer and broom, and initiated the pinboys and staff on their jobs. No beer would be served in his establishment, he said. And the place was air-conditioned to be "healthful as well as morally wholesome." Following the grand opening, which drew thousands of visitors, Durant hosted a post-midnight breakfast for the pinboys.

Reporters who wandered into the place looking for a story were seldom disappointed. Sure, he would talk to them about the old days. "I once controlled the stock market for two years and never sold a share of stock short," he boasted. Even though most of his money, and many of his friends, were gone, he remained lighthearted. "I haven't a dollar but I'm happy and I'm carrying on because I can't stop. There's much more to life than money," he once remarked. He told one interviewer: "Many people value money too highly. I'm trying now to do good for as many people as possible. After all, money is only loaned to a man. He comes into the world with nothing and he goes out with nothing."[15]

When Frank Rodolf interviewed him at the bowling alley, Durant declared that he believed business opportunities were greater than ever before. Discussing the recreation business, he said that "clean recreation for the ladies, for their daughters, for the whole family, will attract greater and greater crowds. I'd like to see recreation in an entirely different atmosphere and on a higher plane than it has always been considered."

A year later he added a drive-in restaurant, described as a swanky "hamburger heaven," in connection with the bowling alley. On the day it opened Durant and his secretary, Scrobogna, both pitched in to wash dishes and serve hamburgers. It is said that one automobile dealer enjoyed taking his salesman to the restaurant so that the founder of General Motors could serve them a hamburger.

Yet most of the ribbing was good-natured and Durant "could put people down in a nice way," recalls Mrs. Anabel Haskins of Flint. He had hired her to help manage the restaurant, the Horseshoe Bar, though she insisted she knew nothing of restaurant management. "He said it didn't matter, he didn't know anything about it either—and he didn't," she told the writer.

"He never seemed very interested in making a lot of money, and I know the restaurant never made any. But we had a lot of fun. He showed me how to make applesauce and he made his own special spaghetti sauce that took 20 hours of cooking. There were times when we would close the restaurant to the public, and invite some of his friends for a special lunch—Mr. Mott, people from the bank, other old friends. Sometimes we served his spaghetti, other times he brought in a French chef. The counter was shaped like a horseshoe but the stools were on the inside instead of the outside like anywhere else. It was crazy. But he said he wanted it to be different. And it was—it was the first drive-in restaurant in Flint. Mr. Durant dreamed a lot. He would sit there with his eyes squiggled up, talking about things he wanted to do with the restaurant. Then he would get so excited he'd close up and we would head for the restaurant equipment store.

"I remember he insisted that his employees be dressed up when working and that meals be served on plates that were hot. 'That's the only way to serve food,' he would say. And he wanted everything to be very clean. If a customer walked up who looked dirty he would say the place was closed and serve the fellow his hamburger through the drive-in window. He enjoyed making hamburgers. He was 80 years old but still a very lively and interesting man with a good sense of humor. And he didn't smoke or drink or swear. He still had some money. He used to carry an attache case with $1,000 to $1,500 in it, and he paid cash for everything."

These promotions, the restaurant and the more successful bowling establishment next door, were undertaken only to develop the property and make it more salable, he said. When a reporter asked the names of his partners, he replied: "William C. Durant, W. C. Durant, and Billy Durant." Actually he was trying to liquidate the assets of the Pomeroy-Day Land Company, of which he was president.

Durant did not look like a man who had been crushed by the Depression. His small frame was still erect, he always dressed immaculately, almost jauntily, and he was becoming more and more enthusiastic about the bowling business. Bowling was the coming thing, he said, and he talked of plans to build fifty "fun houses" in big cities across the country. Among the attractions would be a mechanical horse for children and roller skating. Back in the 1880s, Durant had once helped operate a roller skating rink in Flint.

Some of Durant's old friends and employees wouldn't go to the bowling alley because it depressed them to think of their onetime leader renting bowling shoes to the sons of the factory workers he had brought to town when he was head of Buick and Chevrolet and General Motors. Yet one General Motors vice-president has a fond memory of meeting Billy Durant at North Flint Recreation. Martin J. Caserio, at this writing the general manager of GM's Pontiac division, was a young General Motors Institute student in Flint in the early 1940s when he stopped into the place to bowl one evening. A pinboy dropped Caserio's new bowling ball and chipped it. Caserio wanted to talk to the manager. Over there, waved the pinboy. Caserio walked over to an old man leaning in a chair with his hat pulled down over his eyes. He tapped him on the shoulder and pointed to the chip in his ball. "Just charge it to my account," said the man. The name? "Durant." Then Caserio remembered. "William Durant?" he asked. As Caserio recalls it, he never did get the bowling ball fixed, but he will never forget the night he met the founder of General Motors.[16]

General Motors also did not forget—not quite. When the corporation celebrated the production of its 25 millionth car on January 11, 1940, Durant was invited to the banquet in Detroit. Alfred P. Sloan brought him on stage for an introduction. "Too often," said Sloan, "we fail to recognize the creative spirit so essential to start the enterprises that characterize American business and that have made our system the envy of the world."[17]

And not long afterward, Durant, in a reflective mood, wrote to Sloan:

I do wish, Mr. Sloan, that you had known me when we were laying the foundation—when speed and action seemed necessary. You are absolutely right in your statement [in the *Saturday Evening Post*] that General Motors justified an entirely different method of handling after the

251

At the program celebrating production of the 25 millionth General Motors car on January 12, 1940, GM chairman Alfred P. Sloan led the aged Durant onstage before 5,000 corporation guests in Detroit and paid him a tribute. It was one of the GM founder's last moments in the spotlight before his stroke, in Flint, in 1942.

units had been enlisted. And you with your experience and training surrounded yourself with competent, reliable men of sound judgment, vision and devotion to the cause, which has enabled you to create the General Motors of today, a truly great institution.[18]

But even at the age of eighty Durant was still looking mostly to the future and he could not be satisfied with bowling alleys and drive-in restaurants. For a time he was interested in wheat contracts. And when an acquaintance from Indianapolis told him of an opportunity to develop a cinnabar (mercury ore) mine near Goldfield, Nevada, Durant headed for Goldfield.

Scrobogna felt that Durant's interest in the mine was an effort to do something for him and his family. "All the glory was gone, but I believe he wanted to do something for me, to break into something big, and so we went to Goldfield," Scrobogna told the writer. "Mr. Durant thought it might be good, because during World War II the government would subsidize the mining of cinnabar. I could see the mine was a dead horse. But he wanted a road built up this hill from the main road to the mine, and so we started to build it."

Despite his years Durant insisted on making the exhausting climb from the main road to the mine opening for a personal examination. He looked it over, liked what he saw, and headed back to Flint and the bowling alley, leaving Scrobogna behind to build the road.

A few days later, on October 2, 1942, Durant awoke in his room, Room 544 of the Durant Hotel in Flint, slid out of bed, and fell to the floor. He was able to get halfway back onto the bed and find the telephone. He called his old associate, Fred Aldrich.

Meanwhile, Scrobogna had just arrived in New York from Goldfield. The trip, following the road-building work, had been exhausting. There was a message from Flint. Scrobogna was to get Mrs. Durant and head for Flint immediately. Scrobogna was used to such "come right now" messages and usually obeyed them, but now he was tired, and slightly irritated. The phone rang. He recognized Durant's voice on the other end, but he could not make out the words. Then Fred Aldrich was on. He was with Durant in the hotel. Durant had apparently had a stroke. Within hours Scrobogna and Mrs. Durant were headed by plane to Flint.

Durant was moved to Hurley Hospital in Flint. His recuperation there, slowed by prostate surgery, lasted nine weeks. But even as he lay partially paralyzed in his hospital bed, he showed some of his old drive. One day a nurse walked in to find him tossing a water glass from hand to hand. "Just trying to see what I can do," he explained. He was trying to recover the use of his left arm. Still in the hospital on his eighty-first birthday, December 8, 1942, he was honored by Michigan governor Murray D. Van Wagoner, who proclaimed his birthday as "W. C. Durant Day" in Michigan. He spent part of the day composing replies to the congratulary telegrams and letters.

A week later, on December 15, 1942, he was taken by ambulance to Detroit and placed on a train for New York. He

Durant with secretary Aristo Scrobogna in what Scrobogna says is the last photo taken of the GM founder.

had left his beloved Flint for the last time. The *Flint Weekly Review*, official publication of the American Federation of Labor, reported:

> W. C. Durant, one of the builders of Flint, has quietly left the community where he built a network of factories giving employment to 50,000 workers in the war industry.

Last Tuesday Mr. Durant was taken in an ambulance from Hurley Hospital to Detroit, where he left by train for his New York City home. He was accompanied by his faithful wife, and by his secretary.

He had fallen in his Durant Hotel room a few weeks ago. . . . He has made no complaint. He never has. Taken to the hospital his brain helped build, from the hotel named in his honor, the founder of the Buick, Chevrolet and the General Motors Corporation quietly expressed his thanks to the members of the hotel staff, and to those who attended him. "He was ever the gentleman," a friend remarked.

After the stroke, Durant made a partial recovery, regaining some clarity of speech and trying to spend some time in his office every day. Yet the dreams were gone. The cinnabar mine proved to be unproductive. There were no more plans for a national chain of bowling alleys.

Occasionally friends would stop by to visit. Some acquaintances came to borrow money, not realizing that it was almost all gone. One man stopped over at the Durant apartment often and talked about the "old days" until Durant was reduced to tears. After awhile Mrs. Durant asked him not to come anymore.

Scrobogna said he feels that Durant did not have one happy moment after he lost his last fortune in 1930.

He was a very proud man, gentle and kind, but he had many moments of remorse, moments of chagrin and resentment. It was almost physically impossible for him to say he was wrong; yet once, I remember it distinctly, he said, "There have been moments when I have recognized that I have been a blundering fool." I remember he said that, because it was so out of character for him to admit he was ever wrong.

Despite infirmities, he talked often of Flint. "We must get back to Flint." In 1946 he and his wife and Scrobogna decided to try. But by the time the train reached Detroit, Durant was so ill they had to turn back.

There was one last moment of public recognition. On May 1, 1946, the Automobile Manufacturers Association and the National Automotive Golden Jubilee Committee named ten automotive pioneers to be elected to the Automotive Hall of Fame. They were Henry Ford, Charles W. Nash, J. Frank Duryea, Ransom E. Olds, Alfred P. Sloan, Barney Oldfield, Edgar Apperson, Charles B. King, George Holley—and W. C. Durant. Each received the Charles Clifton Automotive Award, inscribed, "The Genius of Man; His Mind and His Work."

His health was declining steadily. His speech became so garbled that it was almost impossible to understand what he was saying. He was confined to a wheelchair. Yet his mind was clear and he struggled to communicate. He tried to finish his autobiography, pulling out his notes and scribbling in the margins. An indication of what the autobiography might have included had he been able to complete it is a list of chapter headings left in his personal papers: The Purchase of the Heany Patents and Who Benefitted by the Deal; When General Motors Stock Was Cornered—A Startling Incident in the History of the New York Stock Exchange; My Automobile Experience Starting with the Buick Until General Motors Became Reality; My First and Only Meeting with Dwight W. Morrow (a reference to his last days at General Motors); The Invitation Extended to the Du Ponts to Become Interested in General Motors; Midnight Meeting with President Hoover; How I Was Retired from General Motors in 1920 and the Reason; The Industrial Rayon Corporation Reorganization; American Safety Razor Corporation Reorganization; The Story of New Process Gear and How Confidence in Men Can Be Misplaced. . . .

By this time he was broke. It's been said that some of his old associates helped him out on occasion—Walter Chrysler providing him with generous funds for oil explorations, and Alfred P. Sloan and Charles Stewart Mott among others giving assistance. But by 1947 the last of the paintings and fine furniture were gone and Catherine Durant had been compelled to sell her jewelry, piece by piece, to pay living costs and medical bills.

One day in March, 1947, Durant became uncommunicative, apparently lapsing into a coma. A doctor was called, a shot given. A few days later, in the early hours of March 18, Scrobogna was awakened by the telephone. It was Catherine Durant. "It's all over," she said. William Crapo Durant, age

Weather
A Warmer Mostly Forecast
Partly Cloudy, Little
Change in Temperature

Sixty-Fifth Year

Phone 2-1131

The Flint Journal

1:30
Edition

Flint, Mich., Tuesday, March 18, 1947

Twenty Pages   ★

Price Five Cents

WILLIAM C. DURANT DIES

Stalin Holds Long Session With Bidault

Marshall Takes Firm Stand After Hearing Tirade by Molotov

Moscow — AP — Firm indications that Prime Minister Stalin is taking an active, though behind the scenes, interest in the critical world problems now moving toward a showdown here kept the Council of Foreign Ministers meeting to a new pitch today.

The Soviet leader conferred for 95 minutes Monday night with Foreign Minister Georges Bidault of France after a prolonged council session at which Foreign Minister V. M. Molotov of Russia demanded $10,000,000,000 reparations from Germany.

Bidault was the first of the three visiting foreign ministers to call upon Stalin, but Secretary of State Marshall and British Foreign Secretary Ernest Bevin are expected to make such visits in the immediate future.

Marshall's visit in particular is keenly awaited here for the effect it may have on Soviet-American relations which are none too good.

Coal Talks Fail To Bring Break In Strike Here

Union Drivers Make Emergency Deliveries From City Stock Pile; Exchange Refuses Arbitration Plan

Flint's coal strike entered its fourth day today with negotiations at a stalemate after a morning session between the AFL General Drivers Union and the Genesee County Coal Dealers Exchange broke up with no new proposals under consideration.

With no immediate settlement of the differences in sight, City officials announced the establishment of a new emergency delivery service for persons nearly out of coal.

Dr. George Hays, Flint executive health director, said persons without coal either can obtain it themselves from coal yards or, if they have no means of transportation, have it delivered by calling one of five City office telephone numbers 3-2401, 2-4124, 9-9638, 9-2105 and 2-0008.

Union drivers are filling calls to the City by obtaining coal from the City stock pile for $5 per ton, hauling it and shoveling it into coal bins for the City.

Grand Juror Drops Old McKay Case

Seven Others Cleared As Hooper Slaying Removes Key Witness

Lansing — AP — The one-year-old warrants issued by the Ingham County Grand Jury against eight persons, including Frank D. McKay, Grand Rapids politician, were dismissed today.

Special Prosecutor Richard B. Foster said prosecution of the cases was impossible because of the assassination of the late Sen. Warren G. Hooper at Jackson County road Jan. 11, 1945, and the death Dec. 21, 1944, of the late Lt. Gov. Frank Murphy of Detroit (no relation to the former governor and present U. S. Supreme Court justice of the same name).

Charges were dismissed against the following:

McKay, former Republican national committeeman and state treasurer, named in a warrant Dec. 2, 1944, on charges of conspiracy to corrupt the 1943 Legislature.

Fleet to Visit Greek Waters

12 U. S. Warships Awaits Official Word

Athens — AP — An authoritative Greek source said today he had it into coal bins for the City.

Founder of GM Led Industrial Development Here

Flint Wizard, Three Times Toppled From Czardom of Motor Industry, In Poor Health Since 1942

W. C. Durant, 85, founder of General Motors and Flint's "industrial wizard" who three times toppled from virtual czardom in the motor industry, died at 2:15 A. M. today in his Gramercy Park apartment in New York.

Funeral arrangements have not been announced. His wife and nurse were with him when he died.

Mr. Durant, who left in Flint a development, had been in poor health since suffering a slight stroke here Oct. 2, 1942. While in Hoiles Hospital, where he was confined until Dec. 15 that year, he underwent a major operation.

Despite his condition, he was in Detroit briefly a year ago. Three in their heads of the position which he bore has continually valued him as a physician him taking place when the Chevrolet assembly line here.

Although his actual residence had been in New York for many years he always considered Flint home, the place he first found success here.

Tax Cut Bill Revision Seen

Special Relief Favored For Small Incomes

Washington — AP — House GOP leaders gave increasing signs to-

Dec. 8, 1861 . . . William C. Durant . . . March 18, 1947

Another view of the impact of Durant on Flint was written by Arthur Pound, one of the best of the auto historians, who was married to a daughter of Flint vehicle pioneer William A. Paterson and who lived for a time in Flint. In *The Iron Man in Industry*, one of the first studies of the social significance of automation, published in 1922, he discussed a man from Flint he identifies only as Duke Billy:

> He was a mighty seller of goods, not primarily a financier; and, in order to have goods to sell, he built, it seems, somewhat too fast and furiously. In building factories he also built a city—from 13,000 to 100,000 in twenty years.
>
> Ten years ago or so he left us for New York, thereby becoming an absentee duke; but occasionally he returned on flying trips. . . . Even in absentia he remained our leading citizen. We leaned upon him in ways that must have tried his patience. We could get no highly important public enterprise under way until he had given it his sanction by telegraph or messenger. Ever and anon we held him up for money.
>
> His name was on our lips oftener than that of any president except [Theodore] Roosevelt. So he was our hero, actual at the start, mythical toward the end—almost our god. In fact, I fancy some of our real estate men prayed to him o' nights, since he so clearly possessed the power to make or break them. . . . Our local autocrat was Billy, yet he graciously kept the velvet glove over the iron hand, and preferred to stand among us rather as a first among equals.
>
> In return we gave him loyalty. . . . Labor troubles were rare. His old workmen knew him and talked about him to the new ones. All were aware that he played baseball as a kid, sold fire insurance as a youth, and battled through to the top by himself. All agreed he was generous and democratic, called folks by their first names, and was not above darting into a quick lunch for a sandwich.
>
> Labor was for him on two counts: first, he paid high wages and never cut them; second, he did not fit neatly with the Wall Street scheme of things. Now the "boys" have a new boss . . . the morale in factories is low. . . . Another myth must grow up around the central figure in

their work-relations before they can forget Duke Billy, and follow confidently their new leader.

Within a month after his death, some of Durant's old associates announced plans to form a William C. Durant Memorial Association. There was talk of placing a memorial in a downtown Flint park. But nothing came of it, and later, when Flint developed its College and Cultural Center, there were plans for an auditorium named for James Whiting and a museum named for Alfred P. Sloan—but nothing for Durant.

Charles Stewart Mott, who had become one of the wealthiest men in the country, building on his initial holdings of GM stock, still lived in a mansion near the cultural center. He told the sponsors that something must be built to honor Durant. "I was always friendly with Durant, although he was tough with me many times," Mott explained to the writer.

> At the same time, in the final analysis he was most friendly with me. He knew I was his friend and that I appreciated what he had done, and I wouldn't have been where I was, or where I am, if it hadn't been for Durant. Durant had his ups and downs, he was not 100 percent perfect. But when they were having this college and cultural thing here, I said that some important thing should be named after him, and they named the plaza [between Whiting Auditorium and the Sloan Museum] Durant Plaza.
>
> There was a big crowd there for the dedication, and I got up and said, "I wouldn't be here talking to you, and you wouldn't be here listening to me, and Flint would be a bush town if it hadn't been for Durant—with the good, bad, and indifferent things Durant ever did.

The memorial is a handsome long block of marble, a base for flagpoles, but somehow insignificant in the scheme of the cultural center. Few citizens of Flint could direct a stranger to the Plaza, though they would certainly be able to point the way to the Durant Hotel, a downtown landmark for more than half a century. The best monuments to Durant in Flint, of course, carry other names—Buick, Chevrolet, the AC Spark Plug Division, Fisher Body.[19]

A few years ago Aristo Scrobogna bought 100 shares of

General Motors stock in Mrs. Durant's name. It was primarily a sentimental thing, he acknowledged; he felt that Durant's name should be among the General Motors stockholders. Shortly thereafter, she received a letter from the chairman of the board—the customary impersonal form letter welcoming new shareholders to the General Motors Corporation. The oversight was understandable; GM had simply grown too large to notice the significance in the name of a new stockholder, even one whose husband had created the business.

GM President Harlow H. Curtice (second from left) and Flint philanthropist Charles Stewart Mott (third from left) among the dignitaries at the dedication of the Durant Plaza in Flint on August 15, 1958. Inscribed in the marble base near his name is this tribute: "In the Golden Milestone Year of the Corporation its Proud Birthplace Dedicates This Plaza in Lasting Appreciation of What His Vision, Genius and Courage Contributed to His Home City and to the Renown of American Industry."

Yet things have a way of righting themselves. The importance of Durant's career will undoubtedly be appreciated more fully some day. Durant himself once remarked to Catherine, referring to General Motors, "Well, they took it away from me, but they cannot take away the credit for having done it."

Epilogue

By Clarence H. Young

(Mr. Young, assistant director of the Manufacturers Association of Flint, has often been cited as a leading authority on William Crapo Durant's career. His impressions of the man, as originally prepared for a General Motors Institute publication, are printed here as a summing up by a man whose talks in the last few years have stirred new interest about the founder of General Motors. Mr. Young is coauthor of *Foundation for Living*, a biography of Charles Stewart Mott.)

In the creation of the Mass Production Age, Durant was not only the presiding genius; he was, indeed, the Titan—and, as was the fate of the original Titans, he was destroyed by the Olympians whom he had created.

It is almost poignant now to tell the beads of carping criticism reiterated against Durant: He lacked or ignored technical mastery . . . he was a good promoter, but no administrator . . . he had no organization . . . he could not delegate authority . . . he made poor choices of executives . . . he was a promoter, a gambler . . . he was wrong in believing in himself. . . .

It is completely true that W. C. Durant had a weakness: He was human. His humanity included love and trust of his associates—the not-always-correct assumption that they were as honorable as he. He gave a degree and quality of loyalty to "his people" beyond any measurement; he expected the same magnitude of loyalty from them.

He surrendered control of General Motors in 1910 to preserve the company for its investors. In 1920, his loyalty to his company and its stockholders drove him to spend more money than he had preserving the value of the company's name, reputation, and stock. As for his feckless choice of executives, he hired and developed Charles W. Nash, Charles F. Kettering, Alfred P. Sloan, Jr., and a few thousand others.

What was Durant? . . . a small-town boy from a broken home who had no advantages at all except his own character. With a borrowed $2,000 he built up the largest carriage company in the world. With a debt-ridden, faltering motor company, he created the world's largest corporation, providing millions of jobs all over the world in the past sixty-five years.

Small in stature, W. C. Durant was larger than life in every aspect of his thought, spirit, and practice. He was, indeed, so much larger in concept that he made the lesser men who surrounded him uncomfortable—he was as unpredictable as an elemental force of nature.

Durant was an original genius who escapes classification and definition; he had an almost godlike prescience; he had the creativity to translate his vision to reality, not only for himself but for his fellow men. He was compassionate, gentle, charming, delightful, considerate, brilliant, generous, ingenious, and infinitely loyal.

Mass production—the greatest servant ever tamed to the uses of mankind—was still only an idea when Durant grasped it. He, more than any other man, implemented this great multiplier of goods and *good* for mankind. He was, indeed, what Dickens called "The Founder of the Feast"—and we are still eating at his bountiful table, although we have forgotten his name.

Chapter Notes

The most important sources of information for this account were two manuscripts, *An Industrial History of Flint*, by Frank M. Rodolf and *The Flint Journal*, and W. C. Durant's autobiographical notes. Other primary source material included letters, papers, and records from Durant's files; corporate records; interviews with Durant's widow and with many others who knew him well; and contemporary newspaper and magazine accounts, particularly those of *The Flint Journal*. Some twenty books and nearly as many magazine articles were also studied. There are many references to Durant in published works, but they are widely scattered.

A major problem in writing about Durant is separating legend from fact. There is hardly a major incident in his career that has not been reported in widely varying detail. The problem was magnified because Durant was a legendary figure in his own time—his contemporaries were often extravagant in their praise of his ability and personality.

CHAPTER ONE

1. The road cart story is a combination of accounts by Rodolf, Durant, and several newspaper accounts indicated in the text. Durant apparently changed minor details in several tellings of the story. Rodolf, who talked with Durant, uses the account of Durant heading toward the gas works to read a meter when he first saw the cart at Saginaw and Kearsley streets. Amy Davis, who wrote down a conversation she overheard between Durant and her father in 1936, gives another version. Writing furiously as Durant talked in an adjoining room, she recorded his words:

> ". . . one afternoon, I was to go to a meeting. I didn't have any way of getting there, but I knew that _____ had a horse

that could step right along and I knew that if I went right over to his house that he would take me to that meeting. So I went over. He had a CART, a two-wheeled cart. The seat wasn't very wide and he was a big man. But we put a blanket on the seat and I managed to hang on. We went over the crosswalks all right. It was a WONDER-FUL ride! . . . "

In one version of his autobiographical notes, Durant wrote that "I had been on the way to my office when a friend drove up and asked me to hop in for a ride. His horse was hitched to a two-wheeled road vehicle then known as a road cart. There was nothing unusual in a road cart, but there was something decidedly unusual about this one. It had a novel spring suspension, and was amazingly easy riding." He identified the friend as Johnny Alger. The more detailed account used in Chapter One may have been related directly to Rodolf by Durant.

CHAPTER TWO

Most of the detail about the Durant-Dort Carriage Company comes from Rodolf, who had the opportunity of discussing the carriage days with Durant, A. B. C. Hardy, and Fred A. Aldrich, all of whom were living in Flint when Rodolf was compiling his *Industrial History of Flint.* Rodolf also relied on many old Flint newspaper accounts and on the handwritten records of the Durant-Dort Carriage Company and the Flint Road Cart Company, which are in the Sloan Museum, Flint.

1. *Lumberman from Flint: The Michigan Career of Henry H. Crapo,* Martin Deming Lewis, Wayne State University Press, 1958.
2. Governor Crapo's letters are on file in the Michigan Historical Collections at the University of Michigan, Ann Arbor. They provide some of the most detailed information available on Durant's early life and explain the conflicts between his father, William Clark Durant, and his grandfather, Governor Crapo. Letters from this source used in this section are dated June 25, 1863; May 10, 1868; and July 30, 1868.

Durant's maternal ancestry is well documented in published Crapo genealogies. He was a descendant of Resolved White, of the original Mayflower Company of 1620. White's granddaughter, Penelope White, married Peter Crapo (Crepaud). Henry Howland Crapo was their great-grandson.

Little was known about Durant's father until 1972, when Clark D. Tibbits, now a planner at University of Michigan-Flint, and Richard P. Scharchburg, an associate professor at General Motors Institute, searched old records in the East to produce the information reported below. Scharchburg plans to publish a more complete Durant genealogy in a pamphlet tentatively titled, *W. C. Durant, "The Boss."*

William Clark Durant was born in Lempster, New Hampshire, in 1827, son of Stephen Harris Durant, an innkeeper, and Ann (Cristy) Durant. He was five when his father died. At age twenty-six he was chosen a collection clerk for the National Webster Bank of Boston. Apparently through the bank's activities in procuring warrants for Michigan timberland, he met the Crapos of New Bedford. For several years he was an agent for Crapo in buying land. After Henry Crapo moved to Flint, Durant assisted in buying various items for the Crapo store and machinery for the lumber business. He had married Rebecca Folger Crapo, daughter of Henry Crapo, in 1855. In the 1860s Durant dealt in stocks in a partnership first with J. P. Hastings and later with a relative, James C. Durant, both in Boston, and had a reputation as a stock speculator. He was also treasurer of Concord Copper Mining Company and was interested in copper in Michigan's Upper Peninsula. After he and Rebecca parted, by 1872, he worked at least part time out of Detroit, and on occasion was an agent for William Wallace Crapo, Rebecca's brother. He was also employed by the Cristy Brothers, cousins on his mother's side, who were manufacturers and wholesale dealers in lumber, lath, and shingles in Detroit. He also apparently had business interests in New York. He was listed in the Detroit City Directory of 1879, but then dropped out of sight. His tombstone in East Lempster, New Hampshire, gives the date of his death as 1883.

3. From one of two letters written to seven-year-old Durant by his grandfather, Governor Crapo, in Durant's personal papers.

4. Joyce S. Cook, *The Flint Journal*, May 20, 1962.

5. W. A. P. John, *Motor* magazine, 1923. John's article, "That Man Durant," was reviewed by Durant before publication and has thus been considered by some historians as the closest thing to a Durant autobiography in print. W. W. Murphy, Durant's long-time personal secretary, told the writer that John's account is the most accurate article he has seen about his former boss. It is perhaps more colorful than entirely accurate, but it does contain important insights into Durant's thoughts.

6. Emma S. G. Ehrmann, *James C. Willson, M.D.*, pamphlet. Also recollections by Mrs. Frances Willson Thompson, Dr. Willson's granddaughter.

7. Crapo papers, Michigan Historical Collections, University of Michigan, Ann Arbor.

8. Durant's high school record, Flint Board of Education.

9. From an autograph book in the personal collection of Clarence H. Young, Associate Director of the Manufacturers Association of Flint.

10. Margery Durant, *My Father*, G. P. Putnam's Sons, 1929. Another version has it that Durant started as a clerk in a grocery store operated in connection with the Crapo mill, then went into the mill as a common laborer, later getting promotions to machine operator and inspector.

11. Arthur Pound, "General Motors' Old Home Town," *Michigan History* magazine, March, 1956. Pound was also author of the General Motors history, *The Turning Wheel*.

12. On March 27, 1936, Durant, then seventy-five, visited Alva Davis, eighty-six, who had joined Durant and Dort as a carriage salesman in 1898. They reminisced in Davis's Flint home and Davis's daughter, Amy B. Davis, sat outside the room and wrote what she could hear of the conversation, which included the cigar-selling story. This unusual document was given by Amy's sister, Carole M. Davis, to Clarence H. Young in 1971. Young made it available to *The Flint Journal*, which published the text on May 29, 1972.

13. Flyer in the Sloan Museum, Flint.

14. Durant, autobiographical notes.

15. *The Flint Journal*, November 30, 1912.

16. Durant, notes.

17. References to Durant protecting Flint investors are in W. A. P. John's "That Man Durant" in *Motor* magazine, 1923, and in an article in *The Flint Journal*, October 26, 1924.

18. Short biography of A. B. C. Hardy in *The Flint Journal* files; also Rodolf, *An Industrial History of Flint*.

CHAPTER THREE

1. Margery Durant, *My Father.*
2. Dort's return to the presidency of the Durant-Dort Carriage Company followed the death of his first wife, the former Nellie Bates, in 1900. Dort married Marcia Webb in 1907. In 1973, Mrs. Dort, now in her early nineties, remains active and alert.
3. Minutes of the Durant-Dort Carriage Company, Sloan Museum, Flint.
4. Testimony in Durant divorce papers, Genesee County Courthouse.
5. A number of letters from Rebecca Durant to her son remain in Durant's personal papers.
6. From references in Durant's autobiographical notes and from a conversation with Donald E. Johnson of Flint, whose wife Alice is Whiting's granddaughter.
7. The Buick information stems largely from the article, "Wouldn't You Really Rather Be a Buick?" by Beverly Rae Kimes, *Automobile Quarterly*, Summer, 1968, which is generally considered to be the most accurate account published on the early history of Buick. Other important accounts include *The Turning Wheel*, by Arthur Pound; *A Financial History of the American Automobile Industry*, by Lawrence H. Seltzer; "The Inside Story of General Motors," by Benjamin Briscoe (these sources are more fully identified in the bibliography); and Rodolf's *Industrial History of Flint.*
8. Dr. Hills drove the first Flint Buick for four years and sold it to a superintendent at Buick named George Weber, who drove it three more years and tore it down to sell the parts.

CHAPTER FOUR

1. Related by Donald E. Johnson, husband of Whiting's granddaughter, Alice, to the writer.
2. Frank Rodolf, *An Industrial History of Flint*, which is also a general source for this chapter.
3. Statement by Durant in October, 1911, in William S. Ballenger papers, property of William S. Ballenger, Jr.
4. Beverly Rae Kimes, "Wouldn't You Really Rather Be a Buick?" in *Automobile Quarterly*, Summer, 1968.
5. Walter P. Chrysler, with Boyden Sparkes, *Life of an American Workman*, page 143.
6. Durant, autobiographical notes.
7. Letter from Durant to Nash, January 29, 1942, Durant papers.
8. From a conversation with Mrs. J. Dallas Dort.
9. George H. Maines, *Men . . . A City . . . and Buick*, pamphlet. The late George Maines, a widely known public relations man for Hollywood stars, politicians, and athletes, was the son of Charles T. Maines, a Flint real estate developer who helped Durant acquire property for Buick and who built 1,400 homes for Buick workers. George Maines knew all of the early Flint automotive families and told the writer many of his personal recollections.
10. The Genesee Bank subscription agreement contains this provision: "This subscription is made with the understanding that the Buick Motor Co. will discontinue its Jackson plant and locate its entire business at Flint, commencing work upon its new buildings as soon as plans can be prepared and weather will permit."
11. Maines, pamphlet.

12. Arthur Pound, *The Turning Wheel,* page 85.

13. Pound, page 81.

14. Letter from Durant to John J. Carton, May 16, 1906, Carton papers, Michigan Historical Collections, University of Michigan, Ann Arbor.

15. Related by Mrs. W. C. Durant to the writer.

16. Durant divorce papers, Genesee County Courthouse.

17. Clarence H. Young and William A. Quinn, *Foundation for Living,* Chapter One.

18. From a memo written by Charles Stewart Mott.

19. Clarence H. Young, article in *The Flint Journal,* January 9, 1972.

20. Letter by Durant, May 7, 1902, Carton papers, Michigan Historical Collections.

21. Official Buick statistics.

22. Maines, pamphlet, page 8.

23. Walter W. Ruch, "A Great Chevrolet Named Louis," *Friends* magazine, July, 1971.

24. P. C. Baker, *Detroit News,* quoted in *The Flint Journal,* November 25, 1909.

25. Kimes, page 84.

26. Benjamin Briscoe, "The Inside Story of General Motors," in *Detroit Saturday Night,* January-February, 1921.

CHAPTER FIVE

1. Benjamin Briscoe, "The Inside Story of General Motors," in *Detroit Saturday Night,* January-February, 1921.

2. Letter from Ward, Hayden & Satterlee to John J. Carton, July 1, 1908, Carton papers, Michigan Historical Collections.

3. Letter from Durant to Carton, July 2, 1908, Carton papers, Michigan Historical Collections.

4. Frederic L. Smith, "Motoring Down a Quarter of a Century," in *Detroit Saturday Night,* 1928.

5. Letter from Smith to Durant, July 21, 1908, Durant papers.

6. Letter from Carton to Ward, Hayden & Satterlee, July 29, 1908, Carton papers, Michigan Historical Collections.

7. Letters in Durant papers, July-August, 1908.

8. Letter from Briscoe to Durant, August 4, 1908, Durant papers.

9. Letter from Ward, Hayden & Satterlee to Durant, September 10, 1908, Durant papers. The letter indicates that there would still be an opportunity for Durant to use the International Motor Company name later: "When the inventories and appraisals have been finished, and the other problems involved have been successfully worked out, the plans for developing an international market for the business can undoubtedly be perfected, reserving the 'International Motor Company' for use at the appropriate time."

CHAPTER SIX

1. Letter from Ward, Hayden & Satterlee to Durant, September 15, 1908, Durant papers.

2. Minutes of General Motors board of directors, September 28, 1908.

3. Letter from Durant to William S. Ballenger, September 14, 1908, in Ballenger papers, property of William S. Ballenger, Jr.

4. Leland background from *Master of Precision,* by Mrs. Wilfred C. Leland with Minnie Dubbs Millbrook.

5. Benjamin Briscoe, "The Inside Story of General Motors," in *Detroit Saturday Night,* January-February, 1921.
6. Alfred D. Chandler, Jr., *Giant Enterprise,* page 49.
7. W. W. Murphy, eighty-nine years old, recalled the early days with Durant in an interview with Richard P. Scharchburg, General Motors Institute, in 1972 at Murphy's home in Stony Brook, New York.
8. Arthur Pound, *The Turning Wheel,* page 95.
9. Louis E. Rowley, in *Detroit Saturday Night,* quoted in *The Flint Journal,* December 20, 1909.
10. Rowley, in *The Flint Journal,* December 20, 1909.

CHAPTER SEVEN

1. *Horseless Age,* November 3, 1909.
2. *Horseless Age,* April 27, 1910.
3. Minutes of the General Motors board of directors, March 9, 1911.
4. Lawrence H. Seltzer, *A Financial History of the American Automobile Industry,* page 161.
5. Seltzer, page 163.
6. Arthur Pound, *The Turning Wheel,* page 126.
7. Pound, page 126.
8. Seltzer, page 157.

CHAPTER EIGHT

Frank Rodolf's *Industrial History of Flint* contains the most complete account of the early history of Chevrolet that the writer has seen. It was apparently compiled from direct conversations with Durant and Hardy and contemporary newspaper and industry magazine accounts as well as from Arthur Pound's *The Turning Wheel* and Lawrence Seltzer's *A Financial History of the American Automobile Industry.* The Flint Journal's copy of *The Turning Wheel* contains marginal penciled notes where Durant disputed a point here or there or provided further detail. The writer has reviewed the contemporary published accounts used by Rodolf. A few specific footnotes:

1. *The Flint Journal,* November 29, 1911.
2. Arthur Pound, *The Turning Wheel,* pages 146-147.
3. Walter P. Chrysler, with Boyden Sparkes, *Life of an American Workman,* pages 123-127.
4. Walter W. Ruch, "A Great Chevrolet Named Louis," *Friends* magazine, July, 1971.
5. Related by Mrs. Jay (Frances Willson) Thompson to the writer.

CHAPTER NINE

1. Lawrence H. Seltzer, *A Financial History of the American Automobile Industry,* page 172.
2. Seltzer, page 37.
3. Arthur Pound, *The Turning Wheel,* pages 153-155.
4. Alfred D. Chandler and Stephen Salsbury, *Pierre S. du Pont and the Making of the Modern Corporation,* page 435.

5. *They Told Barron,* edited by Pound and Samuel Taylor Moore, page 101, gives Kaufman's version.

6. Letter from Pierre du Pont to J. A. Haskell, September 17, 1915. Exhibit in *United States of America* vs. *E. I. duPont et al.,* in U.S. District Court for the Northern District of Illinois, Eastern Division.

7. Pound, page 156.

8. Letter from Durant to Nash, January 29, 1942, Durant papers.

9. *The Flint Journal,* November 30, 1912.

10. Letter from du Pont to Haskell, September 17, 1915.

11. Seltzer, page 174.

12. Seltzer, page 175.

13. Seltzer, pages 176-177.

14. Letter from Nash to Durant, 1916, Durant papers.

15. *The Flint Journal,* April 17, 1916.

16. Theodore F. McManus and Norman Beasley, *Men, Money and Motors,* page 190.

17. Brief biography of Nash, American Motors Corp.

18. Pierre du Pont letter to Durant, 1916.

19. Related by Mrs. W. C. Durant to the writer.

CHAPTER TEN

1. Walter P. Chrysler, with Boyden Sparkes, *Life of an American Workman,* page 145.

2. The Frigidaire information in this chapter, except where otherwise noted, is from an unpublished manuscript supplied by the Frigidaire Division of General Motors. Sources credited in the manuscript include an interview by Dan McCoy with Alfred Mellowes in 1954 (Mellowes died January 31, 1960, at age eighty), and *The History of Frigidaire,* 1949, by Tom Shellworth.

3. Alfred P. Sloan, with Boyden Sparkes, *Adventures of a White-Collar Man,* pages 109-110.

4. Alfred D. Chandler,and Stephen Salsbury, *Pierre S. du Pont and the Making of the Modern Corporation,* pages 445-446.

5. Chandler and Salsbury, page 448.

6. Letter from Durant to Raskob, September 12, 1917.

7. Report from Raskob to the Du Pont Company's Finance Committee, December 19, 1917, Government Trial Exhibit No. 124, *United States of America* vs. *E. I. du Pont et al.,* in U.S. District Court for the Northern District of Illinois, Eastern Division.

8. Chandler and Salsbury, pages 451-455.

9. Chandler and Salsbury, page 467.

10. Samson Division material from conversations with Richard P. Scharchburg, associate professor at General Motors Institute, who interviewed Eugene E. Husting, son of former Samson executive Walter E. Husting; also, Jacob H. Newmark, "My 25 Years with W. C. Durant," in *Commerce and Finance,* series, May 16-October 17, 1936.

11. General Motors annual report, 1922. Also see Lawrence H. Seltzer, *A Financial History of the American Automobile Industry,* pages 208-209.

12. Chandler and Salsbury, pages 468-471.

13. Chrysler, with Sparkes, pages 156-157. Also Sloan, with Sparkes, pages 115-117.

14. Chrysler, with Sparkes, page 148.

15. Letter quoted in an article by Alice G. Lethbridge, *The Flint Journal,* March 6, 1973.

16. Sloan, with Sparkes, page 115.

17. Newmark, "My 25 Years with W. C. Durant."
18. Interview by Scharchburg with W. W. Murphy in 1972.
19. Letter in Durant papers.
20. Seltzer, page 200.
21. Letter in Durant papers.
22. Official General Motors minutes.
23. Chandler and Salsbury, pages 467-468, detail the debenture plan. See also Seltzer, page 195, and Sloan, *My Years with General Motors*, page 29.
24. Chandler and Salsbury, page 478.
25. Chandler and Salsbury, page 478, and W. A. P. John, "That Man Durant," in *Motor* magazine, January, 1923.
26. *They Told Barron*, page 108.
27. *They Told Barron*, page 106.
28. Letter from Pierre S. du Pont to his brother, Irénée du Pont, November 26, 1920, which provides the most detailed account by a participant of Durant's last days with General Motors. Exhibit in the *United States of America* vs. *E. I. du Pont et al.*, and published in several histories.
29. *They Told Barron*, page 104.
30. Government Exhibit No. 166, the *United States of America* vs. *E. I. du Pont et al.*
31. Direct testimony by John L. Pratt, the *United States of America* vs. *E. I. du Pont et al.*
32. Frigidaire manuscript.
33. Letter in Durant papers.
34. Sloan, with Sparkes, page 118.
35. W. A. P. John; also, *They Told Barron*, pages 103-104.
36. Direct testimony by Alfred P. Sloan, the *United States of America* vs. *E. I. du Pont et al.*
37. Sloan, *My Years with General Motors*, page 32.
38. Chandler and Salsbury, pages 483-484.
39. Letter from Pierre S. du Pont to Irénée du Pont, November 26, 1920.
40. Letter in W. S. Ballenger papers.
41. Sloan, *Adventures of a White-Collar Man*, page 125.
42. Scharchburg interview with W. W. Murphy, 1972. Also W. A. P. John. Durant's formal resignation as a GM director was in April, 1921.
43. Margery Durant, *My Father*. Catherine Durant believes Margery's account is overdramatic. Catherine remembers that her husband had an air of forced cheerfulness on his departure from General Motors, and a determination to roll up his sleeves and get back to work.
44. Direct testimony by Pratt, the *United States of America* vs. *E. I. du Pont et al.*
45. *They Told Barron*, page 108.
46. Letter from Sloan to Durant, March 17, 1921, Durant papers. Letters solicited by Durant from other GM officials regarding his feelings about the Durant Building are also preserved in the Durant papers.
47. Letter in Durant papers.
48. Pretrial brief by U.S. government attorneys, the *United States of America* vs. *E. I. du Pont et al.*, October 15, 1952, page 29.
49. Reprinted in pretrial brief, October 15, 1952, pages 29-30.
50. *They Told Barron*, page 104.
51. Letter from Durant to Pierre S. du Pont, March 18, 1921, Durant papers.

CHAPTER ELEVEN

1. Jacob H. Newmark, "My 25 Years with W. C. Durant," in *Commerce and Finance*, series, May 16-October 17, 1936. One of the most detailed sources on the Durant Motors era.
2. Frank T. Snyder, "The Princeton—Bill Durant's Paper Tiger," in *Old Cars*. October, 1971. Other Durant vehicles quickly forgotten included the Eagle, introduced at the New York Auto Show in January, 1924, but which became the Flint "40" a few months later, and the Rugby truck.
3. *They Told Barron*, pages 109-110.
4. Arthur Pound, "General Motors' Old Home Town," in *Michigan History*, March, 1956, pages 90-91.
5. Train collision described to writer by Catherine Durant. A witness to the collision wrote this recollection in a letter to Durant on July 28, 1930:

> The engine was piled up on your private car and they had just taken you out through the window with a gash on the top of your head. They then proceeded to get Mrs. Durant out. I will never forget as long as I live how pitiful she seemed because she had my arm, or rather I had hers, trying to pull her up the track to get her out of the rain and to the car you were in. She was as nervous as could be and several times she broke loose from me and would run back and scream for you because it seems as though she was under the impression that you had not gotten out of the car, and I will never forget after we tried one or two cars and found them stove in looking for you I then got her to the right one and how delighted she was and the smile you gave her because I was under the impression as she was that she would find you dead.

6. Interview by the writer with Mrs. Durant.
7. John B. Rae, "The Fabulous Billy Durant," in *Business History Review*, Autumn, 1958, page 268.
8. Circular in Durant papers.
9. Press release in Durant papers.
10. From an anonymous interview manuscript in Durant papers.
11. Text of radio broadcast in *The Flint Journal* files.
12. Interview by the writer with Mrs. Durant.
13. Interview by the writer with William S. Ballenger, Jr.
14. Archie Campbell was also long-time manager of the Elks Club in Flint, of which Durant held the first membership card.
15. David J. Wilkie, Associated Press, June 8, 1940.
16. Interview by the writer with Martin Caserio.
17. Alfred P. Sloan, with Boyden Sparkes, *Adventures of a White-Collar Man*, pages 126-127.
18. Durant letter to Sloan, September 13, 1940, Durant papers.
19. A quarter century after his death, none of the Flint houses where Durant lived for any length of time remains. The Federal Building is on the site of his mother's place at Church and W. Second streets, where Durant lived from age 13 to 23—from 1875 until his marriage in 1885. The home at W. Fourth Avenue and Garland Street, where he lived with his wife from 1885 until sometime before their divorce in 1908, was torn down a few years later and several houses stand on the property. A small horse barn converted into a garage behind the home of Ernest Gardner at 116 W. Fourth may be a survivor from the Durant properties there. The house at 415 Stevens Street where Durant boarded in 1908 and later, which was then owned by his daughter Margery and her husband, Dr. Edwin R.

Campbell, has also been razed. A portion of the top floor of the Durant Hotel in downtown Flint was planned as a residence for Durant, but he resigned as president of General Motors shortly before the hotel opened, and it is believed he never occupied the suite. The Flint City Club now uses those facilities. Prominently displayed in the club is an oil portrait of Durant, loaned by Gerry Fauth.

An almost forgotten section of Flint, along W. Water Street between the old Water Street Bridge and Grand Traverse Street, close to downtown, still holds traces of the great carriage industry which gave Durant his impetus in vehicles. The once elaborate Durant-Dort Carriage Company office building at 315 W. Water, a survivor from the 1890s, is a private tavern for a veterans' club. A warehouse across the street, almost on the site of Flint's first trading post (started by Jacob Smith in 1819), is said to be the cotton mill Durant and Dort converted into the Flint Road Cart Company in the 1880s—the starting point of Durant's vehicle career. Among the weeds in nearby fields are foundations of other buildings of the Durant-Dort complex.

Bibliography

Primary source material is indicated in the Foreword and the Chapter Notes. Listed below are the books and magazines which were also useful.

BOOKS

Adventures of a White-Collar Man. Alfred P. Sloan with Boyden Sparkes. Doubleday, Doran and Company, 1941.

Automotive Giants of America. B. C. Forbes and O. D. Foster. B. C. Forbes Publishing Company, 1926.

Birth of a Giant: The Men and Incidents That Gave America the Motorcar. Richard Crabb. Chilton Book Company, 1969.

The City of Flint Grows Up. Carl Crow. Harper & Brothers, 1945.

A Financial History of the American Automobile Industry. Lawrence H. Seltzer. Houghton Mifflin Company, 1928.

Foundation for Living: The Story of Charles Stewart Mott and Flint. Clarence H. Young and William A. Quinn. McGraw-Hill Book Company, Inc., 1963.

The Gasoline Age: The Story of the Men Who Made It. C. B. Glasscock. Bobbs-Merrill Company, 1937.

Giant Enterprise: Ford, General Motors and the Automobile Industry. Compiled and edited by Alfred D. Chandler, Jr. Harcourt, Brace and World, Inc., 1964.

History of Genesee County, Michigan. Edwin O. Wood. Federal Publishing Company, Indianapolis, 1916. Volume Two.

Life of an American Workman. Walter P. Chrysler with Boyden Sparkes. Dodd, Mead and Company, 1937.

Lumberman from Flint: The Michigan Career of Henry H. Crapo. Martin Deming Lewis. Wayne State University Press, 1958.

Master of Precision: Henry M. Leland. Mrs. Wilfred C. Leland with Minnie Dubbs Millbrook. Wayne State University Press, 1966.

Men, Money and Motors. Theodore F. McManus and Norman Beasley. Harper and Brothers, 1930.

Monopoly on Wheels. William Greenleaf. Wayne State University Press, 1961.

My Father. Margery Durant. G. P. Putnam's Sons, 1929

Mystery Men of Wall Street. Earl Sparling. Greenberg: Publisher, 1930.

My Years with General Motors. Alfred P. Sloan, edited by John McDonald and Catharine Stevens. Doubleday and Company, 1964.

Pierre S. du Pont and the Making of the Modern Corporation. Alfred D. Chandler and Stephen Salsbury. Harper and Row, 1972.

The Plungers and the Peacocks. Dana L. Thomas. G. P. Putnam's Sons, 1967.

Seventy Years of Buick. George H. Dammann. Crestline Publishing, 1973.

Sixty Years of Chevrolet. George H. Dammann. Crestline Publishing, 1972.

Son of New England: James Jackson Storrow. Henry Greenleaf Pearson. Thomas Todd Company, 1932.

The Turning Wheel. Arthur Pound. Doubleday, Doran and Company, 1934.

They Told Barron: The Notes of the Late Clarence W. Barron. Edited by Arthur Pound and Samuel Taylor Moore. Harper and Brothers, 1930.

MAGAZINES AND BOOKLETS

"The Fabulous Billy Durant." John B. Rae. *Business History Review*, Autumn, 1958.

"Flint—Laboratory of the American Idea." Clarence H. Young. *Michigan in Books*, Autumn, 1966.

"General Motors' Old Home Town." Arthur Pound. *Michigan History*, March, 1956.

"General Motors Was My Baby." W. C. Durant. *Aviation & Yachting*, May, 1946.

"A Great Chevrolet Named Louis." Walter M. Ruch. *Friends*, July, 1971.

"The Inside Story of General Motors." Benjamin Briscoe. *Detroit Saturday Night*, four articles beginning January 15, 1921.

"James C. Willson, M. D., 'The Dear Doctor.' " Emma Sandilands Green Ehrmann. Published privately by Frances Willson Thompson, 1950.

"The Lively Life of the Gambling Giant." Booton Herndon. *True*, December, 1958.

"Motoring Down a Quarter of a Century." F. L. Smith. *Detroit Saturday Night*, 1928.

"My 25 Years with W. C. Durant." Jacob H. Newmark. *Commerce & Finance*, May 16-October 17, 1936.

"That Man Durant." W. A. P. John. *Motor*, January, 1923.

"Wouldn't You Really Rather Be a Buick?" Beverly Rae Kimes. *Automobile Quarterly*, Summer, 1968.

"Men . . . A City . . . and Buick." George H. Maines. Privately published in Flint, 1953.

Index

Index